AF867794

PRAISE FOR
THE ROLE OF MOM WILL BE PLAYED BY

"What seems like a candid exploration of early motherhood is actually a front-row seat to the creative process. In these pages we witness a spark that leads to gestation, analysis, and breakthrough, showing us, with humor and heart, that mothers are creativity incarnate."

—KC Davis (@DomesticBlisters), *USA Today* bestselling author of *How to Keep House While Drowning*

"Shawna Lander offers a candid and deeply personal account of how motherhood reshapes a woman's inner world, drawing us into the intimate and often unspoken experience. Her writing reads with the ease of a conversation and the craft of a seasoned storyteller, inviting readers into her thoughts, grounding and reassuring them along the way. With an honesty that feels both intimate and universally recognizable, she gives language to the emotional shifts of early motherhood, allowing readers to feel seen and less alone. What a comfort this will be to new mothers."

—Karen Kleiman, founder of The Postpartum Stress Center and author of *Good Moms Have Scary Thoughts*

"Powerful, curious, and deeply human, this book captures the weird, liminal phase of pregnancy and postpartum so well it should be required reading for all fathers."

—Liz Swenson (@LizSwensonBFF), author and illustrator of *You Got This, Mama!*, *Raising Tiny Humans*, and *Trying*

"*The Role of Mom Will Be Played By* is as unflinchingly introspective as it is raw, funny, and hopeful. With her gift for human insight, Shawna Lander tells a story so personal it becomes universal, reminding us all that we are so much more than the roles we play."

—Amber Estenson (@ThatMidwesternMom), actress, opera singer, and content creator

"Shawna Lander does something rare: she tells the truth about motherhood without making it a cautionary tale or a love letter. It's both, and everything in between.

This book lives inside the dichotomy of a woman who swore she'd never have kids and the woman who aches from how much she loves hers. She writes about the joy that's inseparable from the grief, the version of yourself you lose and the one you didn't know you were waiting to become.

It's funny in the way real life can be funny. But, between the funny moments, sometimes the only other option is crying, and Shawna does that, too, honestly and without apology.

Every mother who has ever felt behind, alone, or quietly certain she's the only one getting it wrong will feel seen by this book. And every woman who's wondered if motherhood is for her will find, somewhere in these pages, the most honest answer she's ever been given."

—Sidra Wali (@SidandListen), influencer

"As a young woman without children, I initially believed I would connect with *The Role of Mom Will Be Played By* only as a content creator, or perhaps it would be a cautionary tale about motherhood. I was wrong. This is not simply a story about being a mother; it is the voice of a woman sharing her lived experience with others who, regardless of if they have children, will recognize themselves in the layered, deeply personal, and yet totally universal reality of womanhood. It offers validation, reassurance, and a much-needed breath of relief for women at every stage of life. I can't explain to you how much this book meant to me as a woman who is unsure if she wants children, and I know reading this will be such a defining moment for so many."

—Sydney Jo (@ThatGirlSydJo), creator of viral web series *The Group Chat*

"*The Role of Mom Will Be Played By* is honestly so great. Sometimes changing your mind requires you to create a version of yourself that didn't exist before. Shawna and this book are glowing examples of that transformation."

—Soogia (@Soogia1), influencer

"A raw, honest, and vulnerable account of the journey to motherhood. Sensitively told by Shawna, it's a book you will want to share not only with expectant mothers, but the tribe who surrounds her."

—Dr. Maryhan, psychologist and host of the *How Not to Screw Up Your Kids* podcast

"Shawna Lander has given mothers both a mirror and a permission slip to be fully human. In taking us into her entry to motherhood, Shawna shows us that we are not alone, that we matter, and that by choosing to be the main character in our own lives, we can better play the most sacred role of mom in our children's lives. This is a book for the mom who feels like she disappeared the moment the baby came along and for anyone who ever side-eyed another mom just doing the best she can with what she knows. Lander's story reminds us that, after all, moms are people, too."

—Libby Ward (@LibbyWard), author of *Honest Motherhood*

THE ROLE OF MOM WILL BE PLAYED BY

THE ROLE OF MOM WILL BE PLAYED BY

The year I had a baby and became myself

SHAWNA LANDER

BENBELLA

BenBella Books, Inc.
Dallas, TX

The events, locations, and conversations in this book, while true, are recreated from the author's memory. However, the essence of the story, and the feelings and emotions evoked, are intended to be accurate representations. In certain instances, names, persons, organizations, and places have been changed to protect an individual's privacy.

The Role of Mom Will Be Played By copyright © 2026 by Shawna Lander

All rights reserved. Except in the case of brief quotations embodied in critical articles or reviews, no part of this book may be reproduced, stored, transmitted, or used in any manner whatsoever, including for training artificial intelligence (AI) technologies or for automated text and data mining, without prior written permission from the publisher.

BENBELLA

BenBella Books, Inc.
8080 N. Central Expressway
Suite 1700
Dallas, TX 75206
benbellabooks.com
Send feedback to feedback@benbellabooks.com

BenBella is a federally registered trademark.

Printed in the United States of America
10 9 8 7 6 5 4 3 2 1

Library of Congress Control Number: 2026019094
ISBN 9781637749623 (hardcover)
ISBN 9781637749630 (electronic)

Editing by Leah Wilson and Clara Tamez
Copyediting by Elizabeth Degenhard
Proofreading by Karen Wise
Text design and composition by Jordan Koluch
Cover design by Sarah Avinger
Printed by Lake Book Manufacturing

Special discounts for bulk sales are available.
Please contact bulkorders@benbellabooks.com.

For my darling boy and my precious girl

CONTENTS

CHAPTER ONE

THE ACHE

AT 1:34 AM ON A FRIDAY night in Austin, Texas, I realized I was in love. I knew it was exactly 1:34 AM because I had just nursed my newborn son back to sleep and was diligently recording the amount he ate on the feeding log I was given at the hospital. It had been four days since my ob-gyn had induced labor, three days since our labor nurse had charted the wrong birth time, two days since my first motherhood all-nighter, and one day since I figured out how to work my breast pump. As I sat in bed, tits out and hair up, the pump whir-whirring little squirts of milk into little bottles, I gazed at my sleeping three-day-old baby. He was so fresh that his vernix hadn't completely rubbed off yet, so when the light from my bedside table lamp hit his plump cheeks, it created a creamy white glow around his perfect little head. It was then that I noticed the ache in my chest.

I remember thinking the ache was odd, but not in a

worst-case-scenario kind of way, which I could attribute to my newly mounting anxiety. No, the ache was odd because it felt like I had always been sore there, near my heart, and I had just never noticed it before. *Why haven't I ever noticed that my heart feels like it could bleed,* I wondered, and as I wondered I watched my tiny baby's tiny lips, glued together with a tiny drop of colostrum, suddenly pop apart. Never having seen a baby's lips smack open in comfortable satisfaction before, I laughed softly. *Ahh, it's love,* I thought. *I've never noticed the ache before because he wasn't here yet.*

As the thought formed, tears stung my tired eyes and the ache swelled, expanding up to grip my throat and pushing down to fill my tummy. I looked from my creamy, fresh newborn to my sweet husband, who slumbered soundly. It suddenly felt like the entire world was asleep but me. I probably could have felt lonely, left behind in that late-night hour to plunge deeper into my feelings than I ever had before, but as I sat strapped to my breast pump, I thought of all the other mothers around the world who had ever sat awake and alone at night, and I wondered how many of them had felt the ache. *Billions,* I thought, and a shiver ran up my spine. In an instant, I understood my connection to every mother who had come before me, to every mother yet to come, and to the very fabric of life itself, which had been stitched together across space and time by the wombs of women just like me, and suddenly, somehow, I knew the ache had purpose.

IT CAME AS A SHOCK WHEN I woke up one sunshiny morning in 2014 and thought to myself, *I want to have a baby*. It was long before I would ever dream of a career in social media, and I hadn't thought

I was the baby-having type. I grew up the middle child in a dysfunctional family of yellers in Southern California. Things at home started off okay—Dad had been a nondenominational preacher and a grocery store manager, Mom was a registered nurse, and my two sisters and I were good girls and happy playmates. But by the time I reached high school, Dad had begun a love affair with methamphetamines that had taken him to NorCal, and after the divorce, Mom, who was struggling to continue to exist, vacillated day-to-day between loving and resenting the hell out of my sisters and me.

On the morning of my sixteenth birthday, Mom was distraught. I'd just had a sleepover with my best friend and was in love with a very cute boy, so by all accounts life felt delightfully full of possibilities, when suddenly Mom burst into my room in tears. She was always doing stuff like that. I discreetly rolled my eyes before looking up.

"Happy birthday!" she said, attempting to sound celebratory through stifled sobs.

"Thanks, Mom," I replied. I wanted nothing more than to be left alone.

"Do you girls want anything special for breakfast?" she croaked.

"I'm not really that hungry." I looked at my friend Christine.

"No, thank you," she said. "We're just enjoying Shawna's birthday morning right now, but I'm sure we'll want to eat a little later."

I smiled at her, grateful to have backup, and looked boldly at my mother, whose face had soured into a mixture of self-pity and contempt, a once-puzzling expression that had become routine since Dad abandoned us.

"Maybe later, Mom," I said, hoping she would leave. Her eyes welled up again and she nodded, closing the door.

A half hour later, she was back weeping in my doorway again.

"Shawna, I'm sorry I couldn't get you a car for your sweet sixteen," she managed, and suddenly we had the reason for her upset. I shared an eleven-by-thirteen-foot room with my two sisters in a two-bedroom apartment, and I hadn't yet taken even one driver's education course, let alone secured a driver's license, so I had no delusion I'd be getting a car that year.

"It's okay, Mom," I said, darting an embarrassed eye at Christine, who simply smiled. Mom choked back sobs as she gazed at a small parcel in her hand.

"Is that for me?" I asked.

"It's not a car, but I thought it was nice." She held the beautifully wrapped package out for me.

"Thanks," I said, retrieving my gift. I slid a finger under the edge of the wrap and tore the paper away, revealing a navy-blue velvet box. I popped it open to see a silver pendant necklace not quite to my taste, and smiled.

"Pretty! Thanks, Mom," I said.

"Oh, I like that," Christine offered in support.

"I had really wanted to get you a car," Mom began, "and I tried to figure out—"

"Mom, it's fine," I interrupted. "I don't even have a permit yet."

"Well, I wanted to do that for you," Mom explained.

"Okay, well. You can't. And I don't need it anyway, so it's fine. It's not a big deal."

"The necklace is so pretty!" Christine said.

"Yeah, Mom, really pretty. Thank you." I hoped my feigned gratitude was enough to make her go away, but she lingered in the doorway, needing more. I took the necklace out of the box and secured it around my neck.

"What do you think?" I asked Christine. She gasped, understanding intuitively that my mom needed us to gush, and I felt grateful.

"It's so, so pretty, Shawna. Oh my gosh, it's gorgeous. Wow." She was really selling it.

"I love it so much. Thank you." I stood and hugged my mother. Her heavy shoulders slumped and she melted into me, hugging me around the middle with her head on my chest. I wanted to let go immediately but endured.

"I'm sorry it's not more," she whispered.

"I know. It's okay," I replied.

"Okay, you girls have fun," she said with a deep breath and finally, she let go. Or so I thought.

Around noon I waved as Christine drove away, and I took the stairs back up to the apartment two at a time, eager to call my boyfriend. I stopped short when I crossed the threshold and saw my mother's weeping face. *Not again*, I thought.

"Shawna, I am so sor—"

"Mom, stop," I said. "I knew I wasn't getting a car. Just stop it." My frustration was hard to conceal.

"I know you knew, but I feel terrible. I never wanted any of this for you girls," she said.

That dreary phrase, with its implication that Mom pointed all blame for our family's difficulties squarely at Dad, was the last straw.

"Mom, I don't care about a stupid car. I can't even drive yet! Stop talking to me about how sad you are on my birthday!" I didn't care how she felt. Apart from dealing with this kind of thing from her on a regular basis, I had a good life. I didn't want to talk about her feelings; I wanted to celebrate finally being sixteen. I tried to push past her, but she grabbed my upper arm, digging her nails into my flesh. The corners of her mouth turned down in contempt, and she yanked hard, drawing me close.

"One day you're going to have kids and then you'll understand," she spat.

I laughed. I shouldn't have done it, but I laughed right in her pissed-off face.

"Are you mocking me, little girl?" her hand squeezed tighter, her nails breaking my skin.

"No," I said, wrenching my arm away. "Stop."

"What are you laughing at?" Mom demanded.

"Why do you think I would ever do this to myself?" I questioned flatly.

"Do what?" she asked.

I motioned back and forth at the tension between us, but she didn't get my meaning. I inspected the scratches on my arm to avoid her gaze; they were mostly surface-level, with a dot of blood clotted at the edge of the deepest one, which was my own fault for twisting my arm away from her. I lifted my eyes from the marks to look her square in the face.

"I am never having kids."

THE DIFFICULT RELATIONSHIP I HAD WITH my mother wasn't the entire reason sixteen-year-old me couldn't fathom wanting children; I had other concerns. First, I had found my calling:

to become a movie star. In third grade, a traveling theater troupe pulled me onstage to perform a scene during a school assembly. I was The Princess in a classic damsel-in-distress caper, and the moment my satin-footed slipper hit the stage, I was hooked. Movie stardom would come first, I mused at eight years old, and if I ever did have kids, it would have to be after achieving fame and fortune. Second, by the time I was a teenager, I wasn't sure I even liked children. I didn't know many, and though the few kids I knew from the neighborhood and my extended family members were cute, I didn't really care about their existence. *I'm not nice enough to have kids,* I thought. *People who want to be moms should probably care about being nice to children.* It seemed logical to my mind. Adding these two points to the painfully confusing third, that I could never tell if my own mother loved or hated me, I deduced that having children was not for me.

I campaigned on my child-free values as an integral part of my identity for nearly a decade and well into my relationship with my now husband, John. I loudly declared, *Ew, I'm never having kids!* whenever the topic arose and always to a response of scattered laughter. John and I were young and dumb when we first started dating, and we were having too much fun being blissfully in love to have such responsible conversations. We began dating in college and spent our early years drunk dancing in nightclubs, bungee jumping off bridges, and gambling with friends in Las Vegas. When we weren't focused on studying or fun, I waited tables and auditioned for acting jobs, and John worked as the front desk supervisor of a popular hotel.

After school, around the two-years-of-dating mark, we decided to backpack through Europe together, saving up for six months beforehand to pay for the trip. While we strolled romantically arm in arm through Milan's cobblestoned streets, I saw a woman holding a pantsless toddler upright so he could pee on a tree outside of a restaurant. I scoffed with disgust. I couldn't believe the mother's entitlement, that she would allow her child to disturb restaurant patrons and pedestrians alike, but when I pointed them out to John, he laughed.

"Ew, it's not funny," I said, judgmentally.

"It's a baby peeing on a tree. That's pretty comical," John insisted.

"We're in public," I explained. "I would never let my kid do that."

"I thought you weren't having kids," John said with a wry smile.

"I'm not, but—"

"Well, he obviously had to go," John said plainly, and I was struck by his easy acceptance of the child's humanity. "Besides," he went on, "maybe that restaurant wouldn't let her use their toilet. Or maybe they would, but the tree was more convenient." I looked again at the woman and son, trying to see what John saw. "Or he was going to pee his pants, and she was just desperate," John concluded, displaying much more empathy for the mother than I had ever considered.

We decided to live together after Europe, moving into our own room in an apartment full of single, twenty-something roommates who also worked in hospitality. While the young, dumb fun of our relationship continued with nightly beer pong parties and roommate movie nights, John's observation from our walk in Milan had softened something in me. I hadn't been aware before our trip that I held resentment toward mothers and refused to attempt any compassion for their experience. But now, I began to secretly wonder what it was like to have a child.

I THOUGHT OF THE ITALIAN MOTHER and her son when my niece was born. My sister Sarah had enjoyed a whirlwind romance with a boy from college, and nine months later she had her own little family. John and I visited when the baby was nearly two months old, and I noticed a marked difference in Sarah's demeanor. She was typically a vivacious and friendly hostess, the life of the party, and she was my baby sister, so she loved asking me for a favor, or twenty. But during our visit Sarah didn't ask for help with the baby, or with the house, or with anything, and she didn't seem very interested in casual chitchat, let alone a party atmosphere. When she did speak, her usual witty banter was replaced with soft-spoken directives to communicate simple needs, like "Could you hand me my water?" or "Will you grab that blanket?" I wondered if the changes I saw in her were because, like in Milan, I hadn't known what was socially acceptable in the foreign territory of motherhood, or if Sarah's behavior was her version of adapting to the desperation of the moment in a peeing-on-a-tree kind of a way.

I saw a glimmer of the sister I knew only once that visit, when I had finally worked up enough tender courage to ask to hold the baby. My niece, Lillybelle, was darling to me the instant she was born, so an odd yearning to have her in my arms had naturally developed, but I had a child-free reputation to uphold, and frankly, I was scared. It took me two days to decide that getting to hold the baby was more important to me than worrying about how holding that baby might make me feel. I took my chance the moment Sarah and I were alone on the couch.

"Can I hold her?" I whispered. Sarah grinned.

"What! Who are you and what have you done with Shawna?" she teased, but I could tell she was touched. She sat up straight and, like an old pro, carefully shifted her tiny newborn into her hands, holding her gently aloft for me to take.

"Wait!" I said, just as John returned from the bathroom. "What do I do?"

"You hold her," Sarah replied with a laugh.

"No, but I mean, how?" I asked. Sarah shook her head as if I was being silly.

"Put your left hand under her head and neck and put your right hand under her back and butt, then slide her into the crook of your arm," she said plainly.

"WHAT?!" I exclaimed.

"I'll take her," John offered, reaching up to steal my moment.

"No!" I said. It had taken a lot of emotional labor for me to ask. I was scared but refused to miss my chance. "Me first." John chuckled and relented.

"Okay, just sit up straight," Sarah said. Tired of my hesitance, she stood up and unceremoniously plopped her daughter onto my lap.

"Ahh!" I exclaimed. "Am I doing it right?"

"No," she said, "but neither am I, probably." There she was: self-aware and self-deprecating as hell, my sister. We all laughed—softly, of course, so as not to wake the baby—and I realized it didn't matter if I understood Sarah's change in behavior because, like the Italian mother I had seen in Milan, she was doing what she needed to do to care for her baby.

On our plane ride home, John told me I looked cute holding Lillybelle. I smiled poignantly and searched his face for signs that he understood the potential depth of his compliment, but he buried his nose in a book a moment later, so it seemed to be only a passing remark.

IT WAS OVER COFFEE AT JOHN'S mom's house three years later that my spark of curiosity about motherhood began to smolder. Thesla, the eldest sister of four girls born in Honduras, was bossy, sassy, and quick to make a joke. She spoke perfect English and ran the office for a prominent plastic surgeon in Orange County, California. By the time I met her she was several years sober after a humbling struggle with alcoholism, so, though she liked to tease, she was the least judgmental person I had ever met. She loved John deeply, too, which meant she loved me, because he did. So, one day, when I was sipping my café con leche and chattering about the many benefits of John and me living life as a dual-income couple with no children, Thesla laughed in my face, and the shock stopped me mid-sentence. I cocked my head at her Cheshire-cat grin.

"What?" I asked.

"I don't care what you two do with your lives, but you aren't going to convince me there will be no babies," she chuckled.

I chuckled, too, awkwardly, afraid to acknowledge how accurately she had read my mind.

"No," I said shyly, "babies scare me."

She laughed again and stood to pour herself another cup. Then, as fresh coffee tinkled into her mug, without even meeting my eyes, Thesla blew my mind.

"That's just because you haven't met yours yet," she said.

Could that be true? I wondered that night. I was lying awake in bed, listening to John snore, and trying to assess my real feelings. I grew up with parents who expected obedience, so I wasn't in the practice of knowing what I wanted to do, apart from always knowing that I wanted to act, and I tended to hide my feelings so well that even I didn't understand them. *Could I really want a baby?*

The next morning, John caught me on Pinterest, looking at pinned pictures of an adorable, brown-haired girl styled as a pint-sized version of Audrey Hepburn. I flushed but he merely chuckled and kissed my cheek.

"Would you want to have kids one day?" I asked, embarrassed.

"Yeah, definitely," he said casually. "I'm not ready now, but one day."

"Really?" I was trying to process his candid admission. While the idea of having a tiny best friend I could play dress-up with had begun to sound appealing, I still wasn't sure I wanted that life. "What if I don't ever want kids?" I asked, completely seriously. "I mean, I just have never really liked them."

John's eyes moved from my face to the curated Pinterest board of adorable cherubs open on my laptop.

"Sorry, baby, but I think you want kids," he said.

We were engaged within the year.

A FEW MONTHS BEFORE OUR WEDDING, John and I received the devastating news that his mom had been diagnosed with late-stage lung cancer. In true Thesla fashion, she didn't want anyone to make a fuss about her news, insisting instead that she was looking forward to a good party. At the wedding, she gabbed the night away with her sisters, retelling stories of their girlhood in Honduras, pushing our wedding day coffee budget to its max, though she paused her conversations briefly for the Mother–Son/Father–Daughter dance.

My dad hadn't wanted to make a speech at our wedding, which hurt, but he did pay for everything, walk me down the aisle, and concede to one super short turn around the floor, mostly because I assured him that John and Thesla would be dancing, too, and since everyone knew about the cancer, they'd pull focus. With Dad's reluctance, it didn't surprise me that he bowed gracefully and backed quickly away when John's dad, Buddy, asked to cut in. I knew in an instant what the interruption meant and whipped my head around just in time to watch, horrified, as my mom attempted to end John and Thesla's moment. She paid for our honeymoon, and we hadn't planned anything else to honor her, so I guess she figured we owed her. John flatly declined her request to dance, a move she never saw coming, but they were center stage, so, to avoid embarrassment, Mom threw her head back in a laugh and joyously embraced her new in-laws for the song's final refrain.

THESLA PASSED AWAY IN NOVEMBER OF 2014, just two years after our wedding. Before she was gone, she was placed on in-home hospice care, and John and I were lucky enough to visit her one last time. She was being kept comfortable, but she was tired, and much of our visit was spent conversationless, as the rhythmic gasp of her oxygen concentrator underscored our grief. I gave John a lot of alone time with her—I thought they could talk more freely without me there—but he later told me he mostly just rubbed her emaciated back and ached at her fragility. When the day came for us to leave her side, I forced myself to speak.

"Thesla, we have to go," I whispered.

"Oh, okay," she said, and struggled up to a seated position.

"I wish we could stay longer," I stalled. I suddenly felt guilty, realizing that Thesla had never acknowledged her terminality out loud, so maybe I shouldn't either.

"I'm okay," she said. She must have sensed my hesitation. "I've had a good life, you know? It's been really good."

I studied her face, lined a bit and pigmented with her fifty-seven years, and I thought to myself that she had not yet had enough of that good life of hers. It didn't feel fair. My throat clenched.

"I love you," I said, choking on a sob. "I'll miss you so much."

"I'll miss you too, mija," she managed through tears. It was the first and last time Thesla called me "daughter."

I SMILED DOWN AT THE SUNLIGHT glittering off the coastal waters lapping against the hull of our charter boat on the sunshiny morning we scattered Thesla's ashes in California. The natural beauty of the day was tinged with a funny melancholy: On the one hand, Thesla did always like to look her best and would appreciate her send-off happening on such a gorgeous day, but on the other hand, she was gone. I wiped a tear from my cheek and looked at John. His eyes brimmed with a mixture of sorrow and gratitude at the thought of saying goodbye to his mom. I watched as he took a handful of ashes from the pouch of her remains and turned to face the small congregation of loved ones gathered to pay their respects. John spoke about the difficult circumstances surrounding his relationship with his mom. Alcohol had stolen much of his time with her from a young age, but from his vantage there was no drink that could forever dilute her obvious, unconditional love for him and his siblings. For that he was grateful, he said, and I was in awe of his compassion for the human condition.

I didn't get unconditional love in my childhood. I was told I was loved, often, but I was also often left wondering if I was even liked. While I grew up tiptoeing around Mom's feelings, John grew up feeling unconditionally loved and accepted. John missed his mom when she drank, like I missed my dad when he left, but when Dad came back, we pretended like nothing had happened, while Thesla apologized and, once sober, was supportive, kind, and generous in her love. I wondered what it would feel like to grow up feeling sure of a parent's love. I wondered what it must have felt like to turn sixteen and get a hug instead of pain.

Suddenly, I thought about the mother in Milan. Because of my childhood, when I looked at that mother, I saw an entitled woman acting with no regard for anyone else and felt judgmental. John, however, easily saw the different scenarios that might have been at play for her, and he found delight in her humanity. I wondered if the difference in our perspectives was love.

A strange pang struck my heart, and for the first time in my life, I wanted something more than I wanted to be a movie star.

I wanted to love a baby.

CHAPTER TWO

THE VISION

JOHN'S THUMB MOVED IN A GENTLE circle, pressing deeply into the ball of my left foot as we lay sprawled out on our chocolate brown sectional. It was an uncomfortable couch, with its sections constantly sliding apart, but its massive size meant that we could stretch out and still leave room for Sarah, her husband Dave, and my seven-year-old niece, Lillybelle, who had moved to Austin a month before and had happily agreed to be our housemates, saving us all a little money. No one else was home, so John and I were taking in an episode of *The Bachelor* and talking about his mom's passing.

It had been two weeks since Thesla's death, and losing his mom had left a longing in John I had never witnessed before. I leaned forward and wiped a tear forming at the corner of his eye. He pressed his head into my hand and I brought him to my chest, hugging him close, stroking his thick, dark hair. He would miss his wellspring of love, he said as he sat up, dropping my left foot and taking my right, and he had never looked more handsome, backlit by the soft twinkle of our Christmas tree. I caught myself wondering whether a baby made with him would have eyes that burst into liquid gold when the light hit them, like his did. I felt sure he and I could be a wellspring of love for a little one of our own, and the thought brought me back to my childhood.

Growing up, I loved my two sisters to the depths of my soul, in a steadfast, never-even-questioned-it kind of a way. We were best friends as girls, with all three of us sharing a love for sports, board games, and family time, and my very identity was wrapped up in being one of a trio. But as we became young women, life took us on different paths. My older sister Erin broke my heart in high school when she flirted with my boyfriend behind my back, but she apologized, and she was an extension of me, so I forgave her. After graduation, Erin pursued the academic route, studying extensively for various college degrees, until she met a man she wanted to marry and curved all her plans around him. With Erin gone, my little sister Sarah and I became closer than ever, living at home with Mom for several years and working in the same restaurant. We spent all of our free time together and had all the same friends, until one random Sunday when I abandoned Sarah to go on a date with a boy named John. I never apologized, and she never addressed it, and because she was an extension of me, I never realized that there could have been any problem. Sarah eventually moved to a tiny Texas town in pursuit of new faces and spaces, which took her down the young mom route, at which point she rightfully curved all of her plans around her daughter. Both of my sisters chose very different lives than I did, so though they were still my best friends, life forced me to disentangle my own identity from who the three of us were together.

Disentangling my identity from being Dad's daughter wasn't any easier. He was my hero when I was a child. He was gregarious, passionate, and charming, a born leader as evidenced at the pulpit every Sunday, where he delivered sermons about God's love to a rapt congregation. A quintessential girl dad, he coached my competitive soccer and softball teams when I was little, donning bright pink jerseys to match my friends and me, and watching youth sports coaching tapes in his spare time. He also gave me legendary pep talks, and I looked forward to listening to his direction during the long car rides to away games.

But I didn't get enough time with him. One morning, when I was around six years old, our family plan to visit Sea World was delayed because Mom and Dad sat us girls down to explain that they were undergoing a trial separation, a break from their marriage. My sisters and I didn't know what that meant, but it sounded scary, so we cried while our parents bickered, and in the end, Dad walked out the door and Mom took us to Sea World alone. I smiled in pictures all day long, wearing a neon fanny pack and coordinating hat, but my heart ached to be near Dad. He was home again that night, like nothing had happened, and thus began a new family tradition of us girls sitting annual witness to our parents' relationship grievances, then pretending to ignore the day-to-day violent fighting they did behind closed doors as a divorce failed to materialize. Dad closed his congregation when I was around seven, and though we frequented other local churches, he never got back into pastoring, instead growing more emotionally distant by the day. Eventually, he turned to drug use and moved half a state away, proving good on the threat of separation. My parents finally divorced two years after Dad left, in December of the year I turned fourteen. By that time the pain of missing him had already begun to subside and though I still loved him with the deep reverence one reserves for their father, he became a background character in my life.

Mom, of course, was my constant growing up. I loved her implicitly, perfectly, because she was my mommy. She was the person I wanted to hug when I was sad or scared, and when I crawled into bed next to her in the still of the night, battling a bout of anxiety, she wrapped me in her warm, safe arms, and I would feel comforted. It was her opinion of me that mattered the most, so I lived for her approval, learning how to make her feel happy when she was sad. Once, when I was five, I fell sick for several weeks. I could tell that Mom was beside herself with worry, so when I felt well enough, I drew myself smiling among flowers on a sunshiny day—a sign to her that I was on the mend. Mom treasured the drawing, and when she praised my sweet, intuitive ability to understand that a hand-drawn picture was the perfect relief for her, I felt loved. She was fun, too; she loved playing games with us girls, and often told and retold funny anecdotes from when we were babies.

But Mom was also stern and traditional, and I often fell short of her definition of a good girl. I was six when she found out that an older neighborhood boy had taken me into his room, shut the door, and kissed me with his tongue, and no amount of trying to explain that I didn't like what happened to me saved me from her furious spankings. In high school she labeled me a bitch when I argued with her about wanting to see Dad and a whore when she found out I had sex with my boyfriend. She told me I was disrespectful and needed Jesus more times than I could count.

But she was the parent who stayed; she was home, so when a very dear friend of mine died in a motorcycle crash, I crawled into bed with Mom and sobbed, and she wrapped me in her warm, safe arms, just like she did when I was little. She was both my safe place and my biggest bully, so eventually, I learned to self-protect in her presence, to keep an emotional distance from her I never wanted to need.

I blinked the bokeh of our Christmas tree into focus and looked at John. I realized he had been watching me. "Where'd you go?" he asked.

"Oh." My cheeks flushed and I bit my bottom lip to keep from smiling. "I was thinking about love."

"Aww, what kind of love?" He grinned suggestively.

"Families." I met his gaze. "My family."

"Mm," he said. "I've been thinking about family, too."

"What have you been thinking?" I asked.

"Just," he dropped my foot and rubbed the back of his neck, searching the ceiling for his answer. "My mom had a hard life, you know? She was incredible when she was sober, just charming and witty, everyone loved her."

"Yeah, I loved her," I interjected.

"Everyone did, but then she'd pass out and piss herself." My heart hurt for little boy John whenever he talked about Thesla. "But even with every hard moment, there was a lifetime of good that came out of knowing her." I nodded, my eyes filling with tears. "And in the end, she was surrounded by love, by family."

"Yeah, it's like, what else do you have in the end?" My question was rhetorical, but John nodded.

"I was thinking the same thing. We all go, this all ends at some point. At the end, ideally speaking, who do you want there with you?"

My heart skipped a beat.

"Yeah, it makes you think," I answered cautiously. "Who do you want there in the end?"

"I mean, ideally, you, if you're alive."

I laughed and fiddled with my wedding ring.

"And my kids," John said, and he looked at me at last.

"Yeah, same page," I said.

"I don't think there's anything else in life." He took my right foot again and rubbed it softly.

"I think we should have a baby," I said, cutting to the chase.

"Oh." John sounded surprised but not opposed. "Do you think you're ready?"

"Yeah, I mean, it's scary," I shrugged and pulled my hair into a ponytail as I stammered. "But it's exciting, it's creating a family."

"It's creating love," he said.

"But someone to give my love to. I've always felt like I had to hold back, you know? I couldn't really love all out," I said. John cocked his head. "I mean not you, obviously I go all out on you."

He grinned. "Yeah you do."

"Stop, not like that," I laughed. "I love my sisters but they have their own lives, you know? I mean, I love my mom and dad, too, but—"

"You have to be a certain way with them," he finished.

"Exactly. But a baby? I'm allowed to love a baby—"

"Shamelessly."

A smile opened wide across my face, threatening to betray the truth of my enthusiasm, so I averted my eyes as I nodded, and we sat in silence for a moment.

"Do you think you're ready?" I finally asked.

"Yeah," he said simply, and my jaw inadvertently dropped open.

"Just like that?" I asked.

"Yeah." He dropped my foot and grabbed my wrist. "So should we get started, or . . ."

I giggled as he pulled me onto his lap.

ONCE A BABY WAS ON THE table, I found myself daydreaming about our future life as a family. I knew we'd have a boy, a simple surety with no logical worldly basis, and I wondered if he would have the same dark eyebrows and wry smile I loved so much on John. I hoped he would inherit John's quick, affable laugh and some of his half-Honduran, half-Argentine blood, so that he'd fare well on sunny days. I was born with the same pale, easily fry-able skin that Dad had, and I always hated having to slather on thick glops of sunscreen to protect myself from wrinkles and age spots. But not John. His skin became a beautiful, tawny shade of brown in the sun. I hoped for that for our future baby—less hassle and more attractive anyway.

There were more practical things to consider, too. Babies were expensive, and though we both had stable jobs, we weren't making a ton of money. I knew we needed a budget and an estimate of what our monthly expenses might turn into, to get a reasonable understanding of what our financial life would become if we added a baby. Sharing a house with Sarah was working okay, particularly because we had been concentrating on paying off our student loan debt and building a savings, but I knew I eventually wanted a space of our own, a space where a baby could grow up. I daydreamed about a suburban new-build, with granite countertops and a yard, in a neighborhood with neighbors who would become friends. *I'm really buying into the whole traditional American family thing,* I laughed to myself as I logged into our bank account to assess our finances.

Our child will get my brain, though, I said to myself, and about that fact, I was sure. I wanted a Lorelai Gilmore experience if I had a baby, with much pithy chatter about books and '90s pop music and classic romcoms, so I knew I wanted to read a lot to my little male Rory. And I hoped our child would be interested in the arts. After all, they'd have a mom who planned to be a famous movie star since she was eight years old, and—

Oh, right. That thought stopped me in my tracks. I had wanted to be an actor my entire life, and a baby never fit into that picture. I knew that actors were famously busy spending long hours on set and doing drugs at parties, not that I was eager to partake in the latter (I knew the dangers from Dad, after all), but I always assumed a movie star would need to at least be present enough at such functions to appear glamorous, and to have clever anecdotes to share on talk shows later, and a baby wouldn't allow for that.

Maybe it would, I argued internally. Maybe the movie star dream I'd held since childhood could expand to include a baby. Maybe I would birth a baby so well-behaved and adorable as to be universally beloved. I could bring such a baby to set. I imagined myself practicing lines in the hair and makeup chair as beautiful, loving, doting John arrived with the baby for a visit. He'd look really hot carrying a diaper bag, and I'd stop production to breastfeed and give my family affection. The cast and crew would be charmed by our loving dynamic and would insist on saying hello, and then after a sufficient, succinct while, John and baby would go. I'd blow kisses and wave goodbye, then take a deep breath and refocus on my work.

It'll be fine, I told myself. A baby would need to slot into our lives. I didn't want to be one of those mothers who made their entire personality about their child. I was clever and artistic and driven, and I didn't want to sacrifice my very favorite parts of myself for a baby.

"Do you feel like you lost yourself when you had Lillybelle?" I asked Sarah one day. She thought for a while, and the pause made me nervous for her answer.

"Definitely," she finally said, and my heart sank. "I think so, at least. I had her really young, though. My self wasn't identified yet anyway."

"Is it as hard as everyone says?" I braced for impact.

"Oh yeah, for sure."

"But only at first, right? It gets easier? As they grow you kind of settle in?" Sarah thought for a moment again, and I could tell that she was choosing her words carefully.

"Not really," she said at last. "I mean, yes. They eventually sleep better, which means you do too, but then it just evolves. It gets more complicated as they get bigger."

"But you're able to handle it, right? You learn and adapt?" I asked.

"Sure," Sarah replied in a tone that meant *no*. "And on the days when you can't handle it, you can always go into the next room and scream into a pillow."

I will never do that, I thought, offended by the idea that a grown-up could ever become so frustrated with a tiny baby that they'd have to bury their unavoidable guttural roaring. I mentally dismissed Sarah's answers as ridiculous. *John and I aren't young and dumb anymore*, I told myself. *We can handle a baby.*

I began researching hospital costs. We had good insurance but never had to use it, so I didn't know anything about deductibles or copays or in- versus out-of-network medical providers, and the learning curve was steep. *Will I even be able to take a maternity leave?* I wondered. I needed to look into how much vacation time I had accrued and if my company would allow me any additional time off to bond with my baby. I wanted John to have some time off, too. I wanted us both to be home with our baby, if we were to have one, to experience the first few weeks of his life as a unit. *Then I suppose I'll need to look into daycare after that,* I thought. A quick Google search produced childcare numbers that dizzied my head.

"How do people do this?" I asked John. "I mean other regular, two-income people. How do we afford this?"

"I actually asked my buddy about that today," came John's reply.

"You did?" My eyes crinkled from my grin.

"Yeah, he and his wife used to go out a lot."

"Like us!" I chirped.

"Exactly like us. He said that whatever you're spending on fun stuff now just ends up being spent on the baby instead," John explained.

"So, the baby is the only fun stuff you get to do?" I asked, and he laughed.

"That's what they say, right?"

"Are you okay with that?" I had to be sure he knew what he was signing up for.

"I'm okay with that. Are you okay with that?" he said in reply, evidently wanting to make sure I knew what I was signing up for, too.

The question made me think about my parents. Their first pregnancy was an accident—a surprise, my mom would always say—and I wondered if that had been hard. It had to have been. I wondered if Mom had any time to look into deductibles, or if Dad had asked a friend for advice on how to budget for a baby. *Probably not*, I thought. John and I were already light-years ahead of them in our parenting preparation. We would do things right.

WE SAT ON THE UNCOMFORTABLE COUCH again a week later, in the light of our Christmas tree. While John laughed at a rerun of *The Office*, I imaged us in a year's time: I would sip holiday coffee, and we would pile gifts around the tree. On Christmas morning, surrounded by a room full of friends and family, we'd merrily revel in the love of our brand-new baby. We would start our own holiday traditions, too: Santa photos at the mall, holiday handprint crafts, and sentimental recipes.

My mind then made the leap from holidays to birthdays, and I imagined those would go much the same: We would be in a room full of love; we would watch as our child blew out his candles; and we would shower him with a responsible, reasonable amount of educational gifts to enrich his mind. *Of course*, I thought, *we would never give him screen time*, because we would be the kind of parents who would be present and engaged at all times, who would actually like talking to their kid, who would plan for his future and help him to thrive. And as he grew, I mused, we would discuss his feelings, naming every emotion and coaching him on how to handle hard things, so he'd never have to make his feelings someone else's problem. We would enroll him in competitive sports and attend weekend tournaments, where John could coach, like my dad coached me.

I could see it all, our whole life stretched out before me in my mind's eye: a glorious vision. And above all, the central theme would be love. We would be the perfect parents. We would love our baby and love each other, too, and we would create a little world for ourselves where family only ever meant love, not pain.

My daydream ended there, and I focused back on reality, on an episode of *The Office* where the actress who played Pam was visibly pregnant. I sat up and gasped.

"See! I can have a baby and still act!" I yelled, to John's amusement.

"Definitely," he agreed. "Tons of actors have kids." I grinned ear to ear at his confirmation.

"And once I'm a movie star you can be a stay-at-home dad," I said.

"Um, deal!" He held his hand up for a high-five.

"So, we're doing this?" I asked.

"Looks like it," John said with a wiggle of his fingers, and when I smacked his hand with mine, he gripped my wrist, and I let him pull me into his embrace.

CHAPTER THREE

THE EFFORT

"I CAN'T BELIEVE WE'RE GOING TO MAKE a baby," John said the evening we decided to try.

"On purpose," I replied with a laugh.

He laughed, too, and I realized I suddenly felt incredibly uncomfortable. Our sex life had always been for pleasure, not purpose.

"You're going to cum inside of me," I said, slightly dumbfounded.

"On purpose," he replied, and we laughed again. Something about the mechanics of getting pregnant suddenly had me feeling childish and unprepared, but John had a way of perceiving and gently easing my anxieties before I'd even voiced them. It was a skill that would make him an incredible father, I thought.

"It makes me feel sort of weird," I ventured. "I've only ever tried to prevent this from happening."

I was instructed on how to be a good girl my entire childhood. Good girls were quiet, nice, and obedient to their parents. The one thing they were not was sexual. I was eleven the first time my parents talked to me about saving my virginity for my husband. It was confusing to have a conversation about the way I should conduct myself in the middle of the breakdown of my parents' marriage, but I was a good girl, so I paid attention. Mom and Dad didn't tell me what sex was, but they did tell me it was sacred, special, and meant to be shared between a husband and wife who loved each other. *That's why it's called making love,* they said. They told me that good girls saved themselves for marriage.

"We want you to be a good girl," Mom and Dad said.

"Did you wait until marriage?" eleven-year-old me innocently asked.

Mom took a sip of her coffee and Dad tried to mask a smile.

"You didn't!" I accused.

"I wish I would have, and I want you to learn from our mistakes," Mom said, and the good girl in me quietly agreed to obey.

It was a promise I didn't keep. I was fifteen the first time I bought condoms. Dad had been living a ten-hour drive away from our house for at least three years, and since he'd left, Mom had brought her new boyfriend to an overnight family trip with us girls, so though I was still as quiet and nice and obedient as possible, my opinion on whether good girls had sex outside of marriage had changed. Having an older, more popular boyfriend with his own car and a generous allowance, I had been regularly sexually active for months. And while safeguarding myself from the potential consequences of said actions had typically been outsourced to said boyfriend, I unexpectedly found myself voluntarily bopping into a seedy convenience store one sunny afternoon to buy our condoms. The boyfriend hated this particular store because they kept the condoms behind the counter.

"You have to ask the guy to hand them to you. It's demeaning, like you need permission or something," he complained. In the grand tradition of fiscally well-endowed California kids, such displays of authority had always bothered him.

"I'll get them," I offered.

"No, you don't have to do that," he said, unbuckling his seat belt.

"I know, I don't mind," I insisted, already out of the car. "I don't have any money, though, so you still have to pay." I held out my hand palm up, and he laughed as he tugged a twenty from his wallet. I could tell he was proud of me.

Once inside the store all confidence drained from my body as the thirty-something-year-old clerk looked me up and down. I wished I hadn't worn such a tight-fitting shirt. I was able to fake confidence, though, so I looked him square in the eyes, smiled brightly, and asked for what I needed.

"Can I get those Extra Ribbed Trojans," I asked, pointing to the wall of contraceptives behind the clerk's head, "and these."

The Altoids tin clanked when I tossed it onto the counter, sending a tiny jolt of surprise through the clerk. He looked at me with mildly amused astonishment and rang me up in silence. I felt his judgment, though, mixed with something else, like jealousy or nostalgia, and the convenience store employee knowing such intimate details as the type of condom I liked and the curve of my underage form in a cotton-elastane blend made me feel ashamed. I suddenly felt every bit the whore Mom told me I was.

"Have fun," the clerk said, handing me the condoms and my boyfriend's change, and with that I was out the door.

Beginning that day, and for the many sexy years to follow, I preferred lovemaking that achieved three aims in equal measure: enjoyment, avoidance of fertilization, and the complete and utter separation of my sex life from all public scrutiny. Having a baby went against two of those. While my enthusiastic participation in the act had on occasion caused me some exposure, such as friends overhearing a college dorm room romp, it produced a manageable cocktail of emotion in me, a shy pride I could laugh away. Pregnancy, however, would be carrying the evidence of my sex life around every day, a level of publicity that felt painfully vulnerable.

"Do you want to *try* try, though?" John asked, just as I began an anxiety spiral toward existential crisis.

"What do you mean?"

"It just seems like a lot of pressure on something so fun," he replied.

John had attended a bachelor party weekend with friends some years back, where he chatted with the only other married guy present. The man, a longtime acquaintance, had recently become a father, and while he was thrilled at having welcomed his baby into the world, he openly lamented the unfortunate experience of trying to conceive. Apparently, the couple encountered some fertility frustrations, so the man's wife would swing from depressed to laser-focused on the mechanics of conception, rendering sex an unhappy chore. I hated this story from the moment I heard it, both for the blatantly disrespectful way the man casually shared private details of his marital sex life and for the embarrassingly melodramatic characterization of the wife once she became obsessed with having a baby.

My older sister Erin experienced a similar baby obsession. Erin's periods were, unfortunately, sporadic, which meant that, when she and her husband started trying for a baby, she'd miss a period, they'd get their hopes up, and then menstruation would spontaneously materialize to dash those hopes, leaving Erin feeling faulty and dejected. As she navigated the thrashing sea of emotions that fertility issues had conjured within her, her husband rolled his eyes because he thought her reactions were ridiculous. Erin would rebound after every failed attempt, diving into research on the nitty-gritty of conception, while her hubby would resign himself to the fact that there would be more boring, obligatory sex in his future.

The lesson of both my sister's experience and the bachelor party story was obvious to me: Overthinking the whole pregnancy thing made for controlling and excessively emotional women, which was unsexy. And I liked being sexy.

"I think it'll get too stressful if we put too much pressure on things," I said in reply to John's question, tossing my hair off my shoulder to seem as go-with-the-flow as possible.

"Yeah. And I don't want sex to become some kind of boring means to an end," John said, confirming all of my fears.

"Neither do I! No, thank you," I said, and meant it.

"And I still feel like our relationship is enough even if we don't end up having a baby," John said, kindly.

My stomach jumped up into my throat at the idea, but I gulped it back down with barely a wince.

"Totally!" I exclaimed. "Yeah, no yeah, same page."

I knew in the back of my mind that I was lying, but the good girl in me really wanted to remain agreeable. So I decided I would save everyone some grief and simply pretend to be extra horny over the subsequent weeks. That way John could have fun, and I could make a baby, and no one had to stress out about the process.

This plan worked beautifully—right up until the day my period came.

My period wasn't due for a few days, but fantasies of learning I'd made a baby on my very first try proved too tempting to ignore, so, with my stomach in knots, I ducked into a pharmacy suggested by Google, in a part of town I didn't frequent, and made my way to the family planning section confident I would be avoiding any awkward public encounters with anyone I knew. The shelf of pink and blue pregnancy tests, which had long been a thing of avoidance, suddenly bore the entirety of my focus. I looked each over, front and back, and read the promises advertised, but I couldn't tell which test was best. I was astounded at the price tags for such little boxes, but then I remembered that the contents held the power to reveal vital sensitive information, information I wanted as accurate as possible. *Better get the most expensive one*, I thought, and grabbed the twenty-dollar two-pack.

When I turned, I saw that the cashier was male and cursed my luck. I headed down the candy aisle as if I had always meant to and hunted around for a sweet treat to give the guy a chance to go on break. I grabbed some taffy, then a soda, and finally a bag of Flamin' Hot Cheetos before deciding I could stall no longer. I turned to face my fears of publicly declaring my recent sexual activity, placed my items on the checkout counter, and felt stupid when the cashier unceremoniously rang me up. He hadn't even made eye contact with me; he clearly didn't care in any way that the woman before him was grappling with complicated feelings about goodness and sex and pregnancy.

"Have fun," he said, as he handed me my bag, which made me laugh. I could tell he meant it—that he was wishing me luck with the results of my test, whatever the desired outcome may be—and I appreciated the moment of levity he provided. I opened my mouth to tell him my life story, but he pulled out his phone and turned away because he didn't care, which made me laugh again.

Maybe I care a little too much about how I'm perceived, I thought.

Once home, I went to the bathroom and looked down in shock and wretched dismay at the blood stain on my undies. I had planned to pee on one of the fancy sticks I bought, but the evil red spot on my white and blue checkered briefs stopped me cold. After a month of pretending I wasn't trying, I also wasn't pregnant.

For a tiny moment I thought about taking a pregnancy test anyway, with the hope that I was experiencing some sort of false period, but then I remembered the cost and changed my mind. Instead, I sat there feeling ridiculous.

I knew I was supposed to be calm. I knew I was supposed to be okay with "letting it happen if it was going to happen." I had been so good at seeming very no-pressure about the process for weeks, but suddenly my intense interest in becoming pregnant was more difficult to conceal. Tears formed as I struggled to swallow my feelings. I peed, wiped, and inserted a tampon before diving onto my bed with my laptop, tears streaming.

The results from my "fertile window explained" search query led me to an online forum full of women who were ttc. I felt a pang of shame when I realized from context that the acronym meant *trying to conceive*. It was not a forum for girls married to their indifference about pregnancy, as I was pretending to be. It was a forum for women sharing information to help other women in their unabashedly emotional pursuit of motherhood. It was the type of forum, with post after post of women moving in solidarity on parallel paths, that my sister had probably perused. I wondered if she, or the wife in the bachelor party story, had read these very words. I didn't like the thought, and something like disgust washed over me. I didn't want to be like these women, obsessing so hard about conceiving a child that they were unable to see how clinical and tiresome they had become. *These women are ridiculous,* I thought. *They're probably making their partners miserable.*

I exited the forum and navigated instead to a website that explained the science of fertile windows in sterile, biological terms. There, I learned what I hadn't been taught in school or during the good girl training days of my childhood.

Day one of my period was day one of my cycle, I read, and a twenty-eight-day cycle meant that I probably ovulated on day fourteen. My stomach backflipped with delight. Day fourteen was just two short weeks away. I marked the date on my cell phone calendar with a cat emoji and went back to my research. Next, I learned that my egg was good for twenty-four hours, but sperm could wait around inside me for up to five days and still fertilize an egg when it dropped. That meant my fertile window was six days long. This blew my mind because I had been having so much sex on so many of the wrong days of the month! I opened my calendar again and added more cat emojis. Satisfied with my new knowledge and feeling sufficiently prepared for six days of banging it out in the month ahead, I closed my laptop with a smile.

When my period came again exactly twenty-eight days later, I felt cheated. The internet's baby-making formula was adhered to with precision: The requisite sperm had been deposited into my fertile female reproductive tract on the specified days. So why the hell was I bleeding? The frustration burned low in my chest and radiated from gut to throat. I felt like I could spit fire. Instead, I opened my laptop and practically sprinted to the Ridiculous Women Forum.

The first useful post I read on the Ridiculous Women Forum offered information about cervical position and feel, including reference links to the original poster's source material. Thanks to that ridiculous woman, I marched into the bathroom, washed my hands, and felt around until I could confirm that one's cervix would indeed be low in the vaginal canal and firm to the touch during bleeding. I grinned at my reflection in the mirror as I washed the blood off my hands and wondered if my sister had checked her cervix, too.

Next, another ridiculous woman had posted about the various changes to the look and texture of her vaginal discharge, otherwise known as cervical mucus, during her cycle. *Fascinating*, I thought, and when my period was over, I marched into the bathroom again. This time, I felt for a cervix that had moved higher in the vaginal canal and was still firm to the touch. I really had to jam my hand up there to find it. If John had walked in at that moment, he would have been ecstatic at my zealous thrusting. I laughed at the idea. The moment was purely scientific, however, so I locked the bathroom door. Then, I moved on to examining my cervical mucus, which was dry and sticky, as expected. I was not fertile at that moment.

The Sisterhood of the Ridiculous Women Forum was brilliant. Over the next two weeks, I diligently stuck my clean hand inside of myself to track the changes in my cervix and discharge. As I neared the ovulation date noted on my calendar, I eagerly awaited the arrival of my own forum-coveted *ewcm*, or egg-white cervical mucus.

According to the brilliant women I had entrusted with my fertility, it was slippery discharge that adhered to and stretched between one's pointer finger and thumb when they were tapped together.

Ewcm signaled ovulation. I checked for ewcm on my calendar's ovulation date, but instead of finding something stretchy I discovered the same old slippery discharge. I tap, tap, tapped my fingers, and noticed the tiniest bit of stretch in the liquid, but it looked nothing like an egg white. Disappointed, I took straight to the internet, where another brilliant woman gave me my answer: Ovulation dates could vary month to month. My jaw dropped in disbelief, and I clicked the source link she provided. There, in black and white, was confirmation. A fertile window was merely an estimation.

When my period came again on the next day twenty-eight, I felt a flood of panic rise in me, like sea water filling a cove. It had been three months of pretending I wasn't trying, and I was starting to forget what had consumed my thoughts before existing in baby-making limbo. I swallowed my disappointment and tapped ten tiny cat emojis into my phone, saving them in my calendar on days eleven through twenty of my cycle. *John will be having so much fun this month*, I thought with a laugh.

"Do you feel like I'm using you?" I asked John after our third coital romp of the month.

"What?! No," came the reply. "Why, are you?" he asked.

"No, not even," I said, and I meant it. John was my best friend and had proven himself to be an understanding person. But I was emotionally raw from my secret fertility journey, and I didn't want my emotions judged and dismissed as ridiculous, as so many women before me had experienced.

It was then I realized, in horror, that I was guilty of judging and dismissing those women myself. I had once judged those women for daring to use sex as an unsexy means to an end. I had once dismissed those women who were unable to control the emotional sea of their deep maternal longing as silly. I had once found it ridiculous that those women couldn't just be quiet, and nice, and obedient for the sake of their partners.

Then, in a moment of brutal self-honesty, I realized I had become one of those women I had always criticized. I laughed, embarrassed by my old, snotty attitude, and said a silent apology to my sister, to the woman in John's bachelor party story, and to the brilliant women from the Ridiculous Women Forum, who had taught me so much. I hoped being one of those women meant I would one day have the bravery to live my emotional experience authentically, visibly, whether the way I chose to conduct myself was agreeable or not.

On day fourteen of that cycle, I saw the unmistakable stretch of ewcm. John was elated by my enthusiasm in the bedroom, so I employed my feminine wiles again on day fifteen for good measure. By day twenty, my nipples were fizzy, a brand-new sensation that felt as though the skin cells that made up my areolas had become carbonated, like a soda. On day twenty-four, I hesitated when John offered me a beer during our weekly episode of *The Bachelor*, and it was then that I knew the month felt different. Day twenty-eight of my cycle came and went without a bleed, and I woke up on day twenty-nine more calm, present, and excited than I had ever felt. Though it was a Friday, my typical day off from work, my eyes popped open at the first blaring tone of John's alarm. I jumped up and made a coffee while John groggily rubbed the sleep from his eyes.

"You don't have to get up yet," he croaked.

"I know. Can't sleep," I said, and danced around to hold my pee.

John showered and dressed and ate his scrambled eggs, then headed out the door. I waved from the front porch, trying not to pee my pants, and just about burst when he doubled back.

"Forgot something," he said, and he let his bag slip from his grasp. It thudded on the pavement at our feet as he slipped his right hand under the back of my shirt and gripped the base of my skull with his left. He planted a deep kiss that froze the world for a moment.

"See ya tonight, cutie," he said, pulling away with a wink.

That guy knocked me up, I thought, grinning ear to ear, and I felt unapologetically sexy.

I ran inside as John drove away and took a pregnancy test with my heart pounding in my ears. I laid the stick flat, face down, and distracted myself with a forgotten novel I found tucked into my bedside table. Once my heart rate had calmed and I felt sufficiently capable of meeting the moment, I dog-eared my page in the book and flipped the plastic test over upright.

"Oh my God!" I screamed.

I was pregnant.

CHAPTER FOUR

THE NEWS

TWO LITTLE PINK LINES, ONE DARKER than the other, stared up at me from the First Response test I held in my hands. Slack-jawed and unable to comprehend the full magnitude of those lines, I stared back. I had wanted to get pregnant and had taken deliberate action to achieve my aim, and now, as I clutched the very proof of the fruitfulness of my endeavors in my hands, I sat rigid and immobile and terrified.

What the hell did I do?

"Oh my God," I finally uttered.

"Oh my God, oh my God, oh my God," I said on repeat.

"OH MY GOD!" I laughed in disbelief. *Okay, Shawna, say something else*, I thought.

I moved from my perch on the edge of my bed to a full-length mirror on the wall. I wanted to see what I looked like now that I was pregnant, but the person who met my gaze seemed to be the same girl I always saw there: dirty blond, bright-eyed, and guarded. I stared for a moment as she turned this way and that, my eyes dropping to her low belly. She lifted her shirt to allow me a peek, but all I saw was the same creamy skin and soft tummy that had always been there. She reached up with her left hand and squeezed one boob and then the other.

"Ow," she squeaked, grimacing. Those things were extra tender to an almost absurd degree, and when she met my eye in the mirror, I remembered why. She tried to keep her face neutral, but a quake of acceptance cracked across her lips and she doubled over with a laugh, looking down at the positive pregnancy test in her right hand. She gasped and covered her astonished mouth, and I could taste the sweat of my palm.

I had to tell someone.

It has to be John first, though, I thought as I walked downstairs, where I found my housemate, my sister Sarah, reading leisurely on the couch. She worked in a dental office that had half days on Fridays, so her weekend had just begun. I inhaled sharply and sat in the armchair to her right without a word.

"Hey," Sarah said, with her face still buried in her e-reader.

"Hey," I practically whispered. She looked at me with concern. I must have looked every bit as emotionally fraught as I felt.

"You okay?" she asked.

"Mhm," I mumbled.

My eyes, however, told her a different story, and she gave me a quizzical look I knew meant *you're full of fucking shit tell me right now* in the secret language of sisters we had been honing our entire lives.

"You sure?" she pressed.

I licked my lips to quell a smile.

"What?!" she said in a hush.

"You have to be really, really quiet," I said, matching her tone. Her husband had taken the day off, too, and was in the next room. He didn't get to know before John knew.

"What?! What's up?" she whispered, ditching her e-reader and scooching closer to me, excited for what was obviously going to be a juicy private chat.

"Okay, you cannot tell anyone." I was wide-eyed and pale with shock, so she knew I meant it.

"Yeah, totally." She meant it, too.

I took a deep breath and grinned ear to ear. "I'm pregnant."

"You're what?" she asked. I'd uttered the phrase so quietly she hadn't even heard me.

"I'm pregnant," I said more audibly.

"YOU'RE PREGNANT?!" she whisper-screamed, and I shushed her with a laugh.

Then, Sarah unexpectedly began sobbing into her hands.

"Oh my God, are you crying?" I asked, choking a cry of my own back down my throat.

She nodded, eyes closed and face hidden, and for a moment we sat in silence and let our shoulders heave. Finally, she wiped her face and looked up.

"When did you find out?" she asked, and I laughed to stifle the guilt of having told her before John.

"Just now. I just took a test."

Sarah sobbed again, this time without hiding her face, and adjusted her seat so that the entirety of her body was facing mine.

"Am I the first person to know?" she asked.

Tears fell from my eyes when I nodded, so she stood up and hugged me to her chest. She swept the hair out of my eyes and kissed the top of my head. I hugged both of my arms around her middle and for a moment we held each other without a word. I had never before been so grateful that my little sister knew how to be a mother.

"When are you telling John?" she asked after she sat back down.

"He gets off work at five."

THE ENERGY SHIFTS FROM MUNDANE TO electrifying whenever John enters a room. It's my favorite thing about him. So, when the hairs on my forearms stood up with a jolt that Friday evening, I knew that he was home. My heart leapt into my throat, and I rushed to stuff one last sheet of bright blue tissue paper into the festive gift bag before me. John was about to learn that he would become a father through an adorably curated gift: three tiny newborn onesies rolled and stuffed into a beer mug with the phrase BEST DADDY EVER etched into its glass.

"Hey, gorgeous," came the greeting as John reached the top of the stairs.

"Hey," I said, breathless in my attempt at appearing casual. "How was work?"

"I don't want to talk about work." He wrapped his arms around my waist and pulled me in for a kiss.

I wondered if our baby could feel the butterflies. I tried to pull away, eager for the big reveal, but he didn't let go.

"I can't breathe," I giggled, and wriggled free.

"So, what did you do all day?" he asked.

"Some pretty exciting stuff, actually," I said, indicating with my eyes that he should look at the gift bag waiting for him on our bed.

"Oh yeah, like what?" John walked past me and into the bathroom, completely oblivious to his looming surprise.

"John!" I called out with probably a bit too much annoyance.

"Huh?" He popped his head past the bathroom doorframe to look at me.

"Well, not while you're peeing!" I said, and shooed him back in.

I sat on the corner of our bed feeling slightly let down that such a significant moment was facing unforeseen delays. When he finally finished, John stepped out of the bathroom and launched himself, torpedo-style, onto our bed. I laughed, but I wanted to yell at him.

"What are you doing?" I asked, again with a bit too much annoyance.

"What do you mean?" he asked, still oblivious.

"Are you serious?" I pressed.

"What?" He somehow had no idea what I was talking about.

I pointed to the gift bag occupying the space between us and spoke slowly. "I got you something."

John's eyes came aglow. "Aw, thanks! That's so nice," he said, making me feel terrible for being annoyed with him, which I still was.

"Did you really not see this beautifully arranged gift bag waiting for you on our bed?" I questioned.

"No, I did, I just figured we were going to a birthday party or something." It was the classic John reply: humble, selfless, and kind. I felt even worse.

"Nope," I squeaked out, "it's for you."

My husband stood and casually pulled the gift that would change his life from its bag.

"Oh, nice," he said simply when he saw the mug. He turned it over in his hand, and I searched his face with my heart pounding in my ears as he read the inscription. I was desperate to no longer be alone on the precipice of our new path. But John laughed, a ridiculing kind of a laugh, which shocked me. He leaned toward me and put his hand under my chin, tilting my gaze to his.

"Mmm, 'Best Daddy Ever,' huh?" he said in a low, sexy growl.

"What?!" I asked in disbelief. The air in the room turned slightly awkward as he slowly let go of my face.

"It says 'Best Daddy Ever.' Like . . . I'm your Daddy," he said in all sincerity.

"John, take the clothes out of the mug," I instructed.

"Oh, I thought that was just some kind of stuffing," he explained, and I began to rethink the many years I had spent devoted to a man so stupid. I bit my tongue, though, because he was unrolling the first onesie.

"Aw, how cute. This must be for, like, a teddy bear or something," was the response.

"It's not for a teddy bear, John," I seethed.

"What? Really? Is it super stretchy or something? I can't wear this."

"Are you doing this on purpose?" I demanded to know. He must have been.

"Wait, sorry. I'm messing your gift up, aren't I?" he asked sincerely. He really was clueless.

"John, that's a onesie. See the snaps at the crotch?" Outwardly, I was exhibiting the patience of a saint, but on the inside I was screaming and clawing the walls like a lunatic.

"Okay, so a onesie. Like for a baby?" he asked, really circling the entire point.

"Yes," I said plainly.

"And the mug . . ." he started and, just when I moved to get the stupid stick I had peed on, he pieced it together.

"YOU'RE PREGNANT?!" he yelled.

"YES! Finally!" I laughed.

"REALLY?!" he yelled again as he torpedoed himself through the air again, this time taking me to the bed with him.

"Don't!" I yelped, and he rolled a quarter turn to my left. Then he held my face in his hands, and with tears in his eyes, kissed my forehead. He was elated, and electric again, as usual.

We lay like that for thirty more minutes, talking logistics: when we thought it happened, what we thought the due date would be, where we thought we could fit a crib.

"It's just one baby, right?" John asked. "Or is it three?"

"What! I hope it's not three!" I chuckled nervously.

"Well, just because you put three onesies in this thing," John turned his new beer mug over in his hands.

"Ohh," I said, following his logic. "No, it just looked stupid with only one onesie."

"What if it's three?" he teased me, grinning.

"I can't even think about that," I confessed, and then after a moment, I asked, "Are you happy?" The question tumbled out of its own volition because I hadn't even realized that I didn't know the answer. But as my lips moved, I felt an urgent need to hear what he would say next.

"Yeah! Oh yeah, I'm so excited," came the response, and with it, a flood of relief. "Are you?" he asked, the question giving my soul whiplash.

"Of course!" I squealed, but the truth was I was feeling a great many emotions I couldn't name, not all of them positive. I didn't have the best experience being mothered, and now, I was willingly accepting the role myself.

"When do you want to tell everyone?" John eagerly asked.

I winced, thinking about my mom.

Mom was sensitive to decisions made without her knowledge or input. When I was eight years old, before Dad had discovered the blissful absolution of crystal meth, Mom took a week-long vacation to Mexico with my aunt and grandmother, a break everyone said she needed. While she was gone, Dad was primary parent for my sisters and me, and he was able to get us out of bed, fed, off to school in the mornings, and to our various sporting activities in the evenings in what was a relatively cheerful week. Mom was due home on Sunday, and I couldn't wait to hug her, to have both of my parents feeling calm and happy at the same time. But on Friday, I got it into my head that I wanted a haircut. Specifically, I coveted the idea of a chin-length bob. I had never had a hairstyle so short before, and I was positive I would love it. Having had an agreeable several days with Dad, I liked my chances, and so presented my haircut case by stating my aim and pleading with all my might. Unfortunately, Dad resisted.

"I don't think Mommy will like that," he said. Mom loved my long hair.

"But why?" I pressed.

"I don't know," he admitted. "Mommy likes what she likes."

"But it's my hair!" I argued, and that got him.

The moment I entered SuperCuts on Saturday morning, however, I felt unsure. I suddenly recalled a scene—I couldn't tell if it was a memory from some months earlier or if I had been given a premonition—where I asked Mom if I could cut my hair short, and she gave me a firm no. I anxiously began to shift my weight from right foot to left and wondered if by getting my hair cut I would be considered disobedient, a descriptor that was threatening to embed itself in my burgeoning sense of identity. I really didn't want to get in trouble with Mom.

"Will Mom be mad?" I asked.

"Nah," Dad lied. "If she is, she'll be mad at me."

"I think Mom would say no," I said, sure Dad would let me back out.

"Well, I'm saying yes." He didn't let me back out, and instead put both of his hands on my shoulders and pointed me to a stylist. I sat in a big leather pump chair and let the woman cut eight inches off my hair.

The next day, when the front door swung open to signal Mom's return, the mood in the house swung as well, and suddenly our cheerful week felt tricky. Mom surveyed the living room, clucking the back of her throat and raising her eyebrows at the tidy state of things, all the while muttering, "Oh, wow," in mock praise. It seemed like she had expected things to run poorly without her and was upset to see that everything was fine.

Then, Mom's eyes fell on me, and my hair. I greeted her with an enthusiastic hug, excited to have her home, but she radiated irritation. I began to explain why I made the decision I had, but Mom wasn't interested in listening to reason. Instead, she accused me of deliberate disobedience and suggested that I should have known that Dad granting me permission to cut my hair didn't nullify her no.

So it was *a memory*, I thought and looked to Dad for backup.

He, however, threw his hands up in exasperation and walked away. Abandoned, I watched Mom press her anger between her lips.

"I can't deny that you look cute, though!" she suddenly said with a smile, absolving me of my guilt.

"Thanks!" I said, beaming at the compliment. Then, feeling bold, I chirped, "I told you so!"

And at that Mom took her suitcase into her room, called for Dad, and shut the door. I tried to believe their screaming match wasn't about me.

Despite having been an adult for more than a decade, I still felt nervous breaking news to Mom, so John and I started our baby news announcement tour right away with the known cheerleaders: our sisters. My older sister, Erin, having given birth to her beautiful baby girl, Audra, thirteen months prior, whooped with delight. We screamed and cried and felt so enthusiastic about all the cousin fun our children would have together. John's younger sister, Thesla, named for his mom, cried tears of joy and congratulations and promised she would be the first to visit whenever we were ready. We were off to a good start.

Next, we told our other roommates. Sarah had begged to be the one to tell her husband, Dave, so we gave her the go-ahead, and when we got home from a movie on Saturday, he greeted us with hugs and a toast in our honor: champagne for John and non-alcoholic sparkling apple cider for me. Lillybelle, though, required a more delicate approach. Being my niece and the first baby I'd ever loved, I didn't want her to feel like she was being replaced—especially because my baby was going to come live in our house, *her* house. And while Lillybelle had spent six long years as the only niece and grandchild on our side of the family, she had recently acquired a baby cousin who was stealing a whole lot of familial attention away from her. These factors combined meant that she was likely to feel a bit sensitive to our news. So, on Sunday morning we gave our sweet niece a sweet treat, sat her down between her mom and dad, and told her the plain truth.

"Lilly, we are having a baby," we said.

"NO!" came the response, as predicted, and desperate tears quickly followed. Lillybelle buried her face in her mom's chest for comfort and sobbed about the inevitable change to our household dynamic.

After Lillybelle's reaction, I was feeling well prepared to share the news with Mom, so a few weeks later, John and I went for a drive. I wanted to see the happy blue sky and the natural world, to buffer against the chaotic response on the other end of the phone line. Our tires hit the gravel parking lot of a scenic hiking and bike trail, and after John swung us into a secluded parking spot, I took a deep breath and tapped the call button on my phone.

"Well, hello there," Mom answered after two rings, sounding surprised—and slightly suspicious—to be hearing from me.

"Hey," I trilled. I was trying to keep things light.

"What's up, stranger?" Mom asked, though it was more of an accusation than a question.

"Well . . ." I began, looking to John, who nodded his reassurance. "I'm pregnant."

"Oh!" Mom said. "Exciting!"

I smiled and waited but there was nothing more.

"Thanks," I said. I wasn't sure what else to say.

"Am I the last to know?" Mom asked, and the issue revealed itself. She was reserving her reaction until she knew the position she held in the hierarchy of important people receiving our news.

"No," I said. "We're calling John's family after you and then probably Dad after them." I included the bit about Dad not yet knowing with the hope that it would satisfy Mom's need to feel like a central figure in the scenario.

"Well, congratulations," Mom finally said. Her tone was ambiguous at best.

"Thanks," I replied. And then I couldn't help myself. I added, "You don't sound very enthusiastic."

"Oh, well, I sort of assumed that was why you were calling."

"What?" I was so confused. "Did Sarah tell you?"

"Oh, so Sarah already knows," Mom noted.

"Well yeah, I live with her," was my excuse.

"Hmm. No, she didn't tell me. I just saw you calling so assumed something big had happened, and this was the most logical likelihood."

I laughed to dodge the three-tiered emotional missile Mom had just launched my way: I laughed because my mom was mad that my sister got the news before she did, I laughed because my mom insinuated that I didn't call enough, and I laughed because my mom reduced my life-changing news to a simple inevitability anyone could have foreseen. Still, I decided that I preferred her lackluster response over something more overtly dramatic and pivoted my approach.

"Oh, that's so funny! You're psychic!" I said in earnest. I didn't pause for her response. "Well, very cool. We're excited, so I'm glad you know now. But I've got to go; we need to call John's family before it gets too late."

"How far along are you?" My mom was an expert at delaying the end of a conversation.

"Eight weeks," I said, purposefully terse in my response.

"Wow, I was expecting you to say twelve. Or more," she replied.

"Yeah, no, we waited a few weeks but ultimately we wanted to tell everyone, so. But yeah, I better get going, we need to call them."

Sometimes I could remind Mom that the conversation needed to end and she would acquiesce, but not this time.

"When are you due?" she asked.

"Uhh . . . I don't remember," I lied.

"You don't remember!" she exclaimed, taking a friendlier tone, and I relaxed in spite of myself.

"Yeah, it's late October but I can't remember if it was the twenty-sixth or twenty-seventh," I fibbed again.

"A Halloween baby," she gushed. "How exciting!"

"Yeah, it's fun," I agreed.

"What will you guys do for Christmas?"

It was a masterful shift in the conversation, and I kicked myself for letting her blindside me.

"Oh, no idea," I stalled. "We'll have a tiny newborn so I can't imagine we'll go anywhere or do anything."

"Well, maybe Sarah will plan something festive," came the reproach, and my signal to end the call before things escalated.

"Yeah, we'll see. I've really got to run, though," I said with conviction.

"Okay," Mom replied. "Well, exciting news."

"Thanks, talk to you later!" I was doing my best to remain chipper and had almost pressed the end call button, when—

"Oh, can I tell Grandma?" Mom threw the question out as if it was an afterthought, and I envisioned my head erupting into flames like a cartoon character.

"No," I snapped, bringing my phone back up to my ear. "This is my news; I want to tell Grandma."

"Well, she'll just be so excited," was her justification. "But I won't if you're going to call her."

"I'm going to call her," I confirmed.

"Okay. Don't wait too long."

"I won't, I'll call her today," I said, demonstrating my obedience.

"Alright," Mom replied. It was her signal that she was ready to let the call end.

"Okay, talk to you later," I said.

"Okay. Will you send me a sonogram photo?"

I was bested again.

"Yeah," I caved. "In a few hours. I don't have it with me." I pinched the spot between my eyes, which was starting to hurt.

"Alright. Very exciting!" she said again.

"Yep. Thanks. Bye."

"Don't forget the sonogr—" was the last thing I heard as I ended the call, exhausted. Immediately, instinctively, I turned to Dad.

"Hey sweetie," he said when he answered my call.

"Hey! Guess what?" I prompted. I hoped I didn't sound upset.

"What?" he replied. Dad never really was one for delaying the inevitable.

"I'm pregnant," I said, straight away. "We are going to have a baby."

"Ahh, nooo," was Dad's crushing response.

I laughed to dodge another emotional missile. "No, Dad, it's a good thing. We're excited," I said, my voice as even as humanly possible.

"It's just . . . oh sweetie, kids make everything harder."

I had never heard Dad speak that way before, and I had no idea why he chose that moment to be so callously honest.

"Thanks," I said, with what I hoped was enough hurt and anger to cut like a dagger through the phone.

"Alright, alright," Dad said, backing off. "Well, okay, woo-hoo! That's exciting news, sweetie. I love being a grandpa." He chuckled, but it was such a vicious one-eighty that I felt like I could puke. I thanked him for his congrats, told him I loved him, and hung up as fast as I could.

I looked over to John, whose mouth hung agape, and pressed my anger between my lips. He leaned across the center console without a word and hugged me to his chest. I knew he'd listen if I wanted to talk about the phone calls with Mom and Dad, but I had nothing to say. Instead, I dove into his emotional calm, finding comfort in the way he brushed the hair from my eyes and kissed the tears off my cheeks. His family was next on our announcement list, so I inhaled deeply through my nose, then sighed in relief that the worst was over.

When we called John's dad, Buddy, he answered on the first ring.

"IS THIS MY SON CALLING?" he bellowed loud enough to be heard by anyone standing within a four-foot radius of our car, as if the call was on speakerphone, though it was not.

I giggled, charmed as always. My father-in-law really did embody the meaning of his friendly name.

Taking a short, nervy breath, John got straight to the work of sharing our news, and only when he uttered the word "grandpa" did Buddy respond. He gave a high-pitched squeal so uncharacteristic of his typical baritone that we all dissolved into fits of laughter.

When we finally came up for air, we found ourselves on actual speakerphone on Buddy's end of the line, sharing the good news with John's stepmom Romi and his two little brothers. The kids didn't care too much, since the baby wouldn't be showing up for another nine months, but they gave us their congratulations anyway so they could go back to playing. Romi, however, screamed, then asked us if we were serious, then demanded a link to our registry and to be the very first person to visit. It was the type of celebratory phone call everyone in the world should get to have when sharing baby news with their family—no mental gymnastics required.

My in-laws said their goodbyes and wisely instructed me to relax, to take care of myself, and to insist that John do all the heavy lifting. I wiped my happy, salty cheeks, feeling like I wouldn't have minded chatting with them forever, as John ended the call.

Sunshine hit my face, and I closed my eyes to absorb its warmth as I stepped out of our car. I watched John get out, too, his eyes glowing in the light, and grinned. Our news was officially out in the world: We were going to be parents.

My phone buzzed in my hand and I looked down to see an incoming call from my grandma. *That's about right*, I thought, and I laughed when I showed John my screen. And though I knew Grandma was calling because Mom had told her I was pregnant, I decided not to make it a problem. Lucky us, that our baby would enter a world where a whole family full of loving, supportive, generous people were thrilled about his or her existence and shouted their congratulations from the rooftops, whether they did it the way we wanted them to or not.

I didn't take the call, though. I wanted to go on a relaxing walk with my husband to celebrate our future baby.

CHAPTER FIVE

THE DISTRACTION

My very first OB-GYN appointment was scheduled eight weeks into my pregnancy. After my positive pregnancy test, I had taken immediately to the most local Ridiculous Women Forum I could find to read recommendations on the best baby doctor in town. Post after post of mothers, some of whom were also labor and delivery nurses—reputable sources, I thought—had suggested Dr. Askari. So, when I nervously called his office the Monday after I peed on a stick, stammering through the reason I desired an appointment with the man, I snapped up the first new patient date available, four weeks later.

The office was beige and drab, and there was a heavily pregnant woman panting in the corner, a sight that frightened me and prompted a secret self-promise to maintain an active pregnancy so that I would never look that shockingly uncomfortable. After twenty or so minutes in the waiting room, which had nothing to do or look at that didn't involve pregnancy or motherhood, I was called back for an examination. A practically adolescent nurse took my height, weight, and blood pressure, and asked me for a urine sample. The heavily pregnant woman was grunting her way into the larger of the two bathroom stalls when I entered mine, and I felt intrusive as I lowered my pants and filled my cup as quickly as I could. I heard the poor woman finally begin to release her obviously bursting bladder as I exited, and it occurred to me that having a second stall in the one small office bathroom of a clinic that mostly serviced pregnant women made a lot of sense.

I waited in a private appointment room, naked from the waist down except for a paper gown and feeling a tiny bit confused and anxious, before *the* Dr. Askari entered my orbit. An older man with a gentle countenance, Dr. Askari shook my hand and said a cheerful hello, and I felt instantly at ease in his presence. He confirmed I was seeking verification of my pregnancy, then explained that a fetus at my estimated gestational stage was likely too small to be seen on an abdominal ultrasound, so he would need to use a transvaginal transducer. I must have looked puzzled, which I was, never having heard many of those words before, so he held up what looked like a dildo with a curly cord attached to one end and instructed me to lie on my back. Suddenly, the pantsless look I was rocking made more sense. As I adjusted my position on the exam table, Dr. Askari cracked the door to my room ajar and spoke a few words into the hallway. I looked in his direction and he turned his gaze to meet mine, his hand still firmly on the doorhandle, and asked me if I would mind having a nurse present. *That's smart of him*, I thought, and nodded my consent. Once the adolescent-looking nurse was in place, our appointment began.

"When did you learn of your potential pregnancy?" Dr. Askari asked, making small talk as he readied his machine. His voice was careful, soft-spoken, and heavily accented.

"Four weeks ago," I said. "I peed on a stick."

"And this was the first appointment available, I assume?" he asked, obviously aware of his in-demand status with the local mothers-to-be.

"Yep," I said. I didn't much feel like chatting.

"Well, at least you had lots of time to prepare," he said, and at that I laughed.

More like freak out, I thought but didn't say.

Finally finished with his prep, Dr. Askari explained what to expect as he did the ultrasound and asked if I was ready. I nodded, took a deep breath, and joined the bottoms of my feet together, sole-to-sole, as I let my knees fall apart.

"Okay, you're going to feel my hand here on your inner thigh, do you feel that?" he asked.

"Mhm," I confirmed, ready to get the show on the road.

"And then you will feel me touch the muscle at the vaginal opening, and I want you to relax." I appreciated how incredibly thorough and informative he was in his approach and did my best to comply.

"Good!" he said, enthusiastically. "You have excellent muscle control." I delighted at his praise.

"Okay, here comes the transducer," he said next, and I felt the skinny non-dildo go in with surgical precision.

Weird, but not gross, I thought with amusement.

"So," Dr. Askari began again, "where is the father?"

It occurred to me at that moment that it was, perhaps, strange that John hadn't joined me on our very first baby doctor appointment. I realized Dr. Askari's clever use of small talk was actually information-gathering, and I marveled at his approach even more. John only had so many days off from work throughout the year, so an appointment confirming what we already knew seemed too insignificant to warrant using any of his allotment.

"He's working," I said, not wanting to overexplain myself.

"Oh, well, you'd better get your phone ready for this next part then, because we're going to hear the baby's heartbeat."

I gasped. I hadn't realized this was *that* appointment.

Dr. Askari handed me a sonogram and then, now finished with the machine portion of our time together, turned his attention to me. He sat on his stool facing me on the exam table, crossed his right leg over his left, opened what I assumed to be my file on his lap, and looked gently into my eyes.

"What questions do you have for me?" he asked.

I inhaled sharply, embarrassed because I had neither the foresight nor the presence of mind, having just witnessed a foreign heartbeat emanating from my uterus, to come up with even a single question for the man who would guide me to the brink of death to deliver life.

"None," I said, sounding as dumb as I felt.

"Are you sure?"

The man was giving me a second chance. I thought quickly.

"No, you answered every question I had, so no, I'm good," I said, cleverly.

"Okay," Dr. Askari replied, jotting a quick note I assumed to be *This woman will make a horrible mother* into my file.

"Then, I will see you at about twelve weeks along," he said, finally. I was shocked. I had already waited four whole weeks just to confirm my pregnancy and now I was going to have to wait four more for an update. And in the meantime I was expected to just . . . gestate. Unsupervised. As if I had any idea what I was supposed to be doing.

THERE WAS AN OLD ADAGE FREQUENTLY used to joke about waiting, one of the more boring aspects of the job, when I worked as an actor in the Austin film scene. I was just starting out, so, for me, acting roles could be infrequent and spontaneous opportunities. Oftentimes I would find myself frantically preparing for my last-minute role, delighted to be given the chance and scared that I'd screw it up and never be cast again. Then, when production day would come, I'd arrive on set early in the morning, as instructed, ready in body, mind, and soul, and wait to be told where to stand and when to deliver my performance. The waiting usually took hours. Sometimes my scene would get bumped and the waiting would continue on the next day. After the flurry of excitement that drove all my preparation and hurrying, the waiting was a huge letdown. This phenomenon was referred to as "hurry up and wait," and it was exactly how I felt about the pace of pregnancy. And all of that waiting was allowing me room to do a whole lot of catastrophizing.

Later that week, while John was studying our first-ever sonogram, I felt emotionally numb but for a nervous pang in the middle of my chest. In the hyperactivity of scientifically testing methods of conception, when for weeks on end all of my time and attention was focused on the task of attaining pregnancy, I was able to convince myself I could have it all: an acting career and a baby. In the slowness of reality, however, I was feeling my certainty disintegrate. Mothers, as I knew them, were stressed out by life circumstances outside of their control yet under the umbrella of their responsibilities. I didn't see how I could create the career I had always dreamed of if I was living life for someone else, as the mothers I knew seemed to do. Looking down the path ahead, I saw an entire childhood stretched out before me: There would be diapers and drool first, then ABCs and 123s, friends and soccer teams, birthdays, schoolwork, holidays, and finally, eighteen years down the line, graduation. The kind of mom I wanted to be would happily be there for all of it.

What have I done? I asked myself. *I don't want this; I want to be an actor.*

John's hand and, in it, our sonogram, slid into my blurry field of vision. I looked up with a smile, masking the intrusive thought I couldn't shake, and let John assume my tearful eyes held joy, not fear.

That night in bed I succumbed to my panic and blurted out what I did not mean.

"What if I don't want to do this?" I demanded, with blame in my voice.

"What do you mean?" John asked.

"This, I mean this." I was impatient and cutting.

He suddenly caught my meaning. "What if you don't want to have the baby?"

"No!" I said, confusing even myself. "I mean, obviously I do, but what if I don't? Is this even a good idea? I just feel like it's bad timing or something. I mean, I haven't done anything in the world."

"Okay," John began carefully, closing his book. "Well, then it's something we should talk about because, yeah, if you feel like it's not the right time, then that's that." His words were too cryptic for my liking.

"What do you mean 'that's that,' what does that even mean?" I was picking a fight.

"Shawna, if you don't want to have the baby then we shouldn't have the baby. If you feel like it isn't the right time then we shouldn't do it."

"Really?" I was testing him.

"Yes." He didn't take the bait.

"Would you be sad?" I asked, my voice cracking in grief.

"Yeah, I'd be sad, but it's your body, so it doesn't matter. I'm married to *you*. I love you. I want you happy, and healthy, and thriving in this life we share. So, if you're telling me now is not the time, then I hear you."

With one quick conversion John demonstrated his unconditional support for me and assuaged my every fear. In that moment I had no doubt that he knew exactly who I was and what I wanted in life, and it was the only reassurance I needed. I thought about my sister Erin, about how her husband had treated her when they were trying to get pregnant, and I wondered if, once pregnant, she was able to share her fears about the massive ways life would be changing. Because even if the changes were welcomed, vehemently pursued, they were still unknown and would require adjustment. I wondered if every pregnant person held my same fears, and for the first time ever, I wondered how my mom felt about becoming a mom. John wanted me to continue to be my own person, to experience life as a multifaceted woman—did Mom have that? I dissolved into a puddle of my own snotty tears, wondering how I had yet to succumb to dehydration.

I woke up the next morning with a new lease on life, a newly again chosen path, and, knowing I had John's unwavering support, a new idea: I was going to make a movie. Dr. Askari didn't need to see me but once a month, and I no longer needed to devote my excess energy to getting pregnant, so I had lots of free time outside of work and an endlessly creative brain to distract.

"I'm writing a short film!" I shouted to John who was just trying to have a moment to himself on the toilet.

"Great!" he replied. "Can you close the door?"

"I have this idea about a pregnant woman who has this sister, this insensitive, intrusive sister, who's kind of like, strung out. The sister finds out that the woman's pregnant and insists she let her move in to help with the baby," I explained.

"Did you talk to your mom?" John laughed.

"Yesterday. She called to request more updates," I said.

"Jesus," he groaned. He had been making a joke.

"But this is not about my mom, this is a sister!" I enthused.

"Okay," came the reply.

"Same themes as real life, but different circumstances! Because life is art!" I was really pumped about my idea.

"Got it. I'm gonna close this," John said, shutting me out.

"I'm going to play the pregnant woman and shoot it when I'm eight months pregnant!" I yelled through the bathroom door.

"Wow! Ambitious," John yelled back.

"I'm so excited!" I said. "It'll be like film school!"

"Cool!" He was really getting tired of me.

"I just know if I keep acting I can—"

"Can we talk about this later?" he begged. And, realizing the man just wanted to poop in peace, I laughed at my own absurdity.

BY MY TWELVE-WEEK APPOINTMENT WITH DR. Askari, I had written the final draft of my short film and had begun the process of production. While Dr. Askari took measurements, both mine and baby's, I planned my audition process. When Dr. Askari asked if I had any questions, I asked how much bigger I could reasonably expect my belly to be at eight months pregnant. He answered patiently that while he couldn't tell me what clothing size I would be wearing, he did know that the typical fundus measured close to twenty-eight centimeters at eight months. I jotted the info down in my notes app, on both my *Baby Stuff* and *Film Stuff* lists.

As my belly swelled, my anxieties about the life I was choosing to build were quelled by rereading my shot list, a technical term for the types of scenes and camera angles a film crew needed to capture visually to tell the story of the film. On the day of my twenty-week anatomy scan, John and I were overjoyed to hear that we would be having a healthy baby boy, and I changed the baby in my script to a boy as well, adding baby boy onesies and sleepers to my prop list. Conveniently, the mom-to-be in my little movie would need to wash and sort baby clothes, so they might as well be mine. When John and I shopped for a crib for our little guy, I looked at the options with the eye of a filmmaker, who planned to feature said crib in their film; the mind of a mother, concerned more about safety and practical use than aesthetics; and the budgetary constraints of both. Each week, I took belly pictures to document my growing bump and rehearsed with the actors I cast to play my sister and husband in the film. If ever I experienced a troubling symptom, like uncomfortable heartburn or baby kicks to the bladder, I infused the experience into my storytelling, growing closer to my production date and more excited for my delivery date in the process.

Making my short film during my pregnancy felt deeply nourishing on a soul level. I felt I was honoring myself as a person worthy of living the life they wanted as I created a new person to bring into the world. I wondered who my baby would be and what they would want for themselves. I knew that, because I was giving myself the experience of chasing my dreams, I could bring support and perspective, even wisdom, to any ambitions my child might have. I had daydreamed about the baby I would someday love for several years, but I had planned, aspired, and hungered for the creative self-expression of acting and filmmaking since I was a child. I was gestating two babies that summer, and for the first time in my entire life I felt like I was doing exactly what I was put on the planet to do.

For three blissful days, at the thirty-four-week mark of pregnancy, I met the challenges of film set life with vigor. My actors were prepared and delivered their performances beautifully, breathing humanity and unique perspective into our story. My director of photography captured my shot list with artistry and technical precision, despite the constraints of my limited scope of knowledge as a first-time director. My assistant director managed our schedule and handled logistics, and called action whenever I was acting in a scene. My sound guy humored me when I requested he capture the sound of water plopping off my hair and body for what would be a ten-second-long shower scene in the film. He had said that I could just use stock shower sound in editing, but I knew what shower water sounded like when it flicked off a pregnant belly, and I wanted that specific sound in my film, so he obliged. My friends and John helped out as production assistants each day, running little errands and holding props just off camera. I paid everyone for their time and efforts and enjoyed every moment of making my movie, and when production was over, I had just six short weeks left in my pregnancy and had successfully avoided the panic of an idle mind.

Unfortunately, I had also avoided preparation of a birth plan and development of any semblance of a newborn care skill set. Immediately comprehending the magnitude of my oversight, I wondered to myself why John, who hadn't been occupying his idle mind in the same fervent manner as I, had neglected to book us any classes. I didn't have time to pick a fight about it, though, so I sighed, opened my laptop, and navigated straight to the local Ridiculous Women Forum for recommendations. I selected a hodgepodge of informative classes held by both our hospital and local doulas I did not know, hoped for the best, and headed out to see Dr. Askari.

At thirty-four weeks, my baby was measuring on the big side of normal, Dr. Askari said. I asked if his size was a problem and was reassured that, though we would keep our eye on his growth over the next few weeks, baby could keep cooking. At thirty-five weeks, Dr. Askari became concerned about the amniotic fluid level–to–fetus size ratio going on in my uterus and ordered an anatomy scan. At thirty-six weeks, my anatomy scan confirmed that, while my baby was in fact likely to be big, I also had a ton of fluid in there, so he probably wasn't as problematically huge as anticipated. At thirty-seven weeks, Dr. Askari still had some concerns about my rapidly billowing uterus and asked me what my thoughts were on being induced into labor.

I hadn't thought for even a moment during my entire pregnancy about the possibility of being induced, so I had no ready opinion on the matter, but it didn't sound fun. I had been wondering what it would be like to experience the onset of labor. I imagined waking up in the middle of the night, belly rounded to capacity and squeezing with the ancient rhythm of childbirth, and shaking John awake with the news that it was baby time. I informed Dr. Askari of my lack of opinion, and my romanticized preference, and he noted both in my chart. The baby was head down and in a good position at thirty-eight weeks but was still measuring extraordinarily large, so Dr. Askari suggested scheduling an induction for my due date. He said I would likely go into labor before then, but if I didn't, it wouldn't be wise, in his professional opinion, to let baby continue to grow beyond forty weeks, as baby's giant head had to make its way through my narrow pelvis.

I hadn't cried over pregnancy fears in more than twenty-five weeks, but with no acting project to distract me, and no earthly idea what to decide, my emotional reservoir hit its maximum and the floodgates opened. The trusty Ridiculous Women Forum was no help, as the opinions expressed there were mostly in favor of allowing labor to follow a natural progression but also noted the reality that there were dangers associated with a baby who grew too large or gestated too long. The internet was split, and ardently so, about the need for induction versus the rate at which doctors ordered inductions, the implication being that sometimes inductions really were necessary, but also doctors preferred the predictable outcomes induction provided despite what nature intended. Then of course, there were the opinions that told me that induction outcomes were anything but predictable. It suddenly seemed like baby and I were doomed to trauma and/or death no matter my decision. The hairs on my forearms stood on end, and a moment later John entered our room, stunned to see teardrops splashing off my swollen, naked body as I bounced on my birthing ball and tugged on my nipples, willing labor to begin.

HEAVILY PREGNANT AND PANTING, BIGGER AT forty weeks on the dot than I ever thought it possible to be, I waddled past a bright-eyed young woman and caught the shocked fright in her eyes as she averted her gaze. She reminded me of myself just eight months prior, stunned at the size and obvious discomfort of the pregnant woman I encountered in Dr. Askari's office. *She'll learn*, I thought. *We all learn*. And then, I put the scared young woman out of my mind and crossed the threshold of our hospital's labor and delivery ward for my induction.

CHAPTER SIX

THE ADMISSION

The hospital walls were gray and the air was acrid with antiseptic, and the intake nurse gathering my patient information kept looking at me with blatant concern and at John with badly concealed wariness, probably because of my puffy, red eyes. I ignored her concern so it wouldn't fuel my own and answered her questions succinctly. Once admitted to the hospital, and in the private room that would be my laboring area, I asked the RN assigned to me, Jessica, if the induction process could be stopped once it had started. Her face changed from pleasant to humorless and she asked me in a loud, pointed voice to confirm that I was, in fact, making the choice to be induced of my own volition. I nodded my agreement, but she wasn't satisfied until a tiny "Yes" escaped my lips, and I looked at the sterile hospital bed across the room so I didn't have to witness her concern any longer.

The process would be fairly simple, Jessica explained, moving on. She would place an IV and take my vitals, and introduce a few monitoring agents on my body and belly, to measure mine and baby's heart rate and my contractions. Once strapped up, I would lie back so she could check the dilation and effacement of my cervix, and then we would be ready to get started. She said she would tell me the next steps once we reached that point and disappeared from the room.

Exhausted already, I changed into my hospital gown and clambered onto the bed as John sat down in a Labor Partner Chair positioned in the corner of the room and pulled out his iPad. My eyes squinted involuntarily, and he must have sensed my ire because without even a glance in my direction he thought better and quickly stowed his iPad away.

Nurse Jessica returned and readied me as described, noting that my cervix had dilated to two centimeters all on its own. I asked if that meant I was soon to go into labor naturally, but she said likely not, and that it didn't matter, as she would next be placing a tiny pill deep in my vaginal canal, which would dissolve and aid my cervix in dilating and effacing. She asked if I was ready, and then, as I stared at the blank white ceiling tile above, she stuck a pill inside me. A few clicks entered onto my computerized chart later, and after a reminder that I could request IV pain medication if needed, Nurse Jessica left the room, advising us to get some rest, if possible.

From where my head lay flat, my mound of a belly, swathed in a light blue poly-cotton blend, jutted out from my sternum three feet into the air, or so it looked like, blocking my view of John and the television set on the wall behind him. I thought about moving, but felt relatively comfortable pressed under the full weight of my baby and belly, and I realized comfortable was a feeling I had been missing for several weeks, so I stayed. After a moment, though, I noticed that the circular fetal heart monitor attached to my belly with a stretchy band jumped a little each time baby kicked, and that the little kicks and little jumps were out of sync with the not-so-little beeps of the maternal heart rate machine blaring next to my head. The competing sensations began to make my teeth hurt. I had to make it stop.

John hadn't uttered so much as a word all evening and, though I was now struggling on my back like a turtle on its shell, didn't offer to help me change positions. Maybe he thought I didn't need help, so I certainly wasn't going to ask. I finally heaved my giant belly over to my left side and, using its momentum, shoved my left arm into the bed underneath me, placing my right foot on the ground in front of me for stability. John laughed as I slowly stood, and I stifled the impulse to kick him in the teeth. *I wouldn't be able to land a kick that high anyway,* I thought. The machine beeping went crazy as I plodded to the en suite bathroom, and Nurse Jessica came running.

Several boring hours later, John snored away in his uncomfortable chair while I counted those stupid beeps. I couldn't stop counting, despite not wanting to count, so I gave up any hope of being able to get some sleep and let my brain rattle on while resentment seethed. Nurse Jessica returned to check my progress, rousing John, which I felt he deserved, and told me it was time to place a second pill.

I lay back, stared at the same plain white ceiling tile as before, and wondered why they hadn't thought to paint something pleasant to look at, like a sunset or a jovial island scene. I wondered how many patients before me had stared at that same stupid tile, listening to the same stupid beeps, and chuckled to myself, bouncing my belly and accidentally squeezing Nurse Jessica's hand, which was still inside of me. She cleared her throat as she retracted her fingers, and I laughed even harder, which made John laugh, though he did not know what we were laughing about. Nurse Jessica knew, though, and she turned her head with a fake cough to give herself a moment to neutralize her facial expression. When she could face me again, she explained that contractions were likely to ramp up with the second pill, and because Dr. Askari had instructed her to begin administration of the synthetic hormone Pitocin, they might become rather painful. Eager to meet my baby, I figured I had felt the bleak, lonely nothingness of that boring room for long enough and a change in sensation might be nice.

I AWOKE AN HOUR LATER WITH a cramp just below my breastbone and groaned with irritation as I struggled to adjust my position in bed. I yelled for John but, unbelievably, he had shoved ear plugs into his head at some point earlier in the night, so he did not hear me. I rocked onto my back and arched to stretch the cramping area, but I couldn't get a good angle. I swung my giant belly back and forth from to side to side to create enough momentum to roll myself over. As soon as I did, though, the breastbone cramp worsened and produced enough pain to catch my breath in my throat.

It was then I realized I had to pee. I yelled at John again, louder this time, and threw the pillow behind my head at him, hoping to smack him square in the mouth. Luckily enough, the pillow smacked him somewhere, and he woke up. He was annoyed for a moment, until he saw my face and remembered where we were. I yelled at him to help me stand up, but he was so groggy from bad chair sleep that it took him a moment to remember how his legs worked. By the time he got to my bedside I had already managed to get my feet on the floor. He offered his hand, but I directed him to grab my IV stand instead. He still wore his earplugs and was having difficulty with comprehension so I grabbed the pole myself and stepped on his foot, waddling past him on my way to the bathroom as that stupid cramp seized again.

When Nurse Jessica came to see what all the beeping was about, I told her I was experiencing some muscle cramp–like pain and asked her to administer the IV pain medication advertised at the start of our journey together. She told me it might be better to request an epidural for pain management, as it was nearing morning and the anesthesiologist would likely hit shift change soon. I reiterated that I was having a muscle cramp under my breastbone and would rather save the epidural for when I really needed it, once labor began. Nurse Jessica looked at me with a mixture of pity and disbelief and asked me to show her the cramping area with my hands. The damn cramp cramped again, harder this time, so that I couldn't breathe at all, so I smooshed my boobs out of the way with my left hand and rubbed the charley horse at the very top of my bump with my right.

"Okay, yeah, I think that's a contraction," Nurse Jessica said.

"No, I don't feel it down here," I insisted, rubbing the underside of my belly. "It's way up here."

"Uh-huh," Nurse Jessica said. "That is your uterus."

"What?!" I was having difficulty comprehending, and I suddenly realized John had gone back to sleep. I wished I could throw another pillow at him but I had to deal with Jessica. "No, it doesn't feel like a contraction; it feels like the muscle cramps and can't relax itself or something."

"Way up there at the top of your belly?" Nurse Jessica began, carefully. "That's the very top of your uterus, which is a muscle. And contractions? Are a muscle squeezing, which can feel like a cramp or a charley horse."

"Oh." I was dumbfounded.

Just then another contraction hit and Nurse Jessica instructed me to inhale forcibly through my nose and exhale slowly out of my mouth to help make my way through it. She helped me hoist my trembling body back into bed and stuck her hand inside me, at my request, to check my dilation. She woke John by yelling loudly near his face that he needed to wake. Then, she paged Dr. Askari to inform him that I was close to delivering.

"Oh man," John said sleepily. "Are you really close?"

"I have no idea," I gasped, trying to breathe as Nurse Jessica had shown me.

"Guess I better wake up," John said, and he began gently tapping his cheeks with both hands.

"Harder," I groaned, and he laughed as though I wasn't serious.

Many moments that felt like hours later, Dr. Askari joined us. Seeing his kind, calm face really pissed me off, and I wondered where he had been all night. He said a few things to me that seemed as though they were important, but my contractions had ballooned into waves that blanketed the vast swath of my belly, so I was struggling to remain conscious. John seemed to get the gist of what was said, though, because he reassured me that the epidural team was on its way when Dr. Askari left the room.

Many more moments that felt like hours later, a congregation of fit, rested-looking men in scrubs huddled in the far corner of my laboring space, and I knew from the way they occasionally glanced at me that they were gossiping. I panted, sweated, and twitched my way through yet another contraction as they gabbed, and felt as though I could rip in half, belly first, and still continue to be ignored. I realized that the chickens had finally finished their clucking when I found one of the chiseled young men standing before me, eager to get informed consent to administer my epidural. The man said a lot of things, but all I heard was muffled incoherence so I looked to John for guidance and he motioned for me to sign the papers. I gripped the ball point pen I was offered, scribbled a signature I did not recognize onto a document I did not read, and hoped for the best. The man then got behind me, and Nurse Jessica opened my gown to expose my spine as I attempted to remain still enough for the man to insert a three-and-a-half-inch needle despite the twitching.

And then, blisssssssss.

The white ceiling tiles above my head didn't seem so boring anymore, and the noise of the busy hospital faded into a quiet murmur as my eyelids slowly shut me into darkness. They opened again sometime later because Nurse Jessica had appeared to complete shift change, and she brought with her a beautiful angel of a woman. I didn't catch the new nurse's name, but she smiled sweetly, and when she said hello she spoke softly, and when I looked at her kind face I felt cherished, though perhaps it could have been the drugs, so I named her Nurse Angel in my head. I bid Nurse Jessica a fond goodbye and chuckled when it dawned on me that her hand would never again get to feel the inside of my body.

Nurse Angel took my vitals and showed me how to use my epidural pump, explaining that she liked to show all of her epidural patients how to dispense their own pain relief in case they had been in too much pain during their first demonstration to remember how, and I wondered if, in addition to being an angel, she could also read minds. She then asked me if the beeps of the maternal heart rate machine blaring next to my head were bothering me and showed me the switch to make them stop. Then, dimming the overhead lights, she told me to use my call button if I started to feel any pressure between my legs, and instructed me to try to get some sleep before pushing began.

My eyes blinked open again, though I couldn't remember shutting them, and the first image I saw was John, awake and on his iPad. His lips curved into a smile when he met my gaze and my heart skipped a beat, happy that he was there, and that he had some form of entertainment while I napped. He asked how I was feeling, and if I was having any pressure in between my legs yet. I said no, but after a quick body scan, I changed my mind. I was numb from the waist down, but if I concentrated, I could feel the unmistakable presence of something wanting to exit. I explained the feeling to John as similar to feeling like you needed to poop except that the feeling was not in my butthole. He pushed the call button and told Nurse Angel about the pressure.

I had expected a flurry of activity to swarm around me, but instead Nurse Angel entered the room without any fanfare and came to my bedside. She stroked my hair as I described the growing pressure in general terms, and she softly explained that what I likely felt was baby's head moving the bones of my pelvis. She told me that Dr. Askari was delivering a baby in another room but that we could do a little pushing without him to get baby into position.

"Really?" I felt giddy.

"Yeah, we'll see if we can get any movement," she said in a cute little drawl.

"Is there something I can do?" John asked, eager to help.

"Yep. Dad, you grab that leg, under the knee, and I'll take this one." She grabbed my right leg, bending it, and readied herself. "And while Mama pushes, we brace." John grabbed my left leg, mimicking Nurse Angel's posture.

"Good," she encouraged, then turned to me. "Can you feel the contraction you're having right now?"

"Nope!" I replied with a smile.

"Okay then, I'll need to tell you when one is coming, so when I say go, I'll need you to lean over your belly and use your stomach muscles to push like you have to go to the bathroom."

"Okay," I said meekly, and then to John, "Do not laugh if I poop."

He laughed.

"Don't laugh!" Nurse Angel demanded. It was the loudest I had heard her speak.

"Sorry." John masked his glee and adjusted his grip on my leg.

"Contraction coming in ten seconds, Mama, get ready..." Nurse Angel warned, and I rounded forward, eager to meet my future.

I didn't feel any pain, or even much sensation at all, thanks to my well-placed epidural, except for a slowly shifting feeling of fullness somewhere in my mid- to low pelvis. Every time Nurse Angel began a count of ten, I took a deep breath, leaned forward, and thought about clenching my stomach muscles. The thought and action worked in tandem to make the muscles comply, though I could not feel their engagement, moving what I knew to be my baby but what felt like a slab of meat squishing along a narrow passage. We repeated this exercise five times, and on the last time I felt the baby smoosh up against the catheter in my urethra, and I was positive I had become incontinent.

"Am I peeing?!" I shouted. Nurse Angel looked down and confirmed that I was, but that all fluid was being diverted into a bag via my catheter, so no mess was made. John laughed, though he was not supposed to, but so did I, so it was alright. Nurse Angel stopped our efforts for a moment to check my progress and was shocked to see the top of baby's head mere centimeters away from freedom.

"Don't do anything!" she instructed as she ran for backup.

A squad of blue-scrubbed nurses, who I later learned were called the catch team, poured into the room. They donned booties and skull caps upon entry, and unfurled fold after fold of medical-grade tarping, effectively cocooning a ten-foot diameter catching area in heavy, milky plastic that muffled sound and settled the space into sterile serenity. Then, Dr. Askari joined us at last. He seemed taller and more confident than ever before, and when I saw his kind, calm face, my eyes filled with anticipatory tears of joy.

"I hear we're ready to have our baby," he said in his cheery way.

"I guess so," I managed to choke out, and John wiped a tear away from my cheek.

"Don't cry. We'll make short work of it," Dr. Askari said, and with that he turned to his prep team. Nurse Angel took her place at my right while John remained at my left, and a nurse I didn't recognize cloaked Dr. Askari in a plastic robe. Once sufficiently covered and gloved, Dr. Askari sat between my legs and I could see the top of his skullcap over my belly. He instructed the nurse to his right to adjust his light, and with the flick of his head, flipped a clear shield attached to a visor down over his face. A third nurse moved into position at Dr. Askari's left and a fourth stood to the side, between the third nurse and Nurse Angel. Once all players took their marks, our show began.

"Okay, Shawna," Dr. Askari said. He was the first person at the hospital to call me by my name. "We are going to try pushing just as Nurse Angela showed you before."

I looked to Nurse Angel, who smiled and gave me a nod. I loved that her name was Angela; it fit her.

"Are you ready?" Dr. Askari prompted, and John and Angela braced my legs as I curled over my belly.

"And . . . push!" came the command. I held my breath as instructed and pushed, imagining my stomach muscle squeezing a water balloon through a funnel. The image was nonsensical, but I knew if enough of the balloon (baby) could squish through the tiny mouth of the funnel (vaginal canal), gravity and momentum would do the rest.

"Good!" Dr. Askari encouraged as Nurse Angela finished her ten count. I paused for a moment and noticed the calm quiet surrounding me.

"This is nothing like the movies," I said to the amusement of my audience.

"And now another deep breath," Dr. Askari instructed—rather quickly, I thought. I inhaled deeply and doubled my efforts, eager for more praise.

My eyes bugged wide and I instinctively eased off pushing though Angela was only at eight. I had long heard tales of the ring of fire, an intensely painful sensation a woman feels when a baby's emergence stretches her to the brink, but I had never heard anyone describe feeling the pressure I was feeling in my clitoris. I wondered for a moment if Dr. Askari hadn't grabbed each flap of my labia minora and yanked. I was furious and horrified at the pain, positive the entire apparatus was about to rip off, when another contraction hit.

"Push, slowly now," Dr. Askari instructed, and, deciding I had no option but to accept the pain, I took a deep breath and imagined the balloon easing through the funnel. I was profoundly relieved to realize the pressure of baby's arrival had angled itself away from its previous terrifying trajectory and toward the stretchy skin of my vaginal opening. And then I felt a pop.

"The head is out," Dr. Askari said as Angela counted four.

"And here is our first shoulder," he said as we reached six.

"And there we go," he concluded, and I felt the last of baby whoosh into the world, along with forty weeks' worth of amniotic fluid. An analog clock I had never noticed on the wall across the room came into focus in my field of vision: Baby arrived at five minutes past the hour, after eighteen hours of labor.

God bless the epidural, I thought.

"He's perfect!" Dr. Askari announced, sucking fluid from tiny nostrils with a bulb syringe. Then, Angela opened my hospital gown, Dr. Askari placed my baby on my bare chest, and the entire world turned Technicolor.

CHAPTER SEVEN

THE BREAST

HE WAS HOT AND CLAMMY AND curled naturally against the curve of my breast, but I didn't recognize him. I thought I would—every daydream and fantasy of our meeting I ever had included the instant familiarity I would feel the moment I laid eyes on my child—so my heart ached for that which it did not experience. I loved him instantly, though, because I wanted to love him instantly, so I chose to think and say that I did and hope that I eventually would. I knew I would.

I was absolutely fascinated by him. His face was swollen from having been squashed along the narrow path he traveled to make his way to my chest, but his nose was smashed flat, with flared nostrils, unlike any nose I had seen on my mother's or father's side of the family. I thought his feet would be bony and arched, like mine and my mom's, but they were pudgy and flat and the toes were more nub than phalange. They didn't look like John's either. The only indicators that he really was mine, other than having just come out of me, were his creamy, fair skin and the light, dishwater blond fuzz that topped his round head. And then I noticed his lips: full, with a cupid's bow, and lax, as if ready to expand wide across his face into a charming grin, just like John's.

Ah, I thought, *he really is ours*, and my heart surged.

I labored for fifteen hours to bring him into the world and he seemed just as tired as I felt, sleeping soundly, his bare skin on mine. John stood over us, caressing our boy's head and kissing mine, so I didn't have much desire to change positions. Nurse Angela came by then to bid us a final congratulations. She smiled and gushed over our baby boy, then told us a labor recovery nurse would be by shortly to escort us to our room, and I wept when we said goodbye. John laughed and kissed the top of my head again, and I kissed the top of our son's.

"We have a son," I marveled.

"Can you believe it?" John asked. And though our baby boy was in my arms, it was still hard to fathom.

A WOMAN I DIDN'T RECOGNIZE, EASILY the thirtieth stranger to foist themselves upon me since I stepped foot in the hospital, hovered nearby clutching a clipboard. I vaguely recalled seeing her enter my room from the corner of my eye, to briefly chat just before Nurse Angela left. She caught me looking, so pressed her mouth into a crooked smile, then came our way. I refocused my attention on my baby, desperate for some time alone to absorb the first moments of our new reality, but she spoke anyway. She was middle-aged, with yellow, artfully blown-out hair held stiff with product, and though she was fit, she smelled faintly of old cigarette smoke masked by synthetic florals. She told us she was a lactation specialist, and that the hospital was conducting a study about the effect of early breastfeeding education on breastfeeding outcomes. Then she asked if we wanted to be study participants.

I had intended to breastfeed, having known of its importance from my sister's experience, and had read on the Ridiculous Women Forum that guidance from a lactation consultant was invaluable, so I ignored my instinct to decline and agreed.

The woman handed her clipboard to John so he could sign a waiver, then clapped her hands. "Okay!" she exclaimed. "Let's get that baby latched!"

"Oh, right now?" I asked. I had just pushed a baby out. I hadn't even peed or been moved to a recovery room yet.

"Right now!" she insisted, grabbing at my child. "I'll hold baby, you sit up."

"Can you actually come back when we're in a room?" John asked, sensing my hesitation.

The woman shook her head no.

"Research shows that having baby latch within an hour of delivery is crucial, so if we're doing this thing, we're doing it right," she said, decidedly.

"Well, he's asleep is all," I said, sure the *never wake a sleeping baby* creed would get her to back off.

"Baby needs to eat," she informed me, not backing off. "That's what gets his digestive system functioning, and as his parents, it's important to get that online as soon as we can."

We? I thought. But the new parent guilt trip was a successful angle. I begrudgingly passed the baby to John and struggled my epidural-numbed lower half into a seated position.

"Good, now let's see you hold baby. What's the most comfortable way for you to hold him?" the woman asked.

"I'm not sure," I said, as I carefully took the baby back from John. I had just delivered the dude; I hadn't had time to practice different types of holds.

"Well, try something," she said, a little too impatiently for my taste. I shifted baby until he was curled up on my chest as before and nowhere near a nipple.

"He can't feed in that position," the woman said, a little too impatiently again.

"You told me to hold him," I replied.

"Well, we're trying to feed, so I'm going to need feeding holds. How do you think you'll be comfortable holding him to feed?" Her repeated emphasis on the word *feed* told me she clearly thought I was an idiot.

"I've never had a baby before," I said sharply, my face growing hot.

"Sorry, I didn't catch your name," John interrupted.

"Pam," said the woman, clearing her throat.

"Pam, great. I'm John. This is Shawna."

"Hello." Pam's smile was brusque.

"Can I ask you to speak a little softer? Shawna's been up all night. And I think explicit instructions would help," John said, firm, and I appreciated the backup.

"Okay," Pam started, slowing down. "Go ahead and lie him across your right forearm, I assume you're right-handed?" I nodded and followed directions. She told me to cradle the baby's head and neck with my hand, then shoved a pillow under my arm for added support. Once in position, I guided my son to my breast, but he was too sleepy to eat.

"We need to wake him up," Pam groaned, grabbing the little guy's wrist. She windmilled his arm around like she was trying to break it off and my jaw dropped.

"That's a little much," I said, pushing her hand away.

"It looks harsh, I know, but we have to make him a little mad so that he'll wake up and eat," was her simple explanation.

I looked to John, my eyes begging for his intervention.

"Why don't I take over," he said, and Pam fixed her attention on my breast.

"Are your nipples always this flat?" she asked, squishing my boob like a hamburger. I looked down at my naked breast and erect nipple in confusion.

"Is that considered a flat nipple?" I asked in disbelief.

"Yeah, that's pretty flat, unfortunately. I'll be surprised if he catches a hold of that," she said in consternation. Then, without another word, she dropped my boob and left the room.

"What the hell?" I asked John, who laughed. With Pam gone, I guided my sweet baby to my breast and gently rubbed his lips. He opened his mouth and instinctively latched as Pam returned with three differently sized silicone nipple shields.

"Oh, did you get him on?" she practically shouted.

"I think so," I said.

"Is it working?!" she demanded.

"I have no idea," I said.

Pam sighed with a huff. "Is there pain? You shouldn't have pain," she accused.

"I mean, it's not the most pleasant thing in the world," I said.

"Does it feel like he's pulling anything?" she asked.

"Pulling what? He's sucking, I think," I replied.

"You should feel a sort of internal tugging," Pam insisted.

I tried to notice the sensation but couldn't.

"Is he swallowing?" she asked, putting her head close to baby's face.

"I don't know. I can't tell." Baby was solidly on my boob but everything was new and overwhelming, and Pam's giant coiffed head was blocking my view, so I couldn't see and I didn't know how to describe what I was feeling.

"I don't think he is. He needs to wake up. Dad, go ahead and wake him up so we can get that belly full," Pam insisted.

John pumped baby's arm, but it was no use; he was already asleep.

"I think he must have popped off. Your nipples are too flat," Pam concluded.

"Why don't we let him sleep for a while," John said.

"Yeah, we can try again later," I agreed.

"No," Pam said, her voice stern. She must have seen the shock on my face, because she continued, "I'm sorry, but babies absolutely have to eat. It is imperative to their survival."

"Pam, how about you join us again once Shawna has a recovery room," John offered.

"No, guys, I'm sorry. We have to get him latching and sucking and swallowing. Babies are born with a high concentration of bilirubin that their body can only process if they're eating and pooping." Pam seemed flustered.

"What's bilirubin?" I asked.

"It causes jaundice and baby can die!" she spat.

"Then let's give him formula!" I said, and burst into tears.

MY OLDER SISTER ERIN ALWAYS HAD a sort of furious determination about her that guaranteed success against all odds, no matter her goal. When we were teens, she decided she'd make a great sophomore class president, so she threw together a campaign and gladhanded her school's various cliques at lunchtime to rally votes. She won, of course, because when she had a goal, she made it happen.

So, when the pediatrician discovered Erin's one-week-old daughter had tethers to her lip and tongue that caused difficulty in breastfeeding, Erin had them assessed and addressed. When, at two weeks old, her daughter was struggling to surpass birth weight, Erin doubled her feeding efforts. During week three, when Erin's nipples blanched white while her daughter ate, producing a searing pain throughout her feed and for up to an hour afterward, Erin screamed but did not quit.

For months, while her nipples felt like they were being sliced by razors, Erin called me in sobbing fits about the level of pain she had to endure to continue to nurse her child. She lamented the incredible demand on her body, mourned the romanticized version of motherhood she had foreseen, worried she would fail, and, most of all, raged at the hopeless dread she felt every time her sweet baby girl cried for more milk. But Erin was determined to achieve her breastfeeding goal. So she cried, clawed at the couch, and screamed into a pillow each moment she fed her daughter, from the still, gray cold of January until one day in the hot, sticky balm of June, when the Raynaud's phenomenon she'd been suffering finally let up and her pain subsided. At last, after much suffering and effort, Erin could enjoy the special moments of nursing her daughter. My sister succeeded because she decided to breastfeed.

I had made no such decision. I was interested, sure, but I had been in the young, dumb, fun stage of my marriage and life while Erin was enduring breastfeeding torture, so her phone call candor had been incredibly scary. Because of Erin's experience, I did not directly tie my mental health and self-worth to my ability to breastfeed and instead adopted a will-try-but-will-not-endure-torture mindset. And the idea of my brand-new baby boy dying of jaundice was emotional torture.

Pam made an immediate attempt to backpedal her bilirubin agitation, calling it a natural bodily substance easily processed when baby eats, but the damage was done. I furiously laid on the call button to summon a nurse and, when that didn't instantly work, sent John out into the hallway to grab someone who could bring me formula and order Pam out of my room. She got the hint and slowly gathered her clipboard. Then, handing me the silicone nipple shields, she made one final attempt to persuade me to try again, by complimenting my ability to get baby to latch despite my anatomical deficiencies. Unable to contain my fury, I colorfully requested that she leave my room.

"I understand emotions are high right now. I'll come by your recovery room later," Pam said, no doubt bound by the hospital's breastfeeding study. And then, with her stiff-haired head held high, she left the room without apology.

A half hour passed, and we finally moved to our labor recovery room, where we stayed for three intrusive days full of prods and pokes and suggestions. Pam eventually found our room and popped in to check on us, but we declined her services. A nurse brought us a four-pack of ready-made newborn formula but tucked it away behind our diaper reserves, making it seem a shameful last resort rather than a valid alternative to breastfeeding, so I ignored my instincts and kept trying. Baby continued to latch but the pain in my nipples was excruciating, and no one could tell me if the cause was an improper latch or simply breastfeeding itself. I saw plainly that he was swallowing when he fed but nurse after nurse shared concern for how sleepy he was, how lazily he suckled, and how infrequently he dirtied a diaper. His cries also indicated to me that something was wrong, but when I asked about what I thought was a tongue tie, my recovery nurse doubted the issue.

The morning before we were supposed to be discharged, we received a visit from the pediatrician on duty, who told us the baby's bilirubin levels were too high so he needed to poop before we could leave. My already mounting anxiety skyrocketed at another utterance of the word *bilirubin*, and I thought about the mothers who fed their children from their breast in centuries past. I wondered if bilirubin had killed newborns whose mothers had flat nipples like mine, and I felt like a failure. I cried along with my sweet baby that day, willing some type of motherly instinct to kick in and magically make breastfeeding intuitive in me, but none came. Instead, I thanked the heavens for modern medicine, and fed my baby the formula I requested on day one.

He pooped, to everyone's relief, and we were discharged on time, with a four-pack of newborn formula to take home with us.

THE MOMENT WE GOT HOME, JOHN, who was as delighted to be freed from hospital staff interruptions as I was, settled onto our bed for skin-to-skin bonding time with baby. I thought to lie down with them, but my mind, or perhaps it was my soul, felt electrified and in need of a task. I couldn't fathom resting. The skin of my breasts had pulled tight by day four, as they swelled to double their natural size, aching for release from the gallons of milk they looked to have produced, and I wondered how it was possible that my baby hadn't been getting much, if anything, during our nursing attempts at the hospital.

They were also growing sorer by the moment, so I left the boys where they were and unsheathed my Spectra S2 breast pump.

The small, round machine had a pink face with a digital settings display, and it came with a power cord, flexible rubber tubing, and two breast flanges, which looked like funnels attached to baby bottles. The setup directions were simple, and within ten minutes all pump components were functionally attached. I unclipped my breastfeeding bra and saddled up to my new pump, holding a funnel-shaped flange to each of my nipples. I sat like that for a moment and contemplated my next step.

"I think you have to turn it on," John said, always the wise guy.

"I know I have to turn it on," I informed him, "I just don't know how I'm supposed to do that when both of my hands are full."

I had spent the majority of my pregnancy making a short film and secretly hoping I would turn out to be effortlessly, instinctively maternal, so I hadn't once looked at my breast pump or educated myself about its use. Neither had John, though, I reasoned, so I refused to feel guilty about it. Instead, I decided to experiment. I set the pump on my computer desk, pushed my laptop away, and leaned forward in my chair in an attempt to stabilize the bottles attached to the funnel-shaped flanges that would be sucking the milk from my boobs. Once sufficiently braced, I powered on the pump.

"AHH!" I yelled, as the pump tried to vacuum my sore nipples off my body.

"You okay?" asked John. His concern was touching.

"Too hard," I mustered, and he sucked air through his teeth in sympathetic solidarity.

Luckily, the extreme nipple hoovering incident gave me a fair bit of information about pumping. Firstly, and most self-explanatorily, I learned that I didn't need anywhere near as much suction as previously thought. I gently removed the flanges from my breasts, then powered on the pump to adjust its suction capacity to the lowest possible setting.

Next, my nipples were positioned wrong inside the flanges, which had caused them to rub against the plastic when sucked, which sucked. Double-checking that the machine was off, I repositioned the funnels, lining my flat little nipples up with the middle-most point of each flange corridor, being extra careful to leave room on all sides so that my nipples could successfully be slurped into their most swollen, erect state for lactation.

I leaned forward in my chair again to stabilize the apparatus and powered on my pump. Three successful nipple pulls later, I knew I had the correct placement. My experiment was shaping up.

Finally, I realized I couldn't spend my pumping life leaning against my desk for support. Unfortunately, a hands-free pumping bra would take at least twenty-four hours to arrive via Amazon and, according to the internet, the local maternity stores were already closed for the evening. So, I found a pair of nail scissors and cut holes in my nursing bra. Through a little trial and error, I shoved the pump flanges through the crudely made holes in my bra and jiggled my nipples back into their positions. Then I took a deep breath and started the pump.

"Is it working?" John asked, as the machine exhaled its rhythmic purr.

"I don't know yet," I said. Nothing was producing, and I worried that I had some sort of defect preventing my milk from flowing. The thought made my chest throb. *That happens sometimes,* I thought. I forced myself to relax and tried to think about something else, but just then the baby cried and my heart leapt into my throat. John had it covered, of course, and sprang into action. He soothed our boy in a low, soft voice, offering comfort as he checked that baby was warm and dry. Then, he looked at me.

"Should I just give him formula?" John asked.

Big, wet tears rolled down my face, in an unexpected, constant downpour, but I swallowed enough of the lump in my throat to speak.

"Yeah, feed him," I said, as I ached to be able to do it myself.

John opened one of our hospital-issued formula bottles and cradled our son in the crook of his arm, offering him the synthetic nipple. It wasn't flat, so he took it with no hesitation. I composed myself as baby ate, deciding to feel grateful that John was proving to be as kind and devoted a father as I had expected, and as my body relaxed, beads of thick, yellow colostrum dropped from my nipples.

"Oh my God!" I laughed through more tears.

"It's working?" John guessed.

I nodded, openly sobbing and overjoyed that my flat nipples and I weren't completely useless. I watched as baby ate, knowing without a doubt that I could provide for him, and I hoped he would still be willing to latch to my breast after experiencing the ease of a bottle. Then, I was struck with a sudden realization. *Wow,* I thought, *that consultant really got to me.*

I hadn't intended to marry my maternal worth and identity to my ability to breastfeed my child, but the external authority figures in the hospital did it for me, so it happened anyway. I thought about my sister, and wondered for the first time ever if she had been motivated to breastfeed by external measures of a mother's worth rather than her own intrinsic inclination. I wondered if my own mother felt pressure to feed with perfection as well. And then I imagined Pam herself, lactation consultant extraordinaire, topless and leaking, hair mussed with a crying newborn on her lap, trying in vain to slip a flat nipple into her baby's hungry mouth.

There was no way for me to know if Pam was a mother, of course—I hadn't thought to ask in the hospital—but the curious image made me laugh, and I suddenly felt sure that tender, swollen breasts and unexpected difficulty with learning to nurse was as typical to the experience of motherhood as a crying newborn. I wasn't defective; I was doing my best.

Once thoroughly milked, I poured the ounce of colostrum I had expressed into a sterile bottle, and lay down with my husband and child. I placed my hand on our baby's tiny back, awed to see that the tip of my finger touched his neck as the heel of my palm stretched all the way past his bottom. The boy was so small and snug on John's chest that I wept at the sight of them, grateful to be experiencing a wonder I found so miraculous yet knew to be so absolutely commonplace. I thought about whether my mom, too, had felt a sense of astonishment when she looked at me, her breasts swollen and tender, her chest aching in a way that felt inexplicably foreign and ancient at once, as though every mother who had ever come before was woven into the fabric of her DNA. I imagined what it would be like to be able to call such an experienced woman and encounter wisdom and acceptance on the other end of the line, rather than emotional volatility.

I gazed at my baby, amazed by his perfection, and as my eyes traced the curve of his plump cheek, I realized I was beginning to recognize him. Oddly, my sense of recognition wasn't because his features had become familiar or had begun to mirror mine or John's. It was an understanding of him that felt deeper, more primal. I adored everything about my baby, and though he made no contribution to the world, held no function, put forth no effort, I knew he was worthy of my adoration. I was in awe of him, of his mere existence, and in my awe there lived a recognition of his humanity.

This is a different kind of love, I thought.

I opened my mouth to attempt to explain what I was feeling to John, but there were no words extraordinary enough to illustrate my sudden reverence for the mundane phenomenon of human existence. Instead, I picked up my baby, curled him against the curve of my breast, and delighted in all the feelings I had but could not name.

CHAPTER EIGHT

THE LEAVE

IT HAD BEEN A WEEK SINCE I had given birth, and I had never in my life been so physically, emotionally, or mentally exhausted. My head felt waterlogged, like a sponge bloated to double its natural size, so I closed my eyes and dropped my right ear to my right shoulder, rolling my head forward to stretch my neck. My eyelids lifted to see my phone light with an unknown number calling, and I had to raise my heavy head and focus my eyes on John holding baby across the room on our bed to determine whether the moment was reality or a dream. *Real,* I decided, and I looked at my phone again.

The number calling was local, with my same area code, but it wasn't my doctor or the pediatrician; I had called those numbers so often I had them memorized. I realized it must be the local office of vital records returning my call. We submitted paperwork to obtain baby's birth certificate during our foggy, sleep-deprived days at the hospital, but once home I realized a labor nurse had noted the wrong birth time. I was on minute twelve of my twenty-minute pump, on my seventh day as a mother, and I didn't know the etiquette of answering a phone call while my pump whirred in the background. I picked up my phone and took the call.

"Hi, this is Connor from HR," said the male voice on the other end of the line, and I realized I was talking to my employer. I covered the microphone to muffle the rattle of my pump.

Connor was calling to follow up on my FMLA filing. The Family and Medical Leave Act was a law that required companies with more than fifty employees to provide up to twelve weeks of unpaid, job-protected leave per calendar year for certain family and medical reasons, like childbirth. I was especially fortunate, because my child was born toward the end of the year, which meant I could take leave for the nearly eight weeks from the date of his birth through the end of the year, and then take an additional twelve weeks off from January through March while my position at work remained protected. I would get five whole months at home with my baby. None of the time off was paid, but I figured that was a worry for another time.

Connor disagreed with my understanding of the law.

"You can't do that," he scoffed.

"Yes, I can," I said. "It's the law."

"Believe me," Connor said, voice dripping with condescension, "that is not even remotely what that law says."

I could feel my sleep-deprived blood begin to boil.

"Are we talking about the same law? I'm talking about FMLA, which is a law that states that an eligible employee can take twelve job-protected weeks of leave per calendar year for a qualifying medical reason. That is the law we're discussing, correct?"

"That is correct. We are talking about the same law." Connor's deliberately slow delivery enraged me.

"Fantastic, Connor," I began, before he interjected.

"But you cannot take it consecutively. This is my job. I know what I'm doing here," he reminded me, and I had to mute myself for a moment so I could laugh.

"I'm so sorry, Connor, but you are piss poor at your job," I spat.

"There's no need—" Connor began.

"There is every need when I'm speaking to an utter dickhead. Do you have any idea what medical state I am in?" My voice was deep with fury. I had lost control and begun to shake.

"I am . . . sorry you're having a difficult time." Connor spoke as professionally as he could, but I could tell he was rattled.

"Do I qualify for FMLA?" I asked.

"I will have to look at your case once I receive the proper paperwork, but generally speaking, the birth of a child is a qualifier."

"Okay, so I qualify. That means I can take twelve weeks of FMLA per calendar year. So I would like to take eight weeks to finish out the rest of the year, and then, beginning in January, which is next year—when it is, in fact, a new calendar year—I would like to take another full twelve weeks." I matched his previous pace of delivery so he could really catch my meaning.

"Yeah, you can't do that," Connor said firmly.

"Yes, I can!" I insisted.

"That is not how that law works," Connor argued.

"That is one hundred percent how that law works!"

John was on his feet at that and hovered nearby.

"I assure you, you are wrong," Connor said.

"Is there another rep I can speak to? Someone who knows what they're talking about?"

"I am your representative in this matter, and anyone else you speak to in this department will tell you the exact same thing I am telling you."

"No one in your entire department, in this giant nationwide corporation, knows how FMLA works?!" I was shouting.

"Listen, why don't you take a breath and calm down." Connor's voice was annoyingly flat.

"I will *not* calm down! I am dealing with a DICKHEAD who doesn't know how the FUCK to do HIS JOB!" I yelled into the phone.

"Ma'am, I am going to have to insist that you calm down," Connor pleaded.

"I need the name and phone number of your supervisor. You are arguing with an employee who has just undergone a major medical event! TRANSFER ME to your supervisor."

Without another word, Connor pushed some buttons on his end of the call, and I left my complaint in the voicemail box of a woman with a senior HR title as my pump exhaled its final purr.

AFTER A MOMENT MY FURY DISSOLVED into panic. The research I did before getting pregnant included whether we could afford a baby. I had spoken to friends at work who had taken FMLA. I had even spoken to a woman who worked in HR and had taken FMLA leave in two consecutive years, like I was attempting to do, so I'd been confident my leave request would be approved. But I had used language and a tone of voice that violated corporate policy, and

Connor had power of approval over my request, so now I couldn't be sure. I could appeal a denial, but my job would be in jeopardy during the process, and there was always the chance our recorded phone call would get pulled as evidence during the appeal. The whole thing added stress to my already swimming head, and I worried about what would happen if I had to return to work before I was ready, or if I could no longer return at all.

I had a daycare lined up—the best affordable choice I could find—but I had secured a spot in the infant room beginning at what I thought would be the end of my leave, in March. I contacted them to go over our options, but there were none; the infant room was full until March, so if I couldn't stay home until then, I would have to figure out alternative childcare.

This is ridiculous, I thought. *They should approve these things ahead of time so moms can prepare.*

A search of the local Ridiculous Women Forum provided several phone numbers for several more daycares, but the idea of calling around for, and then touring, new spots one week postpartum and leaking from at least seven orifices at once was not appealing.

Instead, I got an idea.

I barely had to glance down at the letters as my fingers moved with uncharacteristic dexterity across the black keys of my laptop, as if they were guided by some otherworldly force. The daycares in our area, and there were many, boasted infant rooms housing babies as young as three weeks old for monthly figures that rivaled my monthly take-home pay and made my stomach lurch. We could afford a spot on the lower end of the cost spectrum, if a spot could be found, but the spot itself wouldn't be the only associated cost. My eyes flicked across the points plotted on the digital map before me as I jotted down the approximate distance from our house to each of the daycares local to us, and the approximate amount of gas we'd use getting to and from them, in pink ink on my monogrammed notepad. I summed the averages to find a monthly daycare transportation total. The number was within spitting distance of my salary.

What's the point of me even working? I thought, suddenly clear-headed, and a secret thrill shivered through my body.

There were other factors to consider, like the fact our lease on the rental house with Sarah would be up by the end of January. We had been living together for more than a year, but things had grown tense lately with the addition of baby. My sister was thrilled when I got pregnant, so I had expected her to be as obsessed with her new nephew as I had been with my niece, but she wasn't. An uncharacteristic timidity had developed in her after his arrival, and I couldn't tell if her caution was because she was giving me space or judging my every decision. I didn't have the time or bandwidth to address it, and there had been no talk of a lease renewal, so we'd probably be moving soon. If I was going to have to go back to work before March, I needed to figure out where we were going to live, and if our new living situation would impact our daycare costs. *We really should have worked all of this out beforehand*, I thought, then chuckled to myself about my use of "we." John hadn't thought about our housing or daycare arrangements for even a second.

After living in a rental house for so long I couldn't imagine going back to apartment living, but the only homes in our budget existed outside of Austin's city limits, I discovered as I started looking through listings. We'd have to live in the suburbs to have a house, and we'd be a fair distance away from both our scheduled daycare and John's work, increasing our monthly transportation budget for both.

"That's cute," John said from behind me. He squeezed my left shoulder, then ran his palm down my arm, and his eyes crinkled with a smile when I looked up at him from my pump chair. He nodded his head at the house on my laptop screen. "Is that for us?"

"Maybe." I flicked through the listing photos. "It's cheap, but it's kind of far."

"That's cheap?"

I laughed at his bewildered tone. "It's in the 'burbs, baby," I said.

"Ah." He closed his gaping mouth. "What's the distance from work?"

I typed in the two addresses on a driving map. "Twenty-eight minutes," I said.

"Pssshh! That's nothing!"

My fingers tapped a different destination into the search field, and the driving map revealed Austin Film Society's studios a mere forty-three-minute drive away.

"Mm, kind of far for auditions?" John asked.

"Not too bad," I insisted. "And auditions happen all over town, anyway."

"Good point. Should we buy it?"

"It's for rent," I laughed. His enthusiasm was infectious, though, so I clicked on a home search that would populate sale prices. "Holy shit."

"Holy shit." John's eyebrows shot up his forehead. "Those are pretty cheap."

I brought up a two-story three-bedroom in the neighborhood I liked and flicked through the interior photos. The home had neutral floor tiles and an open-concept kitchen with an island that could double as a breakfast counter.

"Aww, for cereal before school," I lilted, romantic for the nostalgia of a childhood home I didn't get to experience.

"What would the mortgage be on that?" John asked.

"No idea." The skin tightened across my areolas begging to be pumped. *Already?* I thought, but the clock on my phone told me I had been working on our housing for more than two hours. Baby squawked for a bottle, so John gave me a wink and we each settled in to feed him.

I looked at more home information as my pump worked, my fingers typing phrases like "first-time homebuyer" and "how to buy a house without any money" into search bars that provided pages of proof that we were actually in a better financial spot than I'd realized. According to the internet, we qualified for a Federal Housing Administration loan, which was only available to people who had never owned anything before. *Down payment as low as 3.5 percent*, I silently read and tapped the numbers into the calculator app on my phone. If we could scrape together five grand, and qualify for a teeny-tiny interest rate, and pay for our closing costs with our loan, we could own a home just outside the city. And if we owned a home just outside the city, it would be more cost-effective for me to stay at home with the baby.

"What are you grinning about?" Sarah teased, catching me in a daydream a week later.

I took a quick breath to stall for time but couldn't contain my giddy smile.

"I think we're going to buy a house!" I said.

"Oh, no way!" She was enthusiastic, so I rambled on, feeling the magnitude of the moment.

"I had no idea it would even be possible; I basically stumbled on the information when I was looking at daycare costs."

"That's awesome, I'm happy for you."

Sarah picked a loose string from the cuff of her sleeve and rolled it into a ball between her thumb and forefinger, and I felt a pang of guilt.

"Sorry I didn't talk to you about renewing first, I know it was up in the air." I tried to catch her eye so she'd believe my sincerity, but she was giving a MasterClass on gaze aversion.

"Oh, not even," she insisted with a shrug. "I actually would love to get into our own house, too."

"*Really?*" I didn't mean to sound condescending, so I quickly blurted out the entirety of my limited knowledge on the home buying process to convey my enthusiasm for the fulfillment of all her home wishes, too. "Have you looked into FHA loans? You've never been a homeowner so it should be possible! I think it is, at least. Do you know your credit score? Mine is *way* higher than I would have expected."

Sarah sucked an inhale past her teeth and stretched her neck. "Don't know. I haven't looked at anything, so." She swept the edge of her hand across some dining table crumbs, picking them up, then made her way to the kitchen.

"Yeah. Well, that's cool, hopefully you can," I said, following after her.

"That would be cool." She turned on the kitchen sink tap and sprayed food off three breakfast plates, placing each one in the dishwasher, and I pretended to look at something important on my phone. I wished I could hug her, but the air between us was contaminated with a drama neither one of us wanted to address, so instead I smiled and turned to go.

"Hey, sorry," Sarah called after me.

"Oh, it's fine," I said it as if I hadn't noticed anything.

"Long day, and I'm just stressed about—"

"Life," I finished her sentence, and it broke the ice. We both laughed. "Want a hug?" I asked, as if the hug would be for her.

"Yeah," came the quick reply.

"Good. Me, too," I said, and suddenly we were little girls again, hugging and playing with each other's hair.

I walked upstairs and pushed open our bedroom door to see John standing in the middle of the room with his back to me in rigid stillness. I saw his cell phone cupped to his ear and froze for a moment to listen, but he didn't speak. My eyes darted to baby; he was asleep in his co-sleeper, and tension released from my shoulders. I stepped around John until I could see his face. His eyes were misty and his face was pale, and a moment later he ended his call with a quick, "Okay, thanks."

After a deep breath he told me he had been on the phone with his mom's widower, Dan, who was a nice man but distant, so an out-of-the-blue phone call had been odd. It was good timing, though, John said, because Thesla had named him and his two siblings co-beneficiaries of her life insurance policy. John was entitled to twelve thousand dollars, a chunk of money bigger than either of us had ever had all at once, and more than enough money for a small down payment on a modest house in the suburbs of Austin.

John dropped his phone and cried into his hands. His mom was still loving him even after death.

I KNEW NOTHING ABOUT REAL ESTATE, but luckily, I knew Amanda Ponce. Amanda was barely five feet tall, but she was bigger than life; she wore a perpetual smile and stomped her steps, which gave her the air of a jolly giant despite her diminutive stature. She was a former colleague who had left corporate America to become her own boss as a real estate agent, and everyone said she was an absolute shark. I remembered her profession at nine o'clock in the evening, two weeks after John learned about his mom's money, and shot her a quick text message. I wanted to know, hypothetically, if she thought, in her expert opinion, we might be able to get into our own home by the time our rental agreement ended in January. My phone rang right away, and after a ten-minute conversation, I was compiling financial documents for our meeting with Amanda the following morning.

John slowed the car to a crawl and craned his neck out of his open window to get a better look at the name on the green street sign up ahead as Amanda answered my call.

"Hi, Shawna!" Amanda piped. "I'm at the future resident parking, where are you?"

"Okay, we're turning onto Avocado Lane, so I think we're . . ." I reached past John's hand on the steering wheel and flicked on our windshield wipers to clear the glass of dust.

"I see you!" A tiny Amanda jumped and waved from thirty yards ahead.

"Ah, yay! Okay, see you in a sec." I tapped the end call button, carefully pulled my pump flanges from their holes in my bra, and fixed my shirt. "Four ounces, not bad for a quick pump," I said to John and poured my haul into a clean bottle for baby to eat when he woke. John parked the car and grabbed baby in his carrier, and we greeted Amanda, then headed inside to begin our home search.

We toured four three-bedroom cookie cutters on streets named after fruits. Amanda was adamant that we could afford twenty thousand dollars over what I had estimated; twenty thousand spread out over a thirty-year mortgage wouldn't make much of a difference, even with interest, Amanda said, but it would buy so much more house in the neighborhoods we liked.

"Of course, if you go with something less expensive then you can stay home with the baby," she laughed, and my eyes bugged out of their sockets.

"Oh, ha ha," I stammered. "Well, actually . . ." I was trying to downplay how intensely I wanted to create that reality for my little family.

"Really, you should think about it," Amanda persisted, tickling baby's feet. "You were always really creative; that corporate place will fry your brain if you stay too long."

I cocked my head to get a read on her. I couldn't tell if the praise she was lavishing on me was another sales tactic or if she just got me, but truthfully, I didn't care; I loved it either way. We didn't like any of the homes we saw that day, but Amanda felt confident we would find something if we kept trying.

THE NEXT DAY, AS MY BREAST pump whirred, I fanned my ribs, forced a breath deep into my belly, and let my head fall back, stretching the front of my neck. It felt so good that I leaned further into my chair back and let my arms fall open to either side. I bounced, a quick jerk, and my back cracked in three places. *Ahh,* I thought, and I opened my eyes to check the bottles of milk dangling from my boobs. My back crack hadn't spilled a drop. Satisfied, I returned to neutral and picked up my phone, which was buzzing. I didn't recognize the number calling me, but it was local so I moved to accept the call. It ended before I could tap the little green circle, which was mildly annoying, and I yawned and rolled my neck around to stretch a little more.

My phone dinged a moment later with a voicemail and a belly-deep, profoundly joyful laugh burst from my throat when I looked at the transcription: Connor from HR had approved my leave and wanted to apologize, first for misinterpreting our company's FMLA policy, but also for causing me any undue stress during my postpartum period.

Yeah, you better apologize, you dumb dickhead, I thought.

The pleasure of having been correct about the implementation of a law Connor should have understood gave me more energy than I had in weeks. But even better than that righteous triumph was the fact that I had transformed my fury at Connor into fuel to provide care and safety for my baby in the form of a childhood home. I giggled again, feeling very mama bear, and stretched both arms up high and wide in victory, as my pump finished its last milk pull and my phone buzzed again.

This time it was Amanda, calling to connect us with a mortgage broker, a home inspector, a property lawyer, a notary, and a flooring guy who also painted, in case we needed to make any cosmetic alterations to the interior of our future home. It had taken three months of house hunting, countless phone calls, four virtual meetings, and eight in-person home tours, all arranged and attended by Amanda, plus a month's extension on our rental home lease while we waited for escrow to close, but we officially owned our own home, in the neighborhood we liked and right on budget. I was going to be a stay-at-home mom. And eventually, when I was ready, maybe I could get back to acting.

CHAPTER NINE

THE INSTINCT

The sun was warm and bright where I sat, and it bathed the world around me, and my son in my arms, in a gentle golden hue. I heard a car door close somewhere behind me, and I rose from the splintered wood of the picnic table when I saw my grandmother's blue flowered pedal pushers sauntering my way. Grandma Sally wore her silver hair like a helmet and gripped the strap of her shoulder bag like a lead. I loved the way her lithe frame moved quickly toward me. It reminded me of how important she made me feel as a child, and I was eager to introduce her to my son. She commanded such a presence that I almost didn't notice Mom trailing just behind. Mom smiled serenely, gazing at me with adoration, and I knew she was proud.

I felt proud, too, excited to see them both, and smiled brightly as they approached. Grandma hugged me first and kissed my cheek, and I recognized the warmth of her embrace and the sweet smell of her perfume. I felt loved. I turned then to greet Mom, who gave me a gentle hug and kiss, and cupped my face in her hand, inspecting me closely with a tender touch so surprising that my heart filled with gratitude. Then, she looked me up and down.

"Where's the baby?" she asked, and terror ripped through my body as I looked down at my cold, gray, empty arms.

MY EYES SPRUNG OPEN FROM MY nightmare and I slammed into the dark, silent reality of my bedroom, still gripped with panic. I stood and tore the sheets from my bed, positive I was such a terrible mother that I had smothered my baby. I screamed for John to wake, and in a blurry instant he was on his feet. I turned then to see my newborn snug in his bassinet a mere step away from my bedside. I collapsed to the floor and sobbed relief into my hands. I felt John's footsteps pound the ground as he hurried to my side, and I stood to stammer out an explanation. His body relaxed once he realized the baby and I were both okay, and with my encouragement he made his way back to bed. Miraculously, baby slept through my frenzy, so I placed a gentle hand on his chest to confirm that he was breathing. All was well, but the damage to my body was done: I was wide-awake. So, I sighed, peed, then decided I might as well pump some breast milk.

I had left my pump parts on the bathroom counter, where I had created a pump part washing station, including a drying rack. I had a decent output of milk each time, so what had begun as a formula-supplemented feeding journey had become an exclusive pumping crusade, and to produce enough supply to meet demand, I sat for twenty-minute pumping sessions six times a day, around the clock.

I didn't mind, though; I was happy to be able to nourish my baby and have some semblance of control over at least one aspect of motherhood. Except on this occasion, because when I entered my bathroom, I found the pieces of my pump still splattered with four-hour old milk, and suddenly the meaning of my nightmare was obvious. *I'm not very good at mothering*, I thought.

It was the second week of December, six weeks since I had given birth, and John would start back at work again the next morning. John was a hands-on dad and took to our son's care like a duck to water, but I was not as maternally inclined as I had expected myself to be. I had been gifted a babywearing wrap during my pregnancy and, on night twelve of baby's life, when I couldn't get him to settle even though he was clean, fed, and dry, John wove the wrap around his body and took the baby for a walk in the chilly night air, calming him in the process. I was simultaneously relieved that John took the initiative to solve our problem and embarrassed that I hadn't had the same instinct for comforting our baby, and so, heavy with guilt, I sat down and pumped some breast milk. Every day since bringing our boy home, John had offered bodily comfort and bottled nourishment, while I, the mother whose body built the baby and made his food, sat alone in a chair strapped to a plastic milking device, watching. With John's return to work I would be thrust into the primary caregiver role and, according to my dream and the unwashed pump parts on the counter before me, I was unequal to the task. I washed and sanitized the parts, then pumped some milk. I crawled back into bed after twenty minutes as a desperate agitation began to fester in my belly.

Several hours later, the world outside my bedroom brightened, and by the time John's alarm blared I wasn't sure I had gotten any sleep at all. My eyes were gritty from exhaustion, and I wished I had a reset button that would take me back to a time when life felt light so I could get some sleep, but I knew that was only an anxious thought I didn't mean. The baby woke then, ready for food, so I shook John awake by the shoulder. He inhaled deeply and fluttered his eyes as I gave baby a bottle, and I wondered how it was possible for him to turn his brain off long enough to fall asleep in the first place. I didn't have that talent. He eventually woke enough to get ready for work, then kissed baby and me goodbye. I waved as I watched him leave from our front steps, and then, alone with baby at last, I shut the door to the outside world and began our day.

I had skipped my usual morning pump to give John some extra sleeping time, so my breasts were aching for relief. Baby was asleep again, but his position in the crook of my arm blocked access to my nipples, so I gently shifted him to the comfort of his bassinet, inconveniently waking him in the process. He cried, a sleepy, screeching kind of cry, filling my body with dread, so I scooped him up to make the noise stop. It didn't. I offered a bottle, but it just angered him further. Tears dripped from his eyes and beads of milk dripped from my nipples as I walked and jostled him around the house in an effort to calm him down. To keep from going insane, I talked to him.

"This is our couch," I said in a singsong voice I hoped he'd find soothing. "We sit here to watch our favorite shows, like *The Office* and *The Bachelor*."

He screamed, but I felt better, so I continued.

"This is our refrigerator," I said. "When you're older, and you draw pictures, I'm going to stick them on the fridge with a magnet, and it'll be so cute." I smelled something musty as I passed the kitchen sink and made a mental note to ask John to inspect it after work.

"This is the bathroom where I checked the position of my cervix so we could make you," I said with a laugh.

Baby wasn't amused, though, so I made my way upstairs to our bedroom, hoping the familiar environment would trigger sleep. I sat down on my pumping chair and held the boy between my breasts, careful to make sure my nipples were free in case he settled enough to allow me to pump. After a moment his cries dwindled into occasional whimpers, and I was sure of impending victory. I gave a deep sigh of relief—and when I did, I smelled the kitchen sink again.

Puzzled by the lingering damp, buttery odor, I sniffed the air, turning my head this way and that. Mild but unmistakable, the smell was all around me. I wondered how our garbage disposal had caused a trail so pungent it could follow me upstairs and three rooms away. Then, awareness seized my body, and my eyes fell to the bulging swath of white covering baby's bottom.

Are you kidding me? I thought, and headed for the changing table.

A tear rolled off my cheek and plopped onto my son's green onesie as I refastened it over the new diaper, leaving a tiny wet circle on his shoulder, but he was clean and quiet at last. I picked him up, feeling like an idiot for not noticing his dirty diaper sooner, and offered him a bottle, which was hungrily accepted. Grateful to have finally done something right, I sat on my pumping chair hoping he would fall asleep. Instead, he popped off his bottle with a little burp and looked around with curious eyes.

I smiled as a drop of milk trickled from the corner of his satisfied mouth. It amazed me that the tiniest micro expression formed on his beautiful face could make my heart burst with love, like champagne from a bottle, abundant and effervescent and sparkling. It was the greatest feeling I'd ever experienced, looking at him, but after a moment I noticed the feeling also touched something in me that I didn't understand, something more like melancholy, an aching of unknown origin. *Oh right, the ache,* I thought, remembering the first night I sat awake and alone with my feelings after baby was born. I didn't have energy to examine the ache further, so I kissed baby's forehead and the bridge of his nose and resisted the urge to suck on his chubby cheek, though it was difficult. He breathed deeply as his eyes closed and his tiny head rested against my chest. I knew I should take the opportunity to pump but instead rested my head, too, on my chairback, and let the salty stress of the morning pour from my eyes.

Two hours and nineteen minutes later than usual, I finally poked my pump flanges through their bra holes and aligned them to my nipples. I powered on my pump and its gentle suction began. The machine purred with each pull and milk quickly began to pour, tinkling relief into the collection bottles below, amassing a full ounce after just three minutes. And then a low, rumbling trill of poots splattered in baby's diaper, and he awoke with a cry.

I balled my fists and pressed my frustration between my lips but it wasn't enough. I growled and dug my nails into my palms, tensing my whole body.

"Why?" I angrily asked, but there was no one to answer and nothing to be done. With one hand on baby, I stopped my pump and ripped the flanges from their holes. I stood, nipples out, and took baby to our changing station to clean him up. I was seething, too angry to attempt a calming tone, so I didn't speak. I knew it was illogical, but I wanted to yell, to demand to know if he realized what I was doing for him. But when I looked at his crying face, I just felt tired.

Not knowing what else to do, I cleaned his bottom then shoved nipple pads into my bra and walked around the house, chattering about nothing. For the rest of the day, I offered several bottles and changed several diapers and sat for several naps, until John came home to rescue us both from my incompetence.

WHEN THE ALARM BLARED ON JOHN'S second day back to work, I glared at him from my pumping chair, annoyed that he didn't immediately rise. I knew I couldn't blame him for his exhaustion, or my own, but I still felt irrationally angry and looked around for something I could throw at him. He woke a moment later, though, without my intervention, and saw me, already upright and milking myself, and smiled sweetly.

He's a better person than I am, I thought, and I knew it to be true.

Baby woke then, so John greeted him lovingly and popped a bottle in his mouth while I choked back hot tears. They looked adorable, father and child curled up in bed for a morning bottle, but the sight made me rage with fury. I thought motherhood would awaken tender affection in me, but all I could access in that moment was an all-too-familiar maternal anger, and it scared me.

Why didn't anyone tell me it would be like this? I silently wondered.

I told John I'd meet him downstairs and he kissed my forehead on his way out of our bedroom. I stored the fresh milk I had pumped in the mini fridge full of baby's bottles by my bedside, then buried my face in a pillow and screamed until my throat was raw. I thought of my sister Sarah, about how appalled I had been way back before I had gotten pregnant, when she confessed to resorting to the occasional frustrated pillow scream on her motherhood journey, and I felt ashamed for having judged her too harshly. I remembered my dream from the other night and wondered if Grandma Sally had ever screamed into a pillow, or if Mom had.

No, I thought, *Mom just screamed at us*, and for the first time ever I understood that Mom must have been consumed by overwhelm a lot during my childhood. I wondered then if every mother who had come before me had felt unequal to the task at times, if we all raged at our partners and felt the urge to yell at our babies. I thought about the women I knew growing up—my mom, of course, but also my friends' moms, my aunts and grandmas, even teachers—and I realized that every woman I could think of had a ferociousness to her.

Why is motherhood depicted as gentle? I wondered, and I thought about birth itself, which was painful and raw and visceral, not gentle, even when heavily medicated, at least in my experience.

"Hey," John said, snapping me back to reality. "I've got to take off." He handed me the baby and pulled us both close, his hand on the small of my back.

"Now, you two don't have too much fun without me," he said with a grin, and kissed me gently.

"We won't," I admitted, and he chuckled like I had made a joke.

I STEPPED OUT INTO THE WARMTH of the sun and adjusted baby's cap for our walk later that morning, wondering when we might get some winter weather. That brief moment of recalling the pain of his birth had awakened a new sense of determination to understand how to tend to my baby. I knew he liked walking with John, so, despite my exhaustion, I donned my babywearing wrap, curved his small body snugly around my swollen boobs, and set out.

When we turned the corner of our rental home's street, I tripped and stumbled three steps. I didn't lose my balance, but images of rolling an ankle and falling on top of my baby flooded my mind and caused tears to spring to my eyes. I looked around for any neighbors who might have seen my almost-tragedy, but there were none. Baby was tied at boob-height, which meant my field of vision was obscured, so I hadn't seen the crack in the pavement below. I felt too stupid to turn back, having set out with such high hopes just moments before, so I shimmied my wrap, and baby with it, lower on my body, until I could see my feet.

Just go slow, I told myself, and, despite feeling wobbly, I continued on.

We turned a second corner, and the faint scent of crape myrtle filled my nose. I inhaled deeply and happily took in the beauty of the spindly trees that lined both sides of the street and shaded the path before me. Their branches were bare for winter, but they still smelled good, and I couldn't wait to see them in full bloom again, which seemed a metaphor for my journey into motherhood—which often had me naked, smelling of milk, and longing to thrive—and the comparison made me laugh. Then I tripped and fell hard on my knees.

Baby cried this time, and pushed his limbs against the trunk of my body, evidently too snug in the wrap once awake. I did my best to loosen the folds, which calmed him down, but the pain in my knees intensified, making it harder to breathe. I sat on my bottom to assess the purple bruising that was starting to form, and, exhaling through gritted teeth, looked around at the sidewalk below me for what I had tripped on.

Where did you come from? I thought as I rolled a small, sidewalk-colored pebble between my forefinger and thumb.

Sufficiently done with attempting to be outside, I scooted my butt to the edge of the sidewalk and fixed both of my feet flat in the gutter. I shook my legs to wake them up and stamped the pounding heartbeat out of my knees, willing a feeling of stability to return. "Please don't fall again," I muttered, and pushing the ground away with my hands, I stood and limped back along the shady lane the way I'd come.

After a short, uncomfortable shuffle home, I lay down on the couch, humbled, and started an old rerun of *I Love Lucy* while I iced my sore knees. I looked at Lucille Ball executing her physical comedy with perfection and sighed deeply. I wasn't an actress, or any good at being a mother, and suddenly I couldn't even walk either. I felt like an all-around failure.

Baby seemed content to lie on his stomach on top of me, and I reasoned with myself that I had been instructed to encourage lots of tummy-time to help strengthen his back and neck, so our position was probably productive. I looked into his curious face, eyes wide and searching, and the world around us melted away. The newborn-blue tint of his eyes had already begun to lighten to a steel gray, and I wondered if he'd have eyes that matched my shade of green, John's golden, or something else unique to him. I hoped for the third option, so he could always feel like his own person.

I thought about our future, too—John's, baby's, and mine—and wondered what kind of boy he would be. I tried to imagine him as a rambunctious toddler, tall and chubby and chasing birds on a beach, but I couldn't envision a dynamic so different from our everyday. All I could see in my mind's eye were the endless miles of sleep deprivation and nipple stimulation ahead of me, and a feeling somewhere between depletion and depression clouded my vision.

I sighed and watched Lucy stuff a chocolate into her mouth, then looked at my boy again. *He's worth it*, I said in my mind as I traced the tip of my finger along the curve of his button nose, and I was determined to believe it.

DON'T SIT IN THIS FUNK, I told myself after a week of doing just that, and started formulating a plan to assume control of the life I had chosen.

First, I decided I would only pump milk when John was home. Pumping every four hours had become too difficult a schedule to maintain during my days alone with baby, so I needed to let go of my feeding perfectionism to focus on his needs without getting frustrated. *I pump when John is home* became my first mantra.

Second, I decided I would learn what all of baby's noises meant. Instead of picking him up the moment he made a peep, I would pause and watch his facial expressions and body language to learn what he was trying to tell me. *Crying is communication* became my second mantra.

Third, I decided to accept that I was exhausted and probably not functioning at my highest possible competency. If I could respect the need to slow down and quiet the chatter in my head about what I should be doing, my body wouldn't have to feel restless and anxious on top of being exhausted. *I am doing enough* became my third mantra.

On day three of my newly adopted mindset, I noticed my sweet boy was still eating one- to two-ounce bottles every two hours, the same way he had since he had first come home.

Seems like he could eat more, I thought, and a quick search of the

Ridiculous Women Forum confirmed that a seven-week-old tummy could handle three to four ounces at a time.

Baby woke then from his cat nap on my lap, so I put my phone to the side and covered his face in kisses. His eyes scrunched and his lips pulled up at the corners into a gummy expression of glee.

"Is that a smile?" I asked, positive I had witnessed a first, and his eyes focused on mine while the grin widened. "It is! You're smiling at Mama!" I gushed.

I snapped a picture, texted it to John, then got to work making faces that would make more smiles.

After about forty minutes and a diaper change, I noticed little grunts coming from baby. My first instinct was to swoop him up and go for another living room walk, but I resisted and watched instead. *Crying is communication*, I repeated to myself. He wriggled a bit on my lap and moved his head from side to side as he whimpered. He brought his balled fist to his mouth, then rubbed his eye.

Aha! I thought. *Hungry and tired.*

I poured four ounces of breast milk into a sterile bottle and offered it to baby. He dozed as he ate, then arched his back and popped off the bottle after two ounces, smacking his little lips, settling into sleep. I took to the Ridiculous Women Forum again and learned that babies may not eat a full meal if they're too tired. For this reason, said the brilliant women, it's best to offer baby a bottle immediately upon waking.

Oops, I thought, and then quickly countered any negativity by repeating, *I am doing enough.*

Baby slept a mere forty minutes, so I quickly had a chance to try again, but when I offered a bottle immediately upon waking, he refused. When I offered the bottle a few minutes later at what

I thought was his first hunger cue, he refused. He refused another fifteen minutes later, and he refused every time after that, until I changed his diaper and we hit the one hour of awake time mark, at which point he ate two ounces, stretched his torso, then fell happily asleep. We repeated the same pattern of wake-and-play, diaper change, then bottle-feed-to-sleep twice more before John came home, and each time the child would not eat more than two ounces.

I pump when John is home, I reminded myself, and handed baby over to sit down, make more milk, and return to the Ridiculous Women Forum.

The space between my eyebrows pinched tight as I scrolled old posts for answers. There had been an expression on my baby's face, something I recognized but couldn't name, whenever he popped off the bottle after a feed, and it made me think there was an obstacle to him eating more. Once sufficiently milked, I had John feed baby while we both watched. When he had his two-ounce fill, he curled his top lip the tiniest bit, spit the bottle out of his mouth, and stretched his head and body backward.

"He's grimacing!" I said.

"He was moving his lip out of the way," John replied, but I knew I was right.

MY PALM WAS SWEATY AS IT gripped the rubber-wrapped handle of my baby's carrier, so I stopped walking and shifted the carrier to the crook of my arm. It hurt to hold it there but I liked how secure it felt, so there it stayed.

I ran through a checklist of important items in my mind as I began to walk again. *Wipes*, I thought, as I arrived at the pediatrician's front desk for my son's two-month well-baby checkup. I gave the receptionist my name, date of birth, and appointment time, and laughed when she asked for baby's information instead. Once checked in, I hurried to the waiting room to rifle through my diaper bag and was relieved to find a sixteen-count sample pack of wipes squashed under other necessities. I checked wipes off my mental list.

A nurse called us back a few moments later, and she noted baby's length and head circumference in his chart. Then, she instructed me to strip baby naked so we could get an accurate weight. I took off his onesie and unstuck the Velcro tabs of his diaper to reveal a mess so massive I was shocked it hadn't been a blowout. Mouth agape, embarrassed I missed the warning signs, I stammered out an apology and tore through my bag for the sample pack of wipes. Five wipes later he was clean, so I laid his naked butt on the countertop baby scale—only for him to pee in a three-foot arc, dousing me and nearly the nurse. I apologized again and could feel my face getting hot, but the nurse simply told me to get baby dressed. I grabbed a fresh diaper from my bag, quickly covering baby's bottom, then snapped his onesie back over his head. I realized then that the diaper *had* been a blowout and removed the soiled garment right away. I cleaned baby off with more wipes, then followed the harried nurse to our exam room, where she left me with the promise that our pediatrician would be right in. I said a silent prayer that the pediatrician would be quick and that baby would stay clean.

Thirty minutes later, I was cleaning up yet another blowout with the last of my precious wipes. I rummaged through my bag for another diaper, which I found, and a second backup outfit, which I did not. I hastily secured baby's fresh diaper and draped him with a backup shirt meant for me as our pediatrician knocked on the door.

"Come on in," I yelled, hoping the feigned confidence in my voice masked my embarrassment.

"Hi, Mama!" came the chipper greeting as the door swung open. Our pediatrician was young but knowledgeable, a new mom herself with a nine-month-old daughter, and I marveled at her clean, brushed hair and the neatly drawn lipstick on her mouth. I asked her once how she managed to look so put together with an infant at home and she laughed, assuring me that she had spent her maternity leave in dirty sweats, and I felt better.

She didn't bat an eye at baby's state of dress but went right to work on his checkup, assuring me that he was developing perfectly. He started to fuss a little, and he'd been awake more than an hour, so I knew he was hungry.

Perfect timing, I thought, and when the doctor asked if I had questions or concerns, I was ready.

"Can I show you how he feeds?" I asked. "He has that tongue tie I told you about, so I pump and we do bottles, and that still works okay, but he never eats more than two ounces."

The doctor was properly concerned at that, and her eyes flitted over baby's chart.

"His weight is okay, so he must be eating around the clock," she concluded.

"Oh yeah, every two hours, day and night," I said, and she looked at me with sympathy.

"You must be exhausted."

I turned my head as I nodded so she wouldn't see the tears forming in my eyes.

"My concern is reflux," I said as I began to feed baby. "It's not bad enough to cause a lot of vomiting, but he does spit up, and I've noticed that he kind of stretches and grimaces right when he pops the bottle out of his mouth, so I don't think he's full; I think he's uncomfortable."

"Have you tried holding him upright to feed?" she asked.

"Yeah, he stops no matter what position he's in," I said.

"Have you tried to pace your feeds?" she asked.

"Yeah, but if I slow him down, he stops at one ounce," I explained.

"Wow, you must be awake every single hour at night," she said, and as she looked me in the eye, I could no longer conceal my crying.

"We take him in shifts," I admitted at last. Baby finished his two ounces, then arched his tiny back, curled his little lip, and pushed the bottle away with his tongue.

"Ah, I see what you mean," the pediatrician said.

"Really?" I asked hopefully.

And then, looking me in the eye again, she confirmed my instinct. "It does look like reflux. Good catch, Mom."

AFTER TWO WEEKS ON PRESCRIPTION FAMOTIDINE, baby hungrily sucked down his first three-and-a-half-ounce bottle, then took his first-ever two-hour nap. I cried as I sat in silence watching him sleep in my lap, intentionally choosing to forgo my pump. I wanted to savor the moment my instincts had led us to. *I pump when John is here*, I reminded myself. I noticed then that my body was still and calm, that I no longer felt agitated deep in my belly, and in that quiet moment alone with my boy, I understood that my restlessness had been fear all along.

I wondered when I had first begun to doubt my own ability, and who had planted those seeds of doubt in me. I wondered if I ever would have realized those doubts had baby not existed. I wondered if those doubts had held me back in other aspects of life, too, like with acting, and I felt an immense surge of gratitude for the boy in my lap. I had been so afraid of pain, his and mine, but sitting with the pain was my path to understanding what he needed. *Crying is communication*, I thought, and a lump formed in my throat.

The fear had been useful, because experimenting to alleviate it ultimately allowed me to become curious about baby's communication. That I was capable of understanding his unspoken language felt empowering. Because of my baby, I was forced to figure out how to be a better me. *I am doing enough*, I thought, *but MAN this is harder than I thought it would be.* And with that, I let the tears flow from my eyes.

After a moment, I picked up my phone, snapped a cute picture of my sleeping baby, and texted it to Grandma Sally and Mom, knowing deep in my heart that they must have once felt the way I did.

CHAPTER TEN

THE HOLIDAYS

My eyes popped open at 7 am, and despite the bone-deep exhaustion of sleeping next to a newborn who had woken nearly every hour all night for the better part of two months, I was flooded with unmitigated joy. It was my baby's first Christmas, and Dad was coming to visit.

He had texted me at one o'clock in the morning (eleven o'clock at night in California, where he lived) after a very busy day of house hunting back in early November, far too late for anyone to be reaching out to a new mother, which annoyed me until I looked at his message, complete with a screenshot of his flight details: *Hey sweetie! Booked my flight to come see you and meet my grandson!!* He didn't ask, he stated, but I forgave his approach without another thought because, though he wouldn't arrive until December 26, he was coming to stay for four nights, and he was coming at Christmastime.

Holidays were an incredibly big deal in my family growing up. Because I'd been born in November, a day before my Aunt Susie, Thanksgiving often felt like an extension of my birthday celebration. I would have a party with friends a weekend or two before Thanksgiving, and then on that fourth Thursday of the month, my entire extended family would gather. Grandma Sally would spend ten hours cooking a twenty-five-pound turkey plus mountains of potatoes, stuffing, casserole, three pies, and a homemade cranberry sauce that nobody ever ate. Sometimes she would also make her famous buttermilk chocolate birthday cake. Her efforts were rewarded when the entire family would crowd around her table, which she always beautifully clothed in cream linen and lace. We'd tell stories and laugh—Dad's stories dazzling most of all—and pass heaps of food arranged on silver serving platters, and then, after dinner, everyone would sing "Happy Birthday" and Aunt Susie and I would open presents.

Christmas was an equally lavish affair. Though Mom and Dad didn't have a lot of money, Grandma Sally had worked hard to create her own wealth as the owner-operator of a chain of upscale convalescent homes for the elderly, and to make up for a lack of available quality time, gift giving was her love language. One Christmas morning when I was nine years old, I woke before anyone else, crept to the top of the stairs, and peeked out over the banister to see piles of presents for all sixteen of my family members stacked up around the base of our glittering tree. It was magical. Christmas also came complete with its own traditional feast à la Grandma, of course, after which all the kid-cousins would abscond to a back room to play with our new haul of toys, board games, and cards.

My favorite part about family holiday traditions when I was a child, though, was that everyone was happy.

I NEVER KNEW THE FULL BREADTH of Dad's brief crystal meth habit, but holidays were never the same after it took hold. I was eleven years old when, on the morning of Thanksgiving Day, Mom broke the news that Dad would not be joining us for our annual dinner. I didn't know it at the time, but Dad would move to Northern California a year later, and two years after that they'd finally sign divorce papers. But that first Thanksgiving without Dad was unsettling.

"Why can't Dad come?" I asked.

"Because he's a drug addict," Mom said plainly. Having known Dad to be a nice guy and a Christian, and having just completed a D.A.R.E. course at school, I wholeheartedly rejected the premise.

"No, he's not!" I cried.

"Ask him," Mom said. "He said he would call. I'm not sure if he will because being a drug addict makes a person unreliable, but if he calls, you can ask him. He'll tell you."

When we arrived at Thanksgiving, there were three love notes from Dad, one for each of us girls. He called, like he said he would, so I knew he couldn't be using drugs. So, in my bravest eleven-year-old voice, I asked.

"Dad, are you really on drugs?"

"Oh," he started, breathlessly. "Yeah, sweetie, I was. I'm sorry. I'm not right now, but . . ."

"Well, then, can you come?" The words tumbled out, and though I already knew his answer, I hoped I was wrong.

"I'm sorry, sweetie, I can't."

Being a child of divorced parents caused more than holiday difficulty growing up. Mom couldn't stand Dad after all the years of hurt and betrayal, and she insisted my sisters and I should feel the same. Mom was a child of divorce herself, and she knew from experience that forcing children to pick sides was hard on them, but she couldn't help herself: Dad had ruined her plans for a wholesome nuclear family experience and instead abandoned her with three daughters to raise and five years of back taxes to pay. Mom's pain often became too much for her to bear, splashing out of her broken heart and all over my sisters and me. Erin, the eldest daughter, collected Mom's pain in pools of tears in her lap, stroking Mom's head and lending wisdom far beyond her teenage years. Sarah, the youngest, hid from Mom's pain behind sweet doe eyes and a childlike propensity for cuddles. As the middle daughter, I saw the hypocrisy in Mom's contempt for a man who could so damage his family when she herself was guilty of the same. Dad did drugs and left us. Mom stayed and screamed at us until we nursed her pain, forsaking our own.

MOM AND I DIDN'T HAVE A close relationship after so many years of hurt, so I was taken aback when she called one day during my sixth month of pregnancy to tell me that she intended to come for an extended visit once the baby was born.

"You'll need help for at least the first two or three weeks," she told me, "so if you'll let me, I'd love to come stay for a while."

"No, thanks," I said flatly.

"I thought you'd say that," she said. "But honey, a baby is a lot of work. It's much different than you'd expect, believe me. It's a lot."

"John and I are perfectly capable, thank you," I retorted.

"Sweetie, I'd really like to be there for you when you become a mommy," she said, and the subtle shift in intention infuriated me.

"It's not really about what you'd like, actually, because I'm the one having a baby," I said.

"I know that," she insisted.

"So, I'd be much more comfortable with a long weekend. What if you come for my birthday?"

"Your birthday," Mom scoffed, but I was undeterred.

"Baby will be three weeks old by then, and we'll be a little settled. So, it's actually pretty perfect. Do you want to do, like, Friday through Monday?" I asked.

"I'll have to think about it" was the reply, and we hung up shortly after.

Sarah stopped by my room a few weeks later to ask what I thought of Mom's plan.

"Coming out for my birthday? Yeah, it was my idea," I said.

"Okay, and you're okay with her staying here?" Sarah asked with surprise.

"Yeah, it's just a long weekend," I said, and Sarah's eyes went wide.

Mom had called Sarah to coordinate a plan for Thanksgiving dinner. Mom would fly into town on my birthday, the Friday before Thanksgiving, and she'd stay through the Sunday after. That way, Mom had said, she and Sarah could cook a traditional Thanksgiving feast and we could all celebrate my son's first holiday.

I called Mom on the spot.

"I invited you out for four days, Mom," I reminded her.

"I know, but I thought it would be nice to do Thanksgiving," she said.

"Fine, then come for four days at Thanksgiving." I replied. "You can fly in Wednesday night and leave on Sunday."

"Those are ridiculously busy travel days, Shawna," Mom reprimanded.

"You can come for four days. You can come for my birthday and stay for a long weekend, or you can come for Thanksgiving. I do not want to host you from my birthday until the Sunday after Thanksgiving. That is way too long when I'll have a newborn."

"Shawna, I really think you'll benefit from having the help—" Mom started, but I cut her off.

"Mom, we do not have a close relationship. Right?" I waited for her reply. She was silent, so I asked again. "Mom, do you think we have a close relationship?"

"No. We do not," Mom said quietly.

"Okay. Because you and I are not close, I am only comfortable with you being here for four days," I informed her, and the matter of her length of stay was closed.

A few weeks later I asked Sarah if she and Mom had decided what to do for Thanksgiving. It was going to be my first Thanksgiving as a mom, so I wanted to contribute a dessert if they were planning a meal.

"I thought she was coming for your birthday," Sarah said.

"I had originally suggested my birthday but last I heard she wanted to do Thanksgiving."

"No, she's definitely coming for your birthday, she told me," Sarah said.

"Oh. Okay. Then I guess we need to plan what to do for Thanksgiving," I replied.

Sarah looked away. "I think we're going to San Antonio."

"What?" I was shocked. Sarah, Dave, and Lillybelle were the only local family I had, and I couldn't imagine not getting to celebrate my baby's first holiday with them. I had already bought him a tiny turkey onesie with matching pants. I was even more shocked that John, baby, and I didn't factor into Sarah's holiday plans. She loved having family around at Thanksgiving and Christmas as much as I did.

"With Mom," Sarah added. "That's how I know she's coming for your birthday; we're going to do San Antonio with her right after."

"WHAT?!"

I was heartbroken. I was appalled. I was furious. According to Sarah, my mother had planned to come out the Saturday after my birthday and stay through Tuesday, meeting my four-day length-of-stay mandate. Then, she would take Sarah, Dave, and Lillybelle to San Antonio for a long holiday weekend, beginning the Wednesday before Thanksgiving. The plan left John, baby, and new-mom me at home alone on a holiday meant to celebrate gathering. I could not believe my own mother would purposefully make plans to leave me alone on Thanksgiving, and I couldn't believe my sister, my best friend and roommate, would go along with it. I swallowed, barely containing my fury, and called Mom.

"Well, honey, you said you didn't want us to do a big Thanksgiving thing," Mom said, "so, this way I get to come see the baby, and then I'm out of your hair."

"That's not what I said, Mom!" I yelled.

"Yes, you did, you said four days," Mom insisted.

"You're doing this on purpose!"

"Doing what, Shawna? Who do you think I am?"

"OH MY GOD, MOM!" I felt like I could spit fire. "You know what, you are UNINVITED. I don't want to see you. Not for my birthday, not for Thanksgiving, not at all!"

DAD'S TEXT MESSAGE THAT NIGHT IN early November, with his Christmas itinerary, forced my hand. It was bad enough that I was letting him visit on a holiday, but I knew from experience that if Mom found out Dad was on the books before she was, there would be hell to pay. There was still a tiny part of me that wanted to be a good girl so, to mitigate any future emotional damage, I replied to Dad's text, went to bed, woke up, then called Mom.

"Well, hello," she said in surprise.

"Hi, I was wondering when you want to come visit," I said, cutting right to the chase.

"Oh," Mom said, doubling down on the surprise in her voice. "Well, I hadn't thought about it. Last I heard you didn't want to see me at all. Has that changed?"

I sighed but attempted to fix my voice so that it didn't sound as thoroughly irritated as I felt. "I didn't want you to come out when the baby born, and we had been talking about you coming out when he was three weeks old, but then that went to shit, right?"

"Right," Mom replied.

"But I'm sorry if I miscommunicated. I didn't mean to banish you forever; I just wanted to make it clear that I wasn't okay with what you were trying to plan."

"Shawna, I wasn't trying to plan anything devious," Mom said, her tone mocking.

"Okay, I don't want to talk about that, but I was thinking you would probably want to come visit sooner than later, while he's still little," I said quickly. The words were easier to get out if I spoke in a rush.

"I would love to visit," Mom said at last. "I'll have to look at the calendar."

THANKSGIVING CAME AND WENT. SARAH DECIDED against her San Antonio trip after much pleading from me, and though she and I worked together to cook our traditional family meal, me through exhausted, bleary eyes, the tension Mom created hung in the air between us. While it was clear to me that Mom's behavior had been inappropriate and hurtful, Sarah didn't agree, and that hurt even worse. Neither of us talked about it, though, so baby's first Thanksgiving was weird: obligatory and quiet instead of communal and festive. So, with Dad's visit, I was excited to create some family holiday magic at last. I opened our front door the day after Christmas and sank into Dad's embrace. I breathed in the rich, woody scent of his cologne. He smelled like home, which made me sad, and he must have spied John over my shoulder, holding baby, because he let out a breathy "Oh, oh, oh!" and patted me on the back to signal the end of our hello. I chuckled, touched that he was so excited to meet my boy, and let him go.

We made our way inside, and Dad went straight to the sink to wash his hands without even being asked. Again, I felt touched that he knew and respected the baby rules. Dad gave a quick hug hello to Sarah and Lillybelle, and asked after Dave, who was working, then settled onto the couch ready to receive his grandson. John handed over our chubby two-month-old and Dad chuckled deeply. He stared at my baby in awed silence, turning baby's body this way and that, looking closely at his face.

"I'm trying to see who he looks like," Dad said, and the debate was on.

"Me, obviously me," I said.

"No, he's all John," Sarah countered.

"People keep saying that, but I don't see it," John said.

"I think he looks like a little baby," Lillybelle added.

"Mmm," Dad nodded. "Definitely a baby."

Lillybelle giggled.

"I think he's a combo," Dad said at last, looking from me to John and back again. It was the best description, in my estimation.

We rose early the next day to celebrate as though it was Christmas morning. Dad had sent packages ahead of time, and we got him a few things as well, so the tree was festively piled with presents. Sarah made cinnamon rolls and her famous Christmas morning egg bake, and we drank peppermint cream–flavored coffee, but the feeling in the room was off. I was so tired I felt like my head was moving through water, and the tension between Sarah and me remained unspoken, so despite Dad's jovial mood, John's easy laugh, and baby's calm demeanor, our fake Christmas felt nothing like magic. The visions I'd had, of baking holiday cookies and showing Dad the beautifully decorated neighborhoods we had discovered during our house hunting, no longer seemed fun; I wanted to shut myself in my room and cry.

Dad offered to hold the baby after presents, so I took the opportunity to pump. As I sat, alone in my room, I wondered how many other mothers in the world were feeling sad and isolated, surrounded by people, on their favorite holiday. I wondered if it was the postpartum hormones at play, or something deeper. Nothing about my motherhood journey up to that point had unfolded the way I'd expected, and so much change in such little time was disorienting. While the rest of the world operated business as usual, *my* world had been flipped upside down, like a snow globe, and though I had done it to myself, the shake-up felt startling and difficult.

When I rejoined the group, Dad was feeding baby a bottle. He looked so tiny on Dad's lap, which warmed my tired heart, and I felt grateful that our boy was so loved.

"Hey, you're just in time," Dad said, and I smiled, remembering that I was loved, too. *Maybe it is just the hormones,* I thought. John, Sarah, Dave, and Lillybelle were all crowded around Dad, who was just about to begin story time. Dad and Mom were both animated storytellers, and while Mom's typical style was quick anecdotes, Dad had a great memory and loved recounting significant funny moments in detail. He was charming and laughed easily, so he always amassed an enthusiastic crowd keen on his every word. His storytelling was one of my favorite things about Dad, so I got another cup of coffee and took an eager seat next to John.

Dad began by talking about Mom's pregnancy. Mom and Dad were married young and pregnant with my older sister Erin before they were even twenty-one. Mom had an okay go of it during the pregnancy, but her labor was exceptionally tough. Erin's head was crooked as she descended the birth canal, and she was in there a long time, so Mom's quack of an OB performed an unmedicated episiotomy that left Mom in incredible pain for months afterward. On top of a traumatic birth, Dad said, Mom also hated breastfeeding. Her breasts ached so intensely that her shirt shifting in place had her crying in pain. This, Dad explained, coupled with too much gummy enthusiasm from newborn baby Erin, left Mom bloodied and miserable, so they decided to switch to formula. Of course, that didn't mean Mom stopped producing milk immediately, so although she had been looking for relief, she then had to deal with the pain of incredibly engorged breasts.

One day, Dad recalled, he made an untoward remark about the attractive look of Mom's painful boobs, then trotted off to work. Dad had been a grocery store assistant manager at the time and worked a busy, full day, forgetting all about what he had said. He finished work and went home, eager to see his loving wife and child, but when he crossed the threshold of his bedroom door, Mom shot him in the face with a stream of hot breast milk from across the room.

I had heard that story told before, from Dad and Mom both, but having just had a baby and being very familiar now with birth and breastfeeding woes, I felt a pang of solidarity with postpartum Mom for the first time ever. I wondered if Dad's remark hadn't felt incredibly insensitive at such a delicate time. I looked at John, who laughed at the story, and thought about what I would say to him in similar circumstances.

Suddenly, I didn't find Dad's story very charming.

THE EARLIEST MOM COULD VISIT WAS the end of January, when baby was three months old. It felt like I had already lived an eternity of sleepless nights and exhausted days mired by near-crippling anxiety by then, plus the Thanksgiving drama and an emotional Christmas, so my nerves about her visit were high. We had just put in an offer on a home we liked and were eagerly awaiting a response, and I felt guilty about not sharing our news, but John reassured me that we could avoid the topic if it felt too vulnerable for me. So, while Sarah was picking her up from the airport, we silenced our phones, put on our best enthusiastic faces, and planted ourselves on the couch for Mom's arrival.

When she entered the house with a smile on her face, I was struck by how glad I was to see her. I held back, protective of myself after a lifetime of hurt, but really, I couldn't wait to hug my mommy. I wanted to hear her tell me everything would be alright. She crossed the room and embraced me with warmth for a brief hug before moving on to John and then, finally, the baby in my arms. She dipped her head low to meet his gaze and smiled broadly, cooing hellos in a singsong voice. Baby cooed and returned her smile, and I felt relieved he did, realizing in that moment that I had been worried about his response to her, since babies don't know how to emotionally regulate grandmas.

It was already getting late, so John and I excused ourselves to put the baby to sleep with the promise that we'd be back downstairs after to visit, in an effort to appear as cordial as possible. Once in our room, I pumped some breast milk while John fed, changed, and bounced baby to sleep.

Watching John care for baby made me feel cared for, too, and I felt a whole new appreciation for him after Dad's retelling of the milk shot story. John had treated me with such tender kindness all throughout my pregnancy and into my postpartum period, and I felt utterly respected and supported by him. I wondered if postpartum Mom had felt cared for, respected, and supported, milk shot story notwithstanding. Or maybe postpartum Mom didn't feel as sensitive as I did. Maybe the milk shot was one big joke I didn't get. I hoped so, for her sake.

Baby didn't take long to fall asleep, and by the time I finished my pump and stored the fresh bottle of milk I had produced, we were ready to rejoin the party downstairs.

Sarah and Mom had a glass of wine each, Dave had a beer, and Lillybelle had been allowed a glass of juice, so John grabbed us drinks as well, and we sat down to play a board game. Mom had a special bond with Lillybelle, her first grandchild, so she was in a friendly mood, and our game play included lots of laughs. I tried my best to be present, but it was the first time I had ever laid baby down to sleep and walked away, so I found myself zooming in on our video baby monitor every few moments to check for the rise and fall of baby's chest. I knew logically that baby was unlikely to spontaneously fail to breathe as he laid flat on his back in his crib, but my heart seized waiting for that tiny inhale and exhale nonetheless.

Once, I couldn't clock any movement, so John volunteered to run up and check on baby, to my great relief. Mom laughed before catching herself and swallowing her amusement, then called us "sweet" in our diligence. I tried not to be hurt by the comment, but I couldn't help it; my innate hyperawareness of Mom's tone of voice and inflection, a means of survival for much of my life, allowed me to recognize her criticisms a mile away, even when masked, and they always cut like a knife.

"Thanks," I scoffed.

"What!" Mom feigned ignorance. "I didn't mean anything by it."

"Okay," I said, dropping it.

"I just never had a voodoo hoodoo video monitor doohickey like that, so my babies were on their own," she insisted with a laugh.

Sarah and Dave laughed, too, but I didn't find it funny.

"You guys are very—" Her eyes widened. "Watchful."

"Ah." I caught her meaning.

"I think it's great," she added, and I nodded to signal I wasn't going to make it a thing.

"We just didn't do it like that in my day," she said in conclusion.

My whole body suddenly ached for the quiet of bed. John returned a moment later with the good news that baby was fine, and I felt equal parts relieved and stupid for worrying in the first place. I managed to play a few more rounds of the game to keep from showing Mom that she had gotten to me before exhaustion overruled will and I excused myself.

The next morning, John fed baby his bottle while Mom looked on. She smiled and cooed as baby ate, and I felt charmed at her delight in spite of myself, so I left to pump some milk.

"Want me to fix you a cup of coffee?" Mom offered, and my mouth watered in anticipation.

Mom joined me in my room with a fresh mug ten minutes into my pump. She had sprinkled cinnamon on the coffee's creamy surface, a garnish I enjoyed but she did not, so its addition was a bittersweet reminder of her sometimes-tender heart. I wished she could be my sweet mom all the time.

Tethered to my pumping chair in front of my desk, I hooked a nearby stool with my foot and, with a bend of the knee, pulled it close so Mom could sit. She did, and she watched through my clear pump flanges, fascinated, as little beads of milk were pulled from my nipples. It was chilly outside of my bedroom window, so we talked briefly about the weather and the neighborhood, then Mom pivoted and my stomach leapt into my throat.

"So, who else has met the baby?" She asked in general, but I knew who she meant.

"John's family hasn't come yet." I pretended to adjust my bra around the left pump flange to avoid her gaze. "But Dad randomly visited a few weeks ago."

Mom nodded but didn't say a word, and I resisted the urge to cause some sort of pump-associated commotion to ease the tension.

Then, to my astonishment, Mom changed the subject. "How do you like pumping?" she asked.

"Um, it's alright." I shrugged. "It doesn't hurt or anything, and I make a lot so we save on formula." I didn't want to go into the emotional complexities of the topic.

"Did you not want to breastfeed, or . . ." Mom trailed off.

"Oh. Um, it wasn't a huge deal to me, although everyone else made a huge deal of it," I said with a laugh. "But yeah, no, this worked out better for us."

"Mmm." Mom nodded.

"Plus, this way John can feed him at night." I knew I was justifying myself, but I couldn't help it.

"I loved breastfeeding my babies," Mom said, and my eyes involuntarily squinted in an expression of perplexity as I recalled Dad's milk shot story.

"I thought you hated breastfeeding."

Mom shook her head. "Unh-uh, no. I loved every minute." She smiled wistfully, then broke into a sudden guffaw. "One time, when

I was breastfeeding Erin, my breasts were so absolutely huge, just super, super engorged, and I was mad at your dad about something."

"Oh, uh-huh." I nodded.

"You remember this story?" she asked with a grin.

"Yeah, I think so," I replied.

"Well, anyway, I was overly engorged, and he walks into the room." She cupped her two hands around her right breast to aim it at imaginary Dad. "And I shot him!" She gave her breast a healthy squeeze and laughed with glee.

I laughed, too. "That's funny," I said. "Dad told that story, too. When he was here."

"Mmm." Her delight faded a little, and she resumed watching my milk collect in bottles.

"So, you didn't want to breastfeed?" she asked again.

"I did," I admitted. "But it didn't work out, so this is fine."

"Oh, honey! If you want to, you should keep trying," she insisted.

"No, he has a tongue tie or a lip tie, something; it was too hard." I hoped my apathy was enough to end the topic.

"It's not, honey. It's not too hard. I could show you." Mom had done a few years' stint as a labor and delivery nurse about eight years prior and she was evidently eager to put her skills to use.

"No, thanks." I hoped my irritation wasn't too obvious.

"It really, really is the best thing for bonding with your baby. There is nothing else that compares."

She was really laying it on thick. I pressed my irritation between my lips.

"We've bonded just fine."

"No, I know. I didn't mean it like that," she said, backing off.

I let silence linger in the air between us, unwilling to rescue Mom from her discomfort.

"It was one of my favorite things when you girls were babies," Mom said at last.

"You guys always said you did formula," I reminded her, laughing.

"No, we did not!" she snapped at me. "I nursed all three of you." She could tell by my face that I didn't believe a word she said, so she continued. "I nursed Sarah the longest but I definitely nursed you all. In fact, it was so sad when Sarah was born," she said, voice softening. "You weren't even two years old yet, so when you saw her nursing, you wanted some, too, and I had to tell you no."

I felt sick. The only breastfeeding stories I'd ever heard as a child were Mom's famous milk shot and baby Erin's infamous gummy boob bite. There was also a story of toddler me and my attachment to my bottle, and a much-regaled sentiment that baby Sarah was clingy like Velcro. And all of a sudden, I realized I couldn't recall if I'd ever actually heard a story about making, shaking, or administering baby formula. Dad had claimed formula feeding on his visit, but Mom was spinning a tale of the opposite being true.

I thought about my own breastfeeding journey and found it hard to fathom that a mother could ever forget such intimate moments. Could Dad have misremembered? Or had Mom actually changed history in her mind? She had clearly learned about the benefits of breastfeeding during her time in labor and delivery, and the timing of her new revelation was convenient, given her desire to teach me to nurse.

I couldn't stop my eyes from finding Mom's face. She held a melancholy expression as she watched my pump churn. I couldn't tell if her feelings of regret were for my refusal to learn to put baby to breast or for her own distant baby-feeding memories, and I couldn't ask. I had no way to know if it was her version or Dad's that was true.

TWO WEEKS AFTER MOM'S VISIT, I was on minute eighteen of my twenty-minute pump and had already produced a full eight ounces of milk. I was proud of my boobs and sat, head down, quietly admiring their output when a small golden box with a red ribbon slid into my field of vision. I looked up at John's sly smile and grinned.

"What is this?" I asked.

He shrugged. "It's Valentine's Day."

Inside the box was a delicate gold bracelet with bold-colored gemstones set in filigree. I loved it immediately.

"And for you—" John picked up baby, who gave a joyful giggle. "You get a new cool-guy stuffy." John offered baby a tiny plush heart, which warmed mine.

I finished my pump, stored my milk, then gave each of my boys a kiss.

"Shall we?" I asked, and we made our way downstairs.

"There she is!" My father-in-law bellowed, his baritone bouncing off the walls of our house. John's dad, stepmom, and little brothers had been in town for a few days, but Buddy always greeted me as if he hadn't seen me in ages. He was a proud, family-oriented man, and I had continued the family line by giving him a grandson, so I seemed to be his new favorite person. He kissed me on the cheek and took baby from John's arms, patting his grandson's belly.

"Did your mother make you milk?" he asked jovially, and baby giggled.

"Acheecheechee," chirped my mother-in-law, Romina. She tickled baby's belly, then looked at me with a clap of her hands. "Are we ready?"

Romi was a woman of action, and John and I had promised to show them our new house. Though our offer had been accepted, we were in the middle of our escrow period. That meant we didn't have access to the place yet, so instead we toured the new neighborhood and local park overlooking the golf course. John's little brothers played at the park while Romi took a call, but Buddy stood atop a hill, in awe at the vista before him. He turned to John and clapped him on the back, no doubt proud of his boy, and I flashed-forwarded in my mind to a future moment with grown-up baby and his new family, smiling at the possibility that John and I would one day be in Buddy's shoes, and I felt loved. John's family was generous with their affection, and though I was bone-tired from the demands of new-mom life, I felt energized by their presence.

Valentine's Day is my new favorite holiday, I thought. And I snuggled into John's embrace and kissed my baby, eager to start our life as a family of three in our new neighborhood.

CHAPTER ELEVEN

THE BEAST

My pink, pointed-toe Amazon flats clacked on the tiles of our new, empty house with my every step, sending an echo that clanged off the ceilings and walls and sent a shiver of delight down my spine. *We bought a house for our baby*, I thought.

Baby was four and a half months old and so smiley, and he had taken to screaming shrieks of glee whenever I clacked, so I clacked as much as possible, assuming the echo must send shivers down his spine, too. I giggled at the thought and triple clacked to his delight. The boy kicked his chubby little legs and smiled up at me from his bouncer, so I scooped him up into my arms and kissed his drooly face all over. John was set to be home from work at any moment, and we had plans to order takeout, watch Netflix, and sleep train our baby boy on our first long weekend as homeowners.

I never in a million years thought I would ever sleep train my baby. I knew from my sisters, and from the self-reports of moms everywhere, and from my research in the Ridiculous Women Forum, that sleep deprivation was on the motherhood docket, so I had mentally prepared during my pregnancy to be tired. But my research glossed over three crucial facts: First, that I would experience a baby who never slept longer than ninety minutes for four and half months straight; second, that I would experience so much new-mom anxiety that I couldn't calm my nerves down fast enough to sleep while the baby slept; and third, that I would be so sleep-deprived for so long, that I would worry I was going to die.

It was all my fault, really. I couldn't sleep at the hospital, thanks first to labor pains, then to the act of childbirth itself, and finally, to all the postpartum recovery nurses who jammed their fingers deep into my low belly to assess the bogginess of my uterus. They were doing it to make sure the dinner plate–sized hole where baby had been wasn't hemorrhaging, a precaution that could potentially save my life, but *oh my GOD* did it interrupt my sleep. Our hospital stay was three nights and four days long, and in total I slept approximately seven hours. By the time we got baby home, I was the kind of exhausted that makes a person irrational, but I was also elated. I was a mom! I wanted to get right to mothering.

I lovingly wrapped baby snug in his swaddle and handed him to John, who placed him into his bassinet. We stared adoringly at our beautiful boy as he slept, then, unsure what to do next, we decided to go to sleep, too. It was six in the evening, so we shared a laugh at how quickly life had changed, then kissed goodnight and rolled over. John began snoring almost immediately, but when I turned off my bedside lamp and pushed my earplugs into place, I began to cry. Fat tears of panic fell from my eyes, so I switched my light back on.

"What's up?" John snorted, rousing.

"I can't see the baby," I said.

"He's right there," John replied, unhelpfully.

"No, I mean, when the light's off, I can't see him. I can't tell if he's breathing." My anxiety was mounting.

"He's breathing; just go to sleep. You're probably too tired." John sounded irritated.

"He's too far away," I concluded. I turned off my light, then shifted my body three feet closer to the foot of the bed, resting my head mere inches away from baby's tiny face. His little body was illuminated in the light of the full moon filtering in through our curtains, so I could see the tiny rise and tiny fall of his little chest. I put my earplugs in again, but when I did my hearing was deadened and the effect made it strangely harder for me to see. I took them out, turned on my side, and stared at baby, listening to John snore as I quietly sobbed. Nighttime was scary; if I was asleep, who was watching baby? I stayed staring at him for an hour, moving in and out of consciousness but not quite falling asleep, willing him to wake for some milk.

Finally, the boy stirred, and I seized him into my arms. I didn't wait for him to cry or fuss, or possibly settle back to sleep, but immediately scooped him up, cooing sweet nothings like a good mother should and nuzzling his face with my nose. I liked it better when we were both awake. I offered a bottle and baby ate hungrily, which I took as a good sign, an indication that I could sense when he was about to cry, about to need something. *Ahh,* I thought, *I'm good at this.* Then, I made a silent vow to always tend to baby's overnight needs at the first sign of him stirring, before he had to wake and cry for me, so that he would never have to experience anything unpleasant. *Good mothers know exactly what their babies need, at all hours*, I thought. And as baby ate, I struggled to hold my head up. I wasn't just tired; I was delirious.

By the time he was three weeks old, a pattern had formed: Baby wanted a sip of milk every hour all night long. I was desperately exhausted, but my heart skipped a beat each time he made a noise, so while baby dipped in and out of sleep, I flip-flopped between wide-awake fretting and semi-relaxed partial consciousness. I wasn't actually sure if I was sleeping at all.

Then, baby had a particularly grunty night, snoring and groaning in his sleep.

"I don't like those noises he's making," John said, "sounds like he's having trouble breathing."

With that, he kissed me goodnight and rolled over to go to sleep while my stomach jumped into my throat. John didn't ordinarily have anxiety about baby's safety, like I did, so if he was worried, I figured I better panic. So, I panicked and sobbed and raged internally at my instantly asleep husband. If baby couldn't breathe, he would die. If baby died, I would die. I was desperately afraid of those things happening, so I shook John by the shoulder and he woke with a start.

"What's up?" he asked, sleepily.

"You can't do that, you can't just say you think he can't breathe and then go to sleep!" I said.

"Oh, sorry. I just said that because it sounded like it. I'm sure he's breathing," John replied.

"Are you kidding me?" I scooped baby up out of his bassinet and handed him to John.

"What are you doing?" he asked.

"Fixing his bed," I spat.

I pushed the bassinet and my bedside table out of the way. I found a screwdriver and took the front bars off baby's crib, creating a co-sleeper, then shoved it into place against my side of the bed. I took baby back from irritated John and laid him flat on his infant mattress.

"Is he breathing better?!" I demanded to know.

John gave my shoulder a sympathetic rub. "Yeah, baby, he sounds okay. I'm sorry."

It was a heartfelt apology, but the damage was done and there was no way I was getting any sleep that night.

"Hey, why don't we take him in shifts?" John suggested.

I whipped my head around to look him in the eye, to make sure I understood what he meant.

"Like, stay up to watch him?" I asked.

"Yeah, you can go to sleep for a few hours, and I'll lie next to him. We can take turns monitoring him tonight."

It was a kind and understanding offer. My eyes welled up with relief.

"No, you lie down first," I insisted, as hot tears lined my cheeks. "I'm up, I won't be able to sleep right now anyway."

The weeks progressed with John and me taking baby in four-hour shifts each night, and, though I felt better knowing someone was always watching him, I was still too anxious to sleep. I didn't know what I was doing wrong. Were baby and I not bonded enough? If I had been able to nurse him, would we all be sleeping better? Why didn't I know what he needed to go to sleep? I didn't tell John I wasn't sleeping, though. I didn't have the energy. Plus, once we'd diagnosed baby's reflux, I had high hopes that the medicine would help.

On a Wednesday night, after administering his prescription for over a week, I changed baby into a clean, dry diaper, zipped him into his sleep sack, fed him, and laid him down in his makeshift co-sleeper as usual, curling my body as close to his as I could. For a moment, all was still as he drifted off to sleep. Suddenly, he screamed an irrational, irritated screech that made me feel like my body was engulfed in flames. I picked him up in utter confusion and fiery rage, offering him the last dregs of his bottle. His tiny face flushed red with anger and his whole body tensed.

"What's up?" John asked, clearly as confused as me.

"Stop asking me what's up!" I yelled.

"What's happening?" John asked instead.

"I have no idea!" I yelled.

I patted baby's back hoping for a burp, but it didn't seem to help, so I administered gas drops to ease his tummy. I pedaled his legs to force a toot, but it made him rage harder. I ripped his sleep sack and jammies off his body, searching every inch of skin for what could be bothering him, to no avail. Feeling utterly hopeless and helpless, I cried along with baby, while John consulted the wisdom of the Ridiculous Women Forum.

"Witching Hour?" John read aloud.

"I don't know, what's it say?" I was hopeful for answers that would end the crying.

"A normal part of development. Babies may experience a period of intense fussiness due to being overstimulated and overtired," John read.

"I'm literally trying to get him to sleep, that makes no sense," I said.

"If all his needs are met it might mean a leap in cognition," John read.

"His brain turned on?"

"Maybe. This says to walk him around." John took our boy and began to pace the floor.

The stress of the moment overwhelmed me, so I decided to make myself useful and saddled up to my breast pump as John gently rocked and swayed. He lulled baby to sleep in ten minutes flat, and my shoulders heaved when I realized once again that John was better at comforting baby than I was. He got me a drink of water to offset my sobs, but his thoughtfulness made me cry harder. He laughed and kissed my cheek, then lay down next to the co-sleeper to take the first shift, and I mentally added "bounce the baby" to our growing list of sleep aids.

Week twelve came and baby graduated from newborn to infant. I was sure the milestone would mean magically better sleep, but instead, things got worse. Baby hated being bounced at naptime, so he would cry and buck in my arms in an effort to resist. It was as if he wanted me to put him down, but when I did, he wailed. I would pick him up again and offer a drink of milk, which he'd accept, only to pop off his bottle after a few quick slugs, screaming again and dizzying my mind. He was mad he wasn't asleep, and he was mad I was trying to put him to sleep. I didn't know what else to do, so, I'd bend my knees deeper and bounce harder for the better part of an hour, when finally, I'd bounce him into oblivion, then sink my own exhausted body down for a brief respite, wondering if a person could die of sleep deprivation. Baby would only nap in my lap, and only for thirty minutes at a time, so when evening finally came, he was so exhausted from terrible naps that he could no longer resist being bounced. But his tiny body was so stressed from lack of sleep that one false move when gingerly transferring him from my arms to his co-sleeper would awaken and enrage him. The boy cried in protest of sleep, and in protest of how we put him to sleep, and in protest of being woken from his sleep, for four hours every single day. My poor baby was as deliriously exhausted as I was.

I loved baby more than life itself. I would have died on the spot if it meant no harm would ever come to him. He was my entire world, and every day I was failing to get him the sleep he needed. I was desperate for help.

Enter sleep training.

I SAT DOWN IN MY PUMPING chair, but I didn't whip my nipples out. Instead, I opened my laptop. The brilliant women of the Ridiculous Women Forum were more divided about sleep than about any other baby topic I had ever looked into. Half of the women said that putting baby in mama's bed and nursing on demand was the way to go, because being near mama was the most natural way for baby to feel comforted, and a comforted baby slept better. But we did the bottle-feeding, safe-sleep equivalent of that and it didn't work, so I couldn't help but wonder if that first half of the forum had magical babies who were born knowing how to sleep and talk and use toilets. Mine was not, and we were exhausted, so I decided to take advice from the other half.

"There will be crying," said the pro–sleep training side of the forum. *There already is crying*, I thought, and read on. The forum explained that baby's cries were communication of his needs. That sounded familiar; when John started back to work at the six-week mark, I was forced to learn what baby was telling me with his cries. I wondered why I hadn't thought to listen to them at bedtime, too.

Instead, I just bounced baby until he shut up. I cringed at my terrible mothering and continued reading. The big need at bedtime, said the forum, was to go to sleep, and baby was going to cry when I changed the way I put him to sleep. Unfortunately, I couldn't go to sleep for him, just like I wouldn't be able to learn to eat solids for him, or go to school for him. He would have to face the difficult task himself. But I could make things easier by adopting a sleep plan.

Step one of the plan was to establish a place that would signal to baby's brain and body that it was time for sleep. *Good thing we have a house now*, I thought with a smile, and I set about making baby's room cozy. First, I hung a bright orange curtain that matched baby's bedding and blocked out any outside light. I hoped the cheery color would add an element of whimsy to our nighttimes. I flipped the switch on the wall to turn baby's light off and was immediately swallowed by deep, dark nothingness. *Excellent*, I thought. Next, I set up a white noise machine near baby's crib. Both the curtain and the white noise would mimic what sleep would have been like for baby inside my womb: dark and noisy. Unlike my womb, though, this dark, noisy place needed to be kept cool, the experts said, because babies slept best in slightly cooled rooms. My heart skipped a beat as I set our thermostat to a nice and chilly sixty-eight degrees and pushed thoughts of baby crying alone and cold in a dark, noisy room out of my head.

Step two of our sleep plan was to create a calming bedtime routine to be completed in baby's new bedroom. The self-reports of many brilliant women on the Ridiculous Women Forum named a nightly bath as the preferred start to bedtime, since the warm water was soothing for baby. We bathed baby on occasion, but *bathing* was close to last on my list of priorities, coming in after *survive the day* and *pump some milk* but beating out *dress baby cute* and *put self together*. However, if it would help him sleep, bath time had to be a new nightly staple, followed closely by lotion, jammies, book, song, and finally, hopefully, bed. And with that, our routine was set.

The third and final step of our sleep plan was to decide how much we wanted to let baby cry before intervening. My stomach flipped and tears stung my eyes. I had spent four and a half months trying and failing to save baby from having to face anything unpleasant. I wanted to be one of those mothers who knew instinctively how to soothe their baby to sleep. I hated that sweet, easy bedtimes weren't part of my new-baby experience and a sick feeling pooled in the pit of my stomach as I thought of the lucky moms with magical babies from the first half of the Ridiculous Women Forum. I didn't have time to dwell on my feelings of guilt and jealousy, though; if we didn't start sleeping soon, I was going to snap. *Baby cries while I bounce him anyway*, I reminded myself.

Back when I was four months pregnant, I'd received a phone call from my sister, Erin, who had successfully sleep trained her one-year-old and wanted to share her triumph. They had used the extinction method, she said, a terrible-sounding technique that required parents to place baby in their crib and leave the room, not to return until a predetermined time, even if baby cried. The idea was that baby would eventually tire and fall asleep independently of any sleep aids. Erin was delighted to report that her previously cranky one-year-old had been sleeping well for the first time ever in her young life, and the rest had been transformative for the entire house.

At the time, the concept of letting a baby cry themselves to sleep sounded like cruelty to me, and I was appalled that Erin could selfishly inflict such torture on her child. But there I was, four and half months postpartum and eating crow. Why did I think I had any idea what my sister had been through during the first year of mothering her child? Why did I think she would do anything other than exactly what her baby needed her to do? What gave me the audacity to assume that I had any right to have opinions about my sister's reality? I was embarrassed by young, dumb me.

John and I agreed that to tame the sleep beast, we needed to get out of baby's way as quickly as possible. We would place him in his crib and let him cry until he fell asleep.

AT SIX-THIRTY IN THE EVENING ON a Wednesday night, we gave baby a bath. I left the door ajar so that the glow from down the hall could filter in softly to light our way. I sang low, soothing songs about sleep as I ran a warm washcloth over baby's chubby body. Baby clenched all his muscles and straightened his legs and arms at his side with a giggle. John tickled baby's little belly to make him giggle more, forgetting entirely that bath was supposed to be soothing. My lips pressed into a smile, and I nuzzled baby's nose with mine and hoped that my undying love for him could be communicated via nostril proximity. John handed me a warmed towel, so I lifted baby out of the tub and dried his pink skin. I massaged lotion in slow circles all over his body and thrilled when he yawned. We went into his room, where John diapered him and popped his arms and legs into jammies as I read our bedtime book aloud. I fed him his bottle and gently rocked him as he drowsily laid his head on my chest. John turned out the light and left us in the deepest black I'd even known. I swayed and patted baby a bit longer, freeing some burps and allowing the boy a few moments of calm, then I made my way to the crib. My heart leaped into my throat as I dipped low over the edge and placed baby on his back, drowsy but awake. I patted his little belly, whispered "I love you," then slipped out of the room and closed the door behind me. Then, all will left my body as baby began to cry.

John hugged me, so I buried my face in his shoulder and tried not to sob. We went downstairs, where John distracted me with drama from work and a fresh grilled cheese, which was faster than ordering takeout, but I didn't hear a word or eat a thing; I just stared at the baby monitor's black-and-white video feed as baby fussed in his crib. He would cry hard for one full minute, then calm down, turning his head this way and that, and I could tell he was looking for a bottle to nurse him to sleep. I had been secretly hoping the boy would be a champion self-soother, that all of his crying during every sleep-bouncing session was really because he wanted to be left the hell alone, but we'd hit the twenty-minutes-of-fussing mark, half of the crying he typically did in my arms, with no end in sight. I choked on the lump in my throat and could no longer keep my tears from flowing. John steered me to the couch and took the monitor from my hands.

"He's just fussing because he's so tired," John reminded me. "His body needs sleep."

I turned on Netflix and hoped for a miracle.

Miraculously, after eight more minutes, baby settled down. In only twenty-eight minutes, his crying had dwindled to intermittent fusses and those calmed even more, until he was quiet, breathing deeply into his belly. We had almost halved his typical bedtime fussing.

I grabbed the monitor again, needing a visual, just in time to watch baby smack his little lips. I laughed, having seen him move his lips like that a thousand times or more as his tiny body lay in my lap, and I loved him so much that it hurt, and I missed him so much that I laughed again, this time at the absurdity of motherhood. Finally calm enough to eat, I crunched into my grilled cheese, and its melty saltiness felt nourishing in my belly. I couldn't remember the last time I had tasted food. I watched the monitor, enthralled, while baby's entire body relaxed, and I felt my own tension release as well. It was working.

Then, baby's tiny arms flailed, and he was awake again. We had left his sleep sack off.

If I had thought to collect my tears, I would have had oceans full at that point. We had to begin again. John slipped into baby's room to zip him into his sleep sack, picking him up and soothing him first, then checking that he was still clean and dry. With his sleep slack on, he relaxed into his Dada's strong arms, and I collapsed my full weight onto our couch, praying for baby's relief. I heard him cry again and knew John had placed him back in bed, and a desperate rage bubbled up from the pit of my belly. *He is fed, warm, and safe*, I reminded myself, but my rage needed someplace to go. I passed the monitor to John as he returned and retreated to our bedroom's en suite, hoping to rinse the rage away with a hot shower.

Another twenty minutes later, John poked his head into the bathroom with bad and good news. I opened the shower door to see him clearly. Baby had settled all the way down, then awakened with cries, twice, for an additional half hour of fussing.

I needed to know: "Was he just frustrated fussing or full-on *help me, I'm scared* crying?"

"It was a little bit, on and off, just little fusses. It wasn't full body-tensed crying at all."

"Okay." I nodded. "That's good."

"Yeah," John agreed. "But he's asleep now."

My head snapped up in shock, and I met John's eyes. He laughed gently and hugged me, and I sobbed, a little mad that he buried the lede. Relief dissolved everything hard in me, and I leaned into John's hug as the shower stream soaked us both. John kissed my cheek, and I could see he was crying, too. He left to change, and my body felt heavy with exhaustion, but my heart was elated. Our baby was asleep! On his own!

I crawled into bed with my laptop and a book of sudoku puzzles, but all I could do was stare at the video feed of my peacefully sleeping baby as happiness streamed from my eyes. I woke up sometime later to a pitch-black room, and it took me a moment to realize the baby must have cried. John was already awake and heading in to feed him a bottle, so I roused myself into a seated position and grabbed my phone.

It had been four hours.

I laughed in utter disbelief, giddy that our gamble had paid off, then got up to pump some milk. I watched the monitor while John put baby back in his crib, and I braced myself for more crying, but to my astonishment, baby smacked his little lips and turned his head to the left, drifting dreamily off to sleep. Fat tears rolled down my cheeks in rhythm to the purr of my pump, and John chuckled when he saw me. He came close and held my face in his hands, kissing my tears away.

"Four hours!" he whispered.

I said a silent thank-you to the universe, or God, or the ancestors, or whoever it was that had heard my desperate cries for sleep and helped, and John and I laughed as we held each other and milk dropped from my nipples.

GOLDEN LIGHT BATHED MY ROOM THE next time I opened my eyes, and I looked over to see John playing a video game on his iPad. I sat up straight in bed with a start and tore around for the baby monitor, but John laughed.

"Still asleep." He shook his head in disbelief and grinned, pointing to the monitor propped up on his bedside table.

I lunged across his lap, clasping my hand around the hard plastic of the monitor and zoomed all the way in for signs of breath.

"I did the same thing," John said, laughing again.

Then, the baby stirred. I bolted upright and paced in circles to allow him a few moments of awake alone time in his crib. To my astonishment, he didn't fuss or whimper but happily babbled to himself instead. I laughed and zoomed in on the monitor I held in my hand, curious about what he must be thinking and feeling after all that sleep. When I could stand it no longer, I tore into his room to retrieve him.

My heart burst when I flipped on the light and the boy's lips stretched into a gummy grin that dimpled his cheeks. I unzipped his sleep sack and his tiny arms shot straight up to his ears for a luxurious stretch and yawn, so I tickled his belly to make him laugh. I scooped him up into my arms and kissed him all over, and he grabbed a fistful of my hair and screeched in my ear with delight.

We continued sleep training for naps that day, and it took only two tries for baby to get the hang of independent sleeping completely.

That was it—one night and two naps, and no more than three hours of crying in total, and baby was sleep trained. There was no torture; there was no leaving baby to cry for hours on end; there was just the sleep we had both needed all along, and as a result, I no longer felt close to death.

That night after our bedtime routine I rocked my sweet boy in the dark, noisy cool of his room. I kissed his plump cheek, and when I stepped toward his crib, he leaned back in my arms, ready to be laid down. I placed him flat on his back, patted his belly, whispered "I love you," then slipped out of his room. I watched him smack his little lips on the video monitor's screen, feeling more deeply bonded to him than ever before, and I was flooded with gratitude for the wisdom of the women who had come before me, my sister included. I no longer felt jealous of those other moms and their magical babies. My boy was magic enough, even if sleep had been hard for us. In the end, sleep training was the best parenting decision we had ever made.

CHAPTER TWELVE

THE BRAIN

THE SOFT, CREAMY SKIN OF BABY'S chubby hand, which fit entirely in my palm even with his fingers fully splayed, was spongy beneath my lips. Kissing his hand made me want to stuff his entire fist into my mouth, which I knew was weird, so I resisted. I moved on to his pink cheek instead, which was rounded and plump like a peach, and I delighted so thoroughly in the way my kisses bounced off his perfect face that I had to actively deny myself the joy of slurping as much of his pudge as I could into my mouth.

I didn't want to actually chew on my child; it was just that he had been sleeping a room away from me for weeks, and I was finally rested enough to notice how often my chest throbbed with a longing to be nearer to him than was physically feasible. The longing manifested itself as an impulse to suck him back into my body via my mouth. I knew it was an impossibility, though, so instead, I gathered him up into my arms and held him against the beat of my heart. I swayed, kissing his gummy smile, his perfect cheeks, and the top of his round head and breathing in his sweet, my-baby scent as he giggled. I hummed a familiar melody and across my mind flashed a cruel vision of future me swaying with future him: tall, broad-shouldered, clad in a black tuxedo, with a room full of onlookers just beyond, to bear witness to the changing of our guard. I choked on my inhale and squeezed my eyes to squeeze the picture out of my mind, but it was no use; sorrow for life's inevitable changes poured from the corners of my eyes.

"What's wrong with you?" John said with a laugh. He had been watching from our bed.

"He's going," I choked on another sob, "to grow up." I handed John the baby, experiencing too harsh a love to continue standing, and sank into my desk chair.

"What just happened?" John asked.

I looked down at my bare desktop amid sobs. "Could you get my . . . uh . . ." I wiped both of eyes with both of my hands.

"Tissue?" John wagered a guess.

"No, my—" I cupped both of my hands to both of my breasts. "My things."

"What?" John laughed, and I wiped a bit of snot from my nose. I couldn't believe he didn't know what I was saying.

"The things, John, I have to . . ." I pulled up my shirt and tapped my boobs. "I need the boob things."

"You need boob things," John said.

"Yes, the things for my boobs to make the . . . The milk sucker things, John!" I was becoming annoyed.

"Ohhh." Awareness dawned in his eyes at last, and he retreated to the bathroom to retrieve my pump parts.

I HAD READ ALL ABOUT THE mysterious "missing word" phenomenon some women experienced postpartum on the Ridiculous Women Forum, and I had rejected it outright. Before baby, I had the kind of mind that could read through a scene for acting class a few times over, then close my eyes and read the words again in my head. I could also replay life events in my mind like my favorite comfort films. It hadn't seemed possible for a whiz kid such as myself to one day lose use of my faculties, but it happened. Postpartum had my brain feeling fuzzy, as if a soft but invasive mold had been allowed to fester, covering the ridges and valleys of my mind with a puffy blanket. I knew there were words and ideas and thoughts somewhere in there, but they were vague or buried or otherwise obscured altogether, so I felt dumb.

It didn't help that John found my newly stunted communication hilarious, nor did it help that he could never guess what I was intimating, proving he needed my words as much as I did. Back when Mom came for a visit, and I noticed we were short a place at our table to put an extra body, I asked John, with much gesticulation and pantomime, to grab another . . . one of those . . . you know . . . things . . . so we could have more people at the table . . . a flat . . . thing . . . where you sit . . . a sitting spot! He laughed at me, mercilessly, because I couldn't remember the word *chair*. It was even worse one evening when I was putting baby to bed (long before sleep training, so I use the words *to bed* loosely here). When baby finished his bottle I lifted him into a seated position on my knee for a nice healthy burp, then laid him down on his back, as usual, for a diaper change. I zipped him into his jammies, then slid my left hand under his neck and head and my right hand under his back and bottom and brought him to my face, nuzzling his nose with mine. He promptly barfed into my nostrils and mouth, and I screamed while John laughed. I shouted at him to stop laughing and to grab me a . . . um . . . one of those . . . you know . . . you throw it over . . . in case they barf . . . a barf wrap! Which, under normal circumstances, would have been called a "burp cloth." I hit a real low the day I replaced the word *diaper* with the much more colorful "baby bathroom thing," and John basically fell on the ground laughing.

It had been six months since I had given birth and baby was sleeping for lovely, four-hour stretches at night and three solid hour-long naps during the day, all in his own crib, so I was better rested and had more free time on my hands than ever before in his short life. I was exploding forth with creative inspiration, having literally just exploded forth the ultimate creation, life itself, and I was desperate to return to acting, but the mold blanket tarping my brain refused to budge. I watched a rerun of *Friends* one day, during which a postpartum Rachel tries to give a fancy restaurant toast to birthday girl Phoebe but is too distracted by her baby's missing sock, and I cried because I couldn't even remember the word *sock*. Instead of getting used to having a baby around so that I could go back to my regular life, like Rachel and all the other TV moms seemed to do, I felt less capable than ever.

IT WAS SATURDAY, SO JOHN WAS at home with baby and me, and the three of us had already enjoyed five lazy hours of cuddling in bed that morning when my mind started to itch. I had to move. I padded downstairs for a glass of water and an excuse, which I found when I opened the fridge: We were out of milk.

Classic, I thought.

Taking our stairs two at a time, I rejoined my boys for a few tummy tickles and arm zerberts (on baby and John both) before announcing that I simply couldn't live another moment without milk. *For my coffee*, I insisted. I bounced into our closet to get changed, pulling my black t-shirt dress over my head. I pinched a black piece of pilled cotton off at the outer part of my left boob, where my arm often crossed to hold baby. There were at least thirty more pill balls in the surrounding area, but the dress matched my black-flowered scarf and the low-top Converses I lived in, and the whole look made me feel pulled together when I definitely was not, so wearing it despite its overuse was a no-brainer, and I needed that.

When I got downstairs the boys were already parked on the couch for a bottle, so I stopped to snap a picture with my phone and made a mental note to ask John to snap some of me and baby at my next feeding. With my phone already in hand, I opened our baby care app to add our morning diaper count and the number of ounces of milk baby had eaten in order to fill those diapers. We hadn't yet had a morning poo, so I warned John to be on the lookout, then turned in a circle, trying to remember what it was that I was going to do. My purse was on its perch on our kitchen island counter, next to the bright pink Post-its I used for occasional laptop bag love notes to John, so I jotted down a quick shopping list: milk, diapers one size bigger, wipes, toilet paper, bananas, avocados, and baby food pouches. John could think of nothing else we needed, so I planted two kisses on two cheeks, one stubbly, the other squishy, then headed for the back door. I stopped to switch the clean clothes over to the dryer but first had to take a dry load to the couch to be folded. At the couch, I gave baby another kiss, wiped spit-up from his chin with the underside of my dress, and guided John's eyes to the diaper blowout that needed addressing. I fished a clean outfit for baby out of the laundry pile on the couch, then ran to the bathroom to relieve myself.

"Go to the store!" John shouted after me.

"He needs to lie down for a nap in thirty minutes!" I shouted back, and once a new load of clothes was in the washer, I was out the door.

I returned a moment later to ask John if he'd seen my . . . jingly . . . little . . . you know . . . starter things, and I said the phrase with a twist of the wrist, acting out the motion of turning over my car's ignition. John didn't laugh, finally having learned better, and I was out the door again a moment later, car keys in hand.

The grocery store bustled with busy people going about their busy lives. The once-familiar errand seemed so foreign and luxurious after baby that it felt as though I was people-watching on a vacation. An old, small grandpa-of-a-man wore three different shades of brown and turned citrus fruits over in his hand near his nose before making his selection at the display of blood oranges. A young woman wore a crisply tailored button shirt and wired headphones, and she grasped her phone with the same hand that held the handle of her basket, where she piled what I assumed would be her breakfast for the week ahead: six strawberry protein yogurts, a loaf of low-carb protein bread, a block of Kerrygold butter, and a container of blueberries. A forty-something woman squeezed avocados and snapped at a teen dressed all in black. The girl rolled her eyes and replaced a prepackaged bag of lemons with individual lemons instead, though she looked like she'd rather be doing anything else. I felt a pang of hurt for both the girl and her mother; the girl likely thought prepackaged lemons would save time and effort, and maybe even money, and her poor mother probably thought she would never get anyone to do anything she asked them to do without first having to lose her temper. The girl lowered her dark eyebrows, then pinched them together as the corners of her top lip lifted into a scowl, but it wasn't until her eyes rolled in disgust away from mine that I realized I had been staring and should probably go to another part of the store.

What the hell is wrong with me? I thought, as I grabbed a twenty-four-pack of paper towels.

"You forgot milk," John said when I arrived home, confused at my haul.

"Are you kidding?" I had picked up diapers one size bigger, wipes, toilet paper, bananas, avocado, and baby food pouches, plus, paper towels, laundry detergent, baby shampoo, and diaper rash cream, but not milk, despite milk being at the top of my list.

What an idiot, I told myself, and sat down to make milk instead. *At least I can do one thing right*, I thought.

With my head in my hands and my eyes closed to the world, I let my breast pump suck me into a state of depression. I couldn't remember what it felt like to have a sharp mind, but I knew my previous feeling of general competency had been stunningly overwhelmed by ineptitude. I sat up, opened my eyes, and studied my nails to change the subject in my brain. I had cut the baby's nails two mornings prior, but I couldn't remember the last time I had tended to my own. The nails on my right hand were longer and stronger than those on my left, most of which were experiencing some level of chipping. The nails of both hands were still streaked with bits of the baby blue manicure I had worn when I was pregnant, feeling ethereally maternal, and wanting to reflect my conscious state with the state of my nails. I scoffed at pregnant me and chipped the remaining paint away as a memory from my old acting class flickered into focus in my mind.

The acting coach I trained with in my twenties, Laurel Smith Vouvray, was an exacting figure, and her passion for performance that spoke truth to humanity was inspiring; when she rose to her feet to emphatically impart a kernel of artistic wisdom, everyone in class paid attention.

"Just name the behavior you see!" Laurel bellowed, pounding her chest with her open palm. "Say it out loud. Let it affect you!"

She was talking about noticing a scene partner's behavior in an acting exercise called repetition, in which two actors are face-to-face with the shared goal of naming the behaviors their partner uses to mask or communicate their true feelings. In an acting context, the feelings are produced by the intimate, awkward nature of the exercise, and later, at more advanced levels, the feelings are manufactured when an actor creates a story about their character in their mind, then lives the truth of those imaginary circumstances in front of an audience. However, as I sat in the isolation of mom life in suburbia, Laurel's coaching seemed unmistakably relevant to my real feelings as well.

"I feel really stupid," I said out loud to no one. My pump whir-whirred in response. Suddenly, I was having a conversation with my most steady companion. "I'm hiding alone in my room because I feel like a stupid idiot who will never feel normal again." *Whir-whirrr.*

"I'm pumping because that's the only stupid fucking thing I can do right, even though I fucking hate it. No offense." *Whir-whirrr.* "But I would feel too fucking stupid and guilty to ever fucking stop, so I'll just sit in my stupid room letting my stupid brain atrophy, and all of my stupid fucking hopes and dreams since I was eight fucking years old will atrophy along with it." *Whir-whirrr.* "But at least I'm making milk! Like a goddamn cow!"

I took a deep breath, but I couldn't stop frustration from flooding my eyes. I hated crying all the time. I loved baby more than I could express, but I hated feeling like a crybaby shell of my former self.

My pump *whir-whirred* her support, snapping me back to reality. I looked around my room to confirm that I was alone, that no one had seen me talking to myself. I imagined what I might look like on a hidden ceiling camera, like I'd seen on reality television shows, and chuckled with embarrassment.

"Oh my God, why are you so psycho?" I muttered. Suddenly, I felt lighter. It was as if naming my feelings made them a little less scary and allowed some room for curiosity, or even levity. I thanked Laurel and acting class in my mind, then picked up my phone to consult the Ridiculous Women Forum.

"Mom Brain" was a phenomenon that began during pregnancy, when the brain would reorganize itself, changing the volume of gray matter, redirecting neural pathways, and shifting hormone production in preparation for baby. The brain changes experienced reflected a neurological recalibration toward the specialized task of caregiving, and they correlated to maternal attachment. These changes were as impactful on the psyche as puberty, according to the internet.

Ohhh, I thought, *So, I'm not dumb; my brain just doesn't care about anything but the baby*. That made sense, because I readily cared so much about things I had never even considered before, like the level of nipple access afforded by any given shirt and the consumable crumb count of any given floor. And happily so! I had never loved anyone like I loved my baby, and because he was my baby, I was allowed to love him to my full, weird capacity. Apparently, I had even been neurologically rewired to do so, to attune to his specific needs.

Actually, that's kind of badass.

The girl in black from the grocery store came to my mind. I could see her clearly: black fingernails and silver jewelry, a black, oversized shirt emblazoned with a picture of the great Ozzy Osbourne in full regalia, and a deliberately reluctant approach to specified citrus selection. But what had registered most of all was the way her shoulders had slumped in dejection when her mother refused her bag-of-lemons suggestion without even meeting her eye. Why I could see the minute details of the relationship dynamics of a stranger in the store was lost on me, but like my inability to recall words, I sensed there was a purpose, an intelligence I didn't yet understand.

I finished my pump and transferred baby's fresh milk to a fresh bottle, then placed it at the back of the line in our mini fridge, marveling at the full eight ounces I had produced. I grabbed baby's next bottle and made my way downstairs.

"Hey! How'd you know he was getting hungry?" John asked, and I smiled.

"Mom brain," I said.

John handed me the baby and I smashed my lips deep into his pink, chubby cheek for a series of kisses. He giggled and I snorted like a pig into the curve of his neck and zerberted his squishy belly.

I sniffed his bottom, then peaked under the elastic at the front of his pants to assess the state of his diaper. He was clean and dry and hungry, and he'd need another nap in thirty minutes, so I snuggled down into the couch with him so he could drink his milk. His eyes looked deep into mine, and I couldn't help but to pull my face into silly expressions, hoping to hear more of his happy little giggles.

"Can you take a . . . with your phone . . . a thing . . . a snap! What's it called?" I asked.

"Oh, a picture?" John retrieved his phone from his pocket.

"Yes, thank you!" I said. "I want to remember this moment."

CHAPTER THIRTEEN

THE BODY

I'D THOUGHT I WOULD HAVE ENOUGH time to shower, but after I threw back a cup of coffee, plus fed baby, changed his diaper, got him dressed, and wiped up an inconvenient barf, I barely had time to throw my hair into a messy bun and pull on a clean hoodie. We were headed to his six-month well-baby checkup, so I didn't need to be precious about my appearance anyway. Realizing we were now running late, I strapped baby into his rear-facing car seat, adjusted the seatback mirror that helped him see my face as I drove, and kissed his drooly mouth. Then I slammed myself into the driver's seat and peeled out of our driveway.

"Of course," I groaned as I hit a red light. As I slowed to an idle, I sighed and turned my head to the left. There, in a dark gray car, was the most gorgeous man I had ever seen. His skin was tanned, his hair was golden and sun-kissed, and when he grabbed an iced coffee from the cup holder of his center console, his full lips parted and his pink tongue found the tip of the straw, guiding it deep into his mouth.

A quick beep of the horn from the car behind me, alerting me to the light changing green, startled me back to consciousness, and I realized I was staring. I quickly looked away. I was sure the man hadn't seen me gawking at him, but my cheeks flushed red anyway. I refocused on my mission of rushing to our appointment as baby cooed in the backseat.

"Great." Another red light. "Almost there, baby," I called, looking into my rearview mirror. Baby's head turned to follow the sound of my voice so I continued cooing, and when his eyes finally locked on mine in his mirror, pure joy lit up his entire face. It was the best feeling in the world.

"Helloooo! Hello, babyyy!" I called in a singsong voice as he giggled and kicked his chubby legs. I vocalized silly noises and suctioned my lips together so I could pop them apart for his amusement and mine, but I lost his attention when he found his chewy rattle.

Suddenly, I became aware of somebody looking at me, and I recognized a dark gray car in my periphery. *Gorgeous Guy's checking me out*, I thought with a gasp. I was a happily married woman, but I was only human, and I never saw an issue with catching the eye of an attractive stranger in mutual appreciation. I couldn't be too obvious about the secret thrill I was having, though, so I dropped my head low and used my left hand to nonchalantly scratch my forehead so I could look through my fingers. Sadly, Gorgeous Guy was not looking at me; he was sipping his coffee again and scrolling on his phone. *That's dangerous,* I thought, and I scoffed my annoyance, though whether I was annoyed at Gorgeous Guy's distracted driving or the fact he wasn't checking me out I couldn't be sure.

I directed my attention back to the streetlight holding us hostage and looped a finger around the elastic at the crown of my head to pull it from my mom bun. I zhuzhed my blond hair and flipped it over my shoulder with a glance back at the dark gray sedan. Gorgeous Guy bobbed his head and drummed his fingers on his steering wheel, completely unaware of my existence. I sat up straight and blatantly stared at him, desperate for some validation, but he didn't care at all. I was invisible. I looked to my right, making brief eye contact with another driver, who was amused at my antics but who also didn't care to check me out, politely averting his eyes instead.

"Oh right, I'm just a mom now," I said out loud, and I flipped down my vanity mirror to gauge what was so uninteresting about me.

MY MOTHER TOLD ME REPEATEDLY AS a child that I was a pretty girl. It was one of her favorite things about me, from what I could tell, because it was the one thing she consistently praised me for. I was told often that when I got older, the boys were sure going to be interested in me, that we would have to "beat the boys off with a stick," and when I grew up the boys were indeed interested. They told me I wasn't just pretty, but sexy, which seemed like a natural progression to me, and I liked being both. I liked that boys' heads turned my way every time I walked by, that they wanted to know my name, talk to me, and do things for me, too: buy me drinks, hold doors for me, help me move. And women treated me just as well; I was pretty, but sweet-looking, an obvious good girl, and the combination inspired admiration, not competition, so I often received compliments on my pretty eyes or skin. My looks provided me a sense of confidence I never really thought about—until I decided I wanted to have a baby.

At the start of my baby research, I was feeling nervous about losing myself to the dreary wasteland of plain-faced, stained-shirted, messy-bunned mom bods who lived on social media, so I started a Pinterest board labeled Mom Goals. During my baby prep period and over the nine months of my pregnancy that followed, I pinned cute photos of cute women whose pregnancy styles I coveted. I pinned staying-fit-for-labor tips that promised quick and easy deliveries. I pinned healthy recipes rich in folate to benefit baby's development and my skin. I pinned "My Cute Hospital Gown" blog posts and exquisite maternity photoshoots that made me feel like pregnant women were capable of pretty, but the pin I liked most of all was an image of a young mom on the beach with her baby. She was beautiful, tanned, and toned, and wore black bikini bottoms and a red bandeau bikini top. Her happy baby perched on her hip in a matching red-patterned swimsuit and a bucket hat. It wasn't an overly curated photo but rather seemed to be a candid shot from the woman's vacation with her little family, so her slim postpartum frame, complete with thigh gap, seemed attainable to me.

As I moved into my second trimester, I became more interested in pregnancy workouts. I pinned a post about a woman who prioritized taking five-mile walks every single evening because walking sounded doable. I pinned another post from another woman who danced for an hour a day during her pregnancy. She wasn't a trained dancer, just a lover of music and movement, and attributed her easy birth to her strong and flexible hips. She even danced in the delivery room. But the pin that really got me moving was a paraphrase of a quote from a renowned midwife I had never heard of; it said, "If you squat three hundred times a day, you are going to have a quicker birth."

Perfect, I thought as I saved the pin, then stood and moved my desk chair out of the way, eager to get started. *Sexy thighs* and *easy labor*!

I started my nineties playlist for a dance warm-up—*Why not combine methods?* I thought—and moving to a few songs by pop star hot girls Britney and Christina got me in the mood to tackle my squat goal. I decided to break up the three hundred squats into sets of fifty and do three different types of squats to target all the muscles I could. A basic squat would hit my glutes, thighs, and hamstrings, a close squat would target my thighs and glutes, and a sumo squat would work my inner thighs. I thought about the cute bikini mom's thigh gap and readied my position.

I was in decent shape, so my first sets of basic squats and close-stance squats were no problem. *I am going to be so fit and cute*, I thought, as I spread my legs apart to begin my sumo squats. I bent low, pushed my knees wide, and squeezed my inner thighs, visualizing the skin there firming on the way up. I squatted deeper with each repetition, feeling the burn, and on rep thirteen I bent so low and so wide that I ripped my vagina skin.

Shock and panic froze me in my stance. My hand shot to the spot between my legs where my inner thigh met my labia majora. *Please no, please no, please no*, I prayed as I dug my fingers under the seam of my boy shorts, but praying was no use. I felt exactly what I thought I had felt: a two-inch-long and half-an-inch-wide stretch mark ripped into the flesh where my thigh gap should have been.

I fell to the ground in instant regret. I climbed into my desk chair, looked at the cute photo of the bikini mom on Pinterest, and cried. There was no way she had a two-inch by half-inch stretch mark next to her labia. John and I didn't have enough money for beach vacations anyway, I had never been tanned a day in my life, and now I had a mangled vagina to boot, so that bitch's life and body and thighs were out of my reach forever. I deleted the evil pin and vowed never to revisit Pinterest again.

Then I redirected my browser to the Ridiculous Women Forum. According to a quick search, pregnancy hormones, particularly progesterone, were known to cause skin to become less pliant on areas like the abdomen and the thighs because of a reduction in elasticity and firmness.

No freaking wonder, I thought, and sent a text message to John to urgently request that he stop at the store on his way home from work to purchase some stretch mark–preventative belly butter.

As my pregnancy progressed, my ribs spread wide to accommodate my growing uterus and my already ample breasts nearly doubled in size, so that I looked like a walking letter B from the side. My hips shifted, too, so that I leaned a little to the left when I stood, my right hip unable to brace against the new weight of my uterus, highlighting a previously unknown muscle imbalance. My nose widened in a biological feat that would improve my ability to smell my newborn, my lips swelled up with no discernible purpose, my jawline softened into two chins, and the entire canvas of my face was spattered with brand-new freckles. All temporary due to hormonal changes, the internet promised, but I looked so ugly I spent the remainder of my pregnancy avoiding mirrors and clinging to my crowning accomplishment: my smooth, creamy, belly-buttered bump had zero stretch marks.

I'D READ THAT JESSICA ALBA, ACTRESS and genius founder of baby wellness brand the Honest Company, credited her body's quick bounce back to wearing a binder throughout the entirety of her postpartum period. So, on the day of my hospital release, I squeezed my squishy belly into a boned corset. Life was so busy with the care and tending of baby that I hadn't so much as taken a shower, let alone looked in a mirror. So, on day ten of baby's life, I decided it was high time I do both. I unhooked the twenty hooks of my corset, tossed it onto my bed, and faced my floor-length bedroom mirror to assess pregnancy's damage on my body.

My face had recovered well but for the freckles, though they seemed to be fading, and the soft chin, which showed no signs of going anywhere. I made a mental note to look up exercises that might help and let my eyes fall to my stomach. It was already pretty flat, which I attributed to the corset, but the ten days of binding had left itchy red indents all over my low belly.

"Thanks a lot, Jessica," I sighed.

After my shower, I felt clean and relaxed but wobbly without my corset, as if the place on my spine where my waist curved in had suffered some structural damage that left my torso unstable. I felt like I might snap in half if I moved too quickly, so perhaps Jessica had been onto something after all. I retrieved my corset from my bed and wrapped it around my body to begin refastening the hook and eyes from the bottom. That's when I saw them: fiery, raging, hideous red lines, zig-zagging from my belly button to my crotch and all the way to the either side of my waistline. My corset hadn't left marks on my stomach; my pregnancy had. My eyes burned as I watched my fingers trace the angry paths of my now bumpy skin, and I couldn't help but think about the cute bikini mom with an embarrassing level of envy. I didn't understand why I had to look so disgusting when she got to look so pretty. So much for bikinis.

I felt stupid and shallow and vapid for caring so intensely about what having a baby had done to my body. But I couldn't stop crying. I was jealous of every single woman who had ever bounced back after baby.

Enough, I told myself, wiping my tears. *You have everything you want. Don't be like Mom.*

MY MOTHER HATED HER BODY FOR the entirety of my childhood. One morning, when I was six years old, I walked into Mom's bathroom as she was getting ready for work. I loved watching her apply her makeup, shading her eyes, blushing her cheeks, and drawing her pout on with a precision I hoped to one day master. Sometimes, after she applied her lipstick, she would hand the tube to me, and I would be allowed to put her creamy mauve lips on my face. I would smack my lips together and rub to spread the color, then smile up at her. When she smiled back down at me, she was the most beautiful woman on Earth. But that day she hadn't seen me slip in behind her while she was leaned in close to the mirror for mascara, and when she finished, she turned, and her pale, squishy apron belly smacked me in the face. She gasped apologetically, but I was fine; her tummy had so much padding that my head had simply bounced off. I grinned up at her, grabbed two fistfuls of her flesh on either side of her navel, and squashed my whole face into her big, soft middle for a hug. Instead of hugging me back, she grabbed me by the armpits and moved me out of her way, clenching and tensing both of her hands as she padded to her closet to find the day's outfit.

I remember watching one day when I was ten as she stood topless in the mirror, turning this way and that. Her breasts were large and drooping, and she picked them up with a tsk of her tongue. She dropped them again and grabbed her apron belly with both hands, moving it out of the way so she could see what her underwear line would look like if her low tummy skin was taut.

"I want to wear a bikini," she moaned, sticking her lower lip out like a toddler. She saw me then, through the mirror, and sighed a little laugh, letting her flesh fall from her hands with a bounce.

"This is your fault, you know." She said it with a smile, but I didn't understand the joke.

"What is?" I asked, an answering grin creeping across my face. I was hoping to be let it on what we were finding amusing.

"This! This big, fat lard belly." She smacked her tummy and a tiny shock wave rippled across its skin.

"How's that my fault?" I laughed.

"Because you were in here! And your sisters. You girls stretched me out. And *these*—" She smooshed her fat flat with her right hand and ran her left fingers along the small, silver squiggles that lined her tummy. "Sarah did these. I was *huge* with Sarah."

Mom sighed, put on a shirt, and went about her day, but I couldn't help but feel terrible for ever having taken up so much space inside of her.

Mom was incredibly supportive of me when I first began to mature into my womanly body, taking me bra shopping and teaching me about menstruation, and when I got my first period at a soccer tournament she gave me pain medication for my intense cramps and walked me to the clean porta potties on the far end of the field to show me how to use a pad. But by the time I was sixteen I was under more scrutiny.

Dad was gone by then, and we lived in a small, two-bedroom

apartment, where I shared a bedroom with both of my sisters, so body boundaries were nonexistent. We often changed and showered in front of each other and walked around in various stages of undress. Whenever Mom caught one of us in the nude, our body was a source of open discussion. My nipples would react to temperature or stimulation but in their normal state they were flat or inverted, and the sight of them caused Mom to scowl or laugh or cock her head for a better look. My labia looked weird to her, too, much too bulbous and oddly shaped, apparently hilariously so, and I was often told to go find some underwear.

It was my flat tummy, though, that she commented on most of all, often with a mixed tone of envy and pride. She'd stare at me wistfully, and it produced a sense of arrogance in me, so I'd strut around to show off my frame. Nothing negative she said about my body bothered me, though: The boys loved it. And even she conceded that positive male attention was the most important thing about having a body.

As I stood in front of the mirror, staring at my newly discovered stretch marks, John stepped behind me. I hadn't seen him enter the room and hover nearby, so he gave me a start. He didn't say a word but kissed my salty cheek, and I watched in the mirror while he put his arm around my waist and ran his fingers over the offensive lines on my belly. I cringed, my bottom lip trembled, and my face grew hot. He pressed his palm into the lines, showing tender affection for my newest insecurity, and hugged me close. When I couldn't bear it any longer, I pulled away from his grip and walked to my chest of drawers, hands clenching and tensing at my sides, to pick out the day's athleisure.

In my young, dumb days, daydreaming of a baby, I knew

logically that my body would have to change with pregnancy, but I always imagined I'd be one of those women who bounced back afterward. When I'd see a diaper ad on TV, where the thin and beautiful mother had clean, brushed hair and long, lithe limbs, I'd envision myself in the role much the same: attractively nuzzling an adorable baby in romantic soft focus.

In the harsh light of reality, though, motherhood was much uglier than I had anticipated. I didn't know that I wouldn't immediately know how to mother, or that the learning curve would challenge my self-worth. I didn't know that challenge would be compounded by a challenge to my very identity, because I didn't know that my identity was so directly intertwined with fitting into the beauty standard. I didn't know my body would become so wildly distorted, and that the distortions would make me feel shame and embarrassment and self-disgust, in a season when I'd already experienced so much difficult change. The effect was unsettling, to say the least.

A LONG BLARE OF THE HORN from the car behind me alerted me to the light changing green. I flipped my vanity mirror away with a sigh and drove the rest of the way to baby's appointment feeling ugly. I missed feeling attractive. I missed my sexy body, how it moved, how I felt in it. I missed how people looked at me before I was just a mom, when I was pretty.

I knew I was being dramatic and self-loathing, but I thought I would be exchanging one type of social currency for another, going from pretty, young girl to mature mother goddess. In a brutal twist of fate, I was now neither. I couldn't even get it together enough to get baby to his checkup on time.

I thought of my mother, who for the entirety of my life was desperate to be beautiful. For the first time, I wondered what she must have gone through as she grew into a woman. I wondered if she had gotten the message that her body was her only source of wealth, too, if she had undergone scrutiny, if she had been envied for her desirability, like she seemed to envy me. Was she afraid to be ugly like I was? Did she feel as though she was losing a sense of power, as I felt? Who taught us that? Her belly was big when I was little, but it didn't disgust me; it just looked like her body. The only opinion I had, before she installed one in me, was that her body's softness was inviting. Mom was worthy to me by her mere existence, and I loved her because she was mine.

As I swung into an empty parking space at the pediatrician at last, I wondered what my self-loathing was teaching baby. *Nothing good,* I thought, and I knew I wanted to make a change.

It took me five long months of intentionally dismissing all self-hating thoughts to finally manage to feel almost neutral about my appearance. I would put on a t-shirt or catch my reflection in a mirror or realize a pair of pre-baby pants no longer fit, and the thoughts would begin. *You're disgusting. How disappointing. Wow, this is bleak.* I took notice of how often it happened, and how bad it made me feel, and then, eventually, I developed the ability to disrupt the thinking. I would screech, or take a deep breath, or trill my lips—anything to change the thought pattern.

It wasn't a perfect system, and I still had plenty of bad days, but I realized it was working on a Monday morning when baby was a rambunctious eleven-month-old. I was lying on my back on the floor of our living room, presenting baby with various noise-making toys in a move that felt both like interactive play and much-needed rest, when he used my belly to stabilize himself during a standing attempt. Once upright, the springiness of my tummy registered in his little mind and, delighted, he immediately bent over, put his head on my belly, and bounced it. I didn't cringe; I laughed. I didn't stop him when he lifted the bottom hem of my shirt, his eyes wide and curious, and examined the stretch marks that tore through my soft flesh. And I didn't recoil when he touched a particularly dark mark with his tiny finger. Instead, I joined him, tracing the lines without so much as a flinch.

I knew he would learn that my belly was gross and ugly from the world around him as he grew, but I refused to contribute to such an opinion. I wanted him to see bellies like mine as normal and neutral, a simple reality with no implication about a person's worth. I wanted to teach baby respect for all bodies, especially those that had become portals for humanity.

I fished my phone out of my pocket to record baby's inspection of the place he once called home. When my camera app opened in selfie mode, capturing me at an angle that emphasized the several soft folds of my chin, I bristled, just for a second. Then, I took a little breath and pressed my lips into a smile. It wasn't that I liked what I saw, it was just that I refused to dwell on it. Moving on felt infinitely better than beating myself up. I flipped the camera's orientation, snapped a photo of baby hugging me across my middle, and was struck with gratitude for the body that grew him.

I decided, then and there, that I would teach baby what it took me too long to learn myself: that a person's intrinsic worth was completely unrelated to how they looked. I would teach him that, because we had bodies, our hearts could love, our minds could think, and our souls could know; my body contained a whole person, and his did, too. Becoming his mother meant a destruction of what once was to allow for the emergence of something new. My body stretched and tore both for baby's existence and for my own expansion, and for the first time in my life, my appearance was the least of any merit by which I measured my worth. I wasn't a pretty, young girl anymore, but I wasn't a mother goddess either, because neither description could encapsulate every fiery facet of my being. No, I didn't bounce back after baby, because I was always meant to keep moving forward.

CHAPTER FOURTEEN

THE BALANCE

I WAS ON MY FEET THE MOMENT I heard the familiar jiggle of our laundry room doorknob. John used that door exclusively to come and go from work, and since the clock on our kitchen stove read 5:45 PM, the jiggle meant he was home—and not a moment too soon, because I had spent nine hours with our grumpy, teething seven-month-old, and I couldn't take another moment.

"Hey," John called cheerfully as the laundry room door swung open.

"Oh my God, take this child!" I yelled back. John chuckled.

"Uh-oh, tough day?" he asked as he came into view.

"Yeah, I need to go sit in silence somewhere," I said, and I held baby aloft for him to take.

"Okay," he laughed. Then he stretched his arms up in a high V and yawned. Once back to neutral, instead of taking baby, John leaned forward and planted a kiss on his chubby cheek. Baby giggled and cooed and reached for him.

"Aww, he's ready for you," I said, trying to get him to *just take the baby already*, a little more irritated than I meant to.

"Okay, just let me poop first." John turned on his heel and disappeared into our half bath while rage bubbled up from the depths of my being.

"John!" I called as the bathroom door closed.

"I gotta go," was the only response. I put baby on my hip and stomped across the room.

"You can hold him while you go," I yelled through the door.

"No, just give me a minute," John demanded.

"Give ME a minute," I yelled as I banged my fist on the door.

"Jesus, calm down," John scolded, and that did it. I stalked into the kitchen, grabbed a butter knife, stomped back, and picked the lock on the bathroom door. I swung the door open and plopped baby on John's bare knee.

"Shawna, what the fuck?!" John yelled.

"Do you know how many times I've taken a shit with him on my lap?!" I yelled back. "You'll be fine." I turned on my heel and stomped away.

"Wow, thanks for the welcome home," he called after me.

"Welcome home, you're a dad now!" I screamed.

I could have sworn there was a time when I liked that man, but I was having trouble remembering it at the moment.

JOHN AND I MET AS FLIRTY teens in high school. He had a girlfriend and I had a boyfriend, and each of us were devoted to our high school loves, so though we talked and laughed in class, nothing ever developed between us. Then, four years after high school, when I was twenty-one years old, we ran into each other again.

My sister Sarah and I were on our way to a rehearsal for Mom's marriage ceremony. Mom had met a kind and loyal man, and my sisters and I had high hopes for her happiness, plus we loved a good party, so we were excited about the wedding. As we walked through the hotel's sliding glass doors and into the lobby, Sarah turned to me.

"Erin said there's a hot guy working at check-in."

Our sister Erin had toured the venue with Mom during her wedding preparations, so she had already met some hotel staffers.

"Oh, really!" I said, thrilled at the prospect of flirting with a cute boy.

I looked over my shoulder toward the front desk, where a handsome young man with tan skin and dark hair stood behind the counter, his eyes trained on a document he held in his hands. He wore a crisp white shirt underneath a black blazer, and the gold flecks on his tie matched the gold of his eyes as they studied the paperwork he held. I recognized him immediately.

"Oh my God! That's John!" I said with a grin. I marched directly over to him and leaned far forward over his desk.

"Hi, John," I said with a toss of my long, blond hair. He looked up from his papers at last and fixed his surprised eyes on mine.

"Hey," he said, and thus began our love affair.

JOHN WAS KINDER TO ME THAN anyone had ever been in my entire life, plus he was funny, charming, a friend to all, and he looked at me with an adoration that made my skin tingle. For the first few days of our relationship, before we even called it that, we hung out in a groups with my friends and sisters, drinking heavily, and only stealing away for a moment of privacy here and there, during which I had to pace myself to keep from immediately giving him my entire being. By the two-week mark I told Sarah, much to her shock, that I would run away and marry him if he asked. He didn't ask, though, so I had to pace myself even more.

For our first proper date, John told me he wanted to take me somewhere nice, just the two of us. I was excited that he seemed to feel as strongly about me as I did about him, though he didn't say it. He wouldn't tell me what we were doing either, or where we were going, beyond that I needed to keep Friday night open for him. On the morning of our date there was a note on my car's windshield: a clue about what I should wear and where I could find more information, sending me on a quest for my next clue, a romantic scavenger hunt that crisscrossed our hometown. When I finally pieced the mystery together, John was waiting by his car with a bouquet of flowers to whisk me away on a surprise weekend trip to a locale I had mentioned in passing during our very first conversation. It was as though I was living in my own personal romcom.

We weren't always showboating, though, and often, time spent together lazing at my house in front of the TV with a few beers was my favorite. On one such occasion, the cast of *Weeds* was encouraging the bad behavior of recently widowed mother Nancy to my left, but I wasn't watching. My head was on John's chest, my eyes were on his face, and my mind was thrashing. I loved him but I didn't know if he loved me, and his lack of commitment was agony. I didn't know how to broach the subject without seeming needy or crazy or desperate, because I was. I didn't know how to tell him that I was all in, so I looked away and cried. I tried to stop myself but was there no dam that could contain my river of emotion, and eventually my drowning splashed John into awareness.

"Are you crying?" His tone was mostly one of concern, but there was a playfulness to him that buoyed me.

"No," I lied.

He laughed and tugged my chin up so he could see my eyes. "Yes, you are. Why are you crying?"

"I don't want to say," I said, an expert at the art of suspense.

"Well, now you have to say," John insisted. He sat up, and sat me up with him, so he could look at my face. The move just made me seasick, so I crashed again into his lap. He chuckled, not knowing what else to do or say, and stroked my hair.

"I'm sorry I'm being crazy." My voice was muffled by the fabric of his sweatpants.

"Hey. Stop," he said, and he flipped me over to lie on my back. He smoothed my hair out of my eyes, then held my head in his hands. "You don't have to do that. I don't think you're being crazy."

I closed my eyes so I didn't have to look at him.

"Something is obviously on your mind. You don't have to tell me if you don't want to. But if you do want to, I want to hear it."

I covered my face with both of my hands so he wouldn't see my emotion swelling again.

"Or you can keep hiding." He stroked my hair again. "That's cute, too."

"Okay, but don't look at me," I insisted from behind my hand screen.

"Alright, I'll close my eyes."

I peeked to make sure he was telling the truth. His eyelashes were dark and fanned in perfect little half circles, ending just above the apples of his cheeks, made more prominent by his Cheshire-cat grin.

"Stop grinning!"

I grabbed at the meat of his ribs, tickling mercilessly, sending him in a fit of laughter. His fingers flew to my sides and inner thighs, touching all the tickle spots that made me jump and flail as he rolled to the floor, pulling me down with him. I let him pin my right hand to the ground with his knee as he peeled my left hand off his ribs and held it motionless to his chest. I giggled when he roared like a lion.

"Oh my God, I love you, you're so funny."

I threw it at him as an aside, as if I didn't mean it, as if I was commenting on the silliness of the moment, but he turned serious. He lay down next to me and pressed his lips into mine, and I could taste the salt of my tears.

"I am so in love with you," he said at last.

We dated for six more years and moved three states away before getting married, and we had been together ten years total when I became pregnant.

I WAS EIGHT MONTHS ALONG WITH a large, round belly that was inconvenient but not yet uncomfortable when John and I sat down for a roommate movie night with Sarah and family. The non-pregnant adults were enjoying some beers while Lillybelle and I had juice. The evening was a welcome distraction for me, from my mounting anxiety about the unforeseeable ways life would change with baby, but when it was over and Sarah's family said goodnight,

I felt a slight panic begin to settle on my chest. John got himself a third beer, cracking it open as he sat down next to me, and he looked at me with the same loving adoration that always made me melt. He smiled his Cheshire-cat grin and rubbed my knee and told me he couldn't wait to have beers with me again.

"Okay," I said with a grimace. He couldn't have known that I was feeling anxious about our impending future, but as we were two months out from having a newborn, he should have known how dumb a statement he was making.

"I just mean I'm excited to get to hang with you again," he tried to explain.

"What are you talking about? We're hanging out now," I said.

"I know, but you don't get to *hang out* hang out."

I raised my eyebrows and pressed my frustration between my lips.

"You don't get to relax is what I mean; I can't wait until you can relax with me again." He rubbed my thigh with the palm of his hand.

"What are you fucking talking about?" I blurted. My heart was beating out of my chest. No way did he actually think we'd be able to have a beer and relax like old times once the baby arrived.

His brow furrowed and his shoulders raised in a defensive shrug. "I'm saying a nice thing here," he insisted. "I'm excited for things to go back to normal a little bit."

"Oh my God," I said, and my hands shot up to hold my suddenly swimming head. Who the fuck did I make a baby with? "John, I'm becoming concerned that you don't realize that we're having a baby." My blood pressure was rising along with my voice.

"Of course I realize we're having a baby," he scoffed.

"Okay, then let me ask again: What the fuck are you talking about?!" I was beyond mad.

"Why are you yelling at me?"

I turned in my seat to face him. "Nothing will 'go back to normal' when the baby comes out! I can't believe I have to say this to you!" I yelled.

"Obviously I know things will be different!" he yelled back.

"Do you? Do you know? Because you are still fucking around like a twenty-year-old while I am creating a goddamn brain in my uterus!"

"Okay." He rolled his eyes and took his hand off my leg. "Wow. Sorry for saying I wanted to hang out with you."

"Don't do that. That is such passive-aggressive bullshit," I spat, narrowing my eyes and bending my head low to meet his gaze. "I'm worried. What you just said worries me. In fact, it fucking scares me. You're acting like this is a momentary hiatus in our life of good times."

He took one last swig of his beer, then set it on the coffee table before us. He crossed his arms over his chest and refused to meet my gaze.

"You're acting like a child. Are you a child? Or are you a grown man building a life with me? I need to know which it is."

He was silent, and I could tell his pride was hurt, but I didn't care. It was the truth.

WHEN MY PREGNANCY OFFICIALLY HIT FULL term at thirty-seven weeks and I found myself facing a possible induction I hadn't mentally prepared for, I fell apart. I came home from my OB appointment in heaving sobs and sought the comfort of John's arms. He was always a level-headed, rational man, so I knew I could count on him to talk plain logistics while I emoted. I flopped onto our bed while he consulted the Ridiculous Women Forum for me. I wasn't due for another three weeks, so unless there was an emergent danger to the baby, an induction wasn't necessary, the internet said.

"They say we can try natural induction methods," John read.

I nodded, and he helped me stand up and put my sneakers on my feet. We walked slowly, for two hours, traversing every side-walk in our neighborhood and talking while I cried. John didn't even mind when, on occasion, my sentences were halted by sobs; he waited patiently for me to choke out what I was trying to say. He was rock solid in his support.

When I asked his opinion about the induction on offer, he instead asked me to tell him about my fears, and I realized with a small smile that I married a deeply kind man. I had been gripped by my fears the moment I heard the word *induction*, so I hadn't thought them through enough to name them.

"Well, think them through now," John coached.

I took a deep breath and let my mind wander through all the terrible scenarios floating around in my brain soup until I found the one that seemed the meatiest.

"I'm not ready," I said. "I'm supposed to have three more weeks; I don't feel ready yet."

"That makes sense," John said with a small smile. "It literally is three weeks until your due date. So, yeah, that's a perfectly logical reaction."

I smiled, too, grateful for the vote of confidence.

"What else?" he asked.

I wiped my eyes and thought up another morsel. "I want to know what it's like to go into labor naturally?" The statement came out sounding more like a question, which made me realize I felt stupid for wanting that experience.

"Yeah, it's a big deal. It's your first time having a baby."

"But, also, if my doctor is saying I might need it, who am I to be like, no, I don't want to?" I blurted out. "I don't know anything about babies or birth, he's the expert, you know? I really want to feel like the doctor who is helping me through this scary, vulnerable thing knows what he's doing."

John put his arm around my shoulder and kissed me on my temple. "Okay, here's what I think," he began.

I inhaled deeply through my nose and held my breath.

"I think we should wait," he said. "We take induction completely off the table until you're forty weeks."

I let go of my breath and, with it, all of the tension I didn't know I was holding in my body. I leaned into his hug and felt truly seen.

But by the time baby was five weeks old, John and I were in survival mode. We were barely sleeping and rarely experiencing a moment without baby wanting to be in someone's arms, and no matter how good John was at soothing baby, I felt like I was constantly running after him to correct his caregiving mistakes.

Once, he propped a bottle with a pillow so baby could continue to eat, giving himself a moment to stand up and stretch. I walked into the room and saw John five feet away from baby, bent over in a hamstring stretch and watching a YouTube video on his phone. I was seized with panic and ran to hold baby. John didn't know why I was angry, but all I could imagine was my helpless newborn drowning in milk while John worked on his mobility. What if I hadn't walked in? I demanded to know. Would John have ignored baby for the entirety of his video? After a heated discussion, he ultimately agreed that baby shouldn't be left unattended with a bottle, even for just a moment.

Another time, John brought the baby in from the car, and I politely reminded him to take the baby out of his carrier before I headed upstairs to pump. Something told me to stop and double-check that John had complied, so I turned around on the stairs just in time to see John put baby on the floor, still in his carrier, and grab a PlayStation controller. I stomped down a few stair steps so he could see me demand to know what the hell he was doing. He rolled his eyes, told me baby was fine, and ordered me to my pumping chair. My entire body tensed as I yelled positional asphyxiation facts at his dumb, dissociated face, but it wasn't until I moved down the stairs to grab baby myself that John finally agreed. It was the same childlike behavior I had seen from John during my pregnancy, and it left me again wondering who I had married.

Baby was two months old when John had to go away for two days for a work trip. Baby was still up every hour all night long at that point, so we usually took him in shifts, and I had no idea how I was going to make it through by myself. On night one, I bounced baby for his requisite forty-five-ish minutes, and when I laid his body down to rest, I cried, too anxious to fall asleep with no one else to keep watch. I moved in and out of sleep that night, my anxiety eventually overpowered by fatigue, and when baby woke for the day, I felt relieved that I only had to go one more night without John.

Night two went better, though. Baby was calmer, slept in slightly longer stretches, and needed less reassurance during wake-ups, and the thought crossed my mind that John and I both juggling his care throughout the night had created some opportunities for miscommunication between baby and us. I couldn't be sure that John was responding to baby on his shift the same way I was responding to baby on mine.

We were still living with Sarah at the time, and she mercifully woke up three hours before she had to for work to watch baby the next morning while I got some solid sleep. I could have cried when I woke to a report of baby sleeping through her entire three-hour watch. I was grateful for her and wondered what she had done differently from me. Nothing, she said when I asked. She just read her book and he slept. I wondered if John and I were disrupting baby's sleep as much as he was disrupting ours.

When John came home, I was thrilled to have him back—until it was his turn to bounce the baby. While he was gone, I'd discovered baby preferred a gentler bouncing motion that involved a bit of swinging, but John hadn't learned the new method, and I could see his face beginning to twist with frustration as he jiggled baby. He had enjoyed two blissful nights of no stress and uninterrupted sleep, a taste of life before baby, so his reintroduction to our sleep issues was a rude awakening. I tried to explain what I had learned, but baby was overtired and hated moving back and forth between us while he was trying to go to sleep, so he cried, and John threw up his hands.

"I'm trying to help here," he snapped.

I hadn't enjoyed the break he had while he was gone, so I found his frustration disrespectful. He took baby out of my arms, stomped over to my birthing ball, and bounced, hard.

"Come on, dude!" he yelled at the baby, and I flooded with rage.

"Stop! Immediately," I yelled.

He did, to his credit, and I calmly took my baby away from him.

"Go take a walk," I directed, then I bounced and swayed baby with my bone-tired body for forty-five minutes until the boy was asleep at last.

Weariness glistened on my cheeks when John returned from his walk. He apologized, but I scolded him anyway.

"You do not get to leave for two days and then come home to yell at my baby," I spat at him in a hushed tone.

"Yeah." He rubbed the back of his neck.

"I get frustrated with him all the time! But you control yourself. *Of course*, things are different from what worked two days ago! Things change all the time!"

I could tell he felt terrible. He hugged me and let me cry on his shoulder. He stroked my hair and thanked me for taking care of our baby while he was gone. And he apologized, and promised he would do better.

"We have to get on the same page," I said at last. "This is a marathon."

"Yeah, it's for the long haul," John agreed.

"No, this is those crazy people who swim the English Channel."

John laughed, but I meant it.

"I don't just mean commitment-wise. I mean this requires everything." I spoke through tears, no longer afraid for him to hear me. "This is physically exhausting, obviously, I'm sure you're as tired as I am. But it's a mental game, too. I won't be mentally capable to be who he needs me to be if I have to scold you like I'm your mom. I'll drown."

He was quiet, but I could tell my words resonated, so I went on. "And it's emotional, you know, when you're that depleted but you care that much and you're trying to tread water but the waves keep coming? That's you invalidating my concerns. You're making waves here."

"I get it," he said at last.

"We're in the water; there's no going back to shore. This needs our mutual dedication."

"I know," he said.

"We have to swim together or we're going to die. I need you to be a grown-up who knows how to swim."

John took my face in his hands and wiped my tears. "I hear you," he said. "I get it. I'm sorry. Same team, always."

I nodded with a sigh, grateful that I was able to help him understand at last. It wasn't entirely his fault, I reflected. My training began the moment I got a positive pregnancy test. He hadn't been forced to evolve in the same time frame.

I EXHALED THE STRESS OF THE day from my body as my pump finished its last milk pull. I could hear John playing with baby downstairs and, from the sound of it, they had made it to the living room. I felt satisfied, realizing he must have finished his after-work poop despite baby's company. The thirty-five minutes I sat alone in silence had been enough to center me, and I missed my boys. I trotted downstairs to see John on the couch, as expected, bouncing baby on his knee. I was still mad at him, but I did feel a little bad for yelling. I flopped down on the couch and leaned into baby's line of vision. His drooly face lit up when he saw me, and John and I laughed. I leaned forward and kissed baby's cheek. Then, in a singsong voice, I asked him if he could say "mama."

"No way, try 'dada.' 'Dada,'" John prompted.

We laughed, and I made mama sounds while John made dada sounds until baby got bored and demanded a bottle.

"Hey, sorry I yelled," I said to John as I stood to ready baby's milk.

"Yeah, me, too," he replied.

"You get to leave the house, you know?" I explained.

"I get it."

"No, like, I never leave the house. I never have a moment away. But you do. So, when I tell you I'm at my breaking point, it's because I'm at my breaking point." I handed him the bottle.

"Understood," John said, but I wasn't positive he did.

"Can you imagine never talking to grown-ups, though? Or never having a moment of quiet, like ever? Never peeing without a baby pulling your hair?"

John nodded. "Probably gets old." He cradled baby and held his bottle as he ate.

"I mean you had been gone for nine hours, and you still wanted a moment to yourself the second you walked in, so I know you know what I mean," I said.

"Shawna. I know what you mean." He met my gaze so I knew he was serious, then added, "We're on the same team."

"Okay," I said, and I thought about all the mothers who had a John who refused to listen. I wondered if Erin had been heard in her frenzied first year of motherhood. I wondered if Sarah had, though I doubted it, since Sarah and Dave were so young when they had Lilybelle. My mom was young when she became a mother, too, and I wondered if my dad had listened to her when she tried to tell him she had hit her breaking point with the baby. *Probably not*, I thought, and it made me feel sad.

What would the world be like, I wondered, *if all mothers had someone who listened before they hit their breaking point?*

I hadn't realized I was lost in thought until John took my chin in his hand and tipped my face his way. His gold eyes flitted from each of mine to my lips. He kissed me, softly, with an adoration that made my skin tingle, then he said the sexiest thing he had ever said to me.

"Do you think you're ready to get back into acting?"

I smiled, breathlessly, in pure exhilaration. *Oh yes*, I thought. *I remember. I like this man.*

CHAPTER FIFTEEN

THE SILENCE

"OKAY, I'M OUT OF HERE," JOHN said, shouldering his laptop bag. It was seven-twenty in the morning and he was on his way to work. He opened the back door of our house, then paused, turning to me and grabbing my waist, and I tipped my face up in anticipation as he leaned in for a kiss. Baby, from his perch on my hip, kicked his legs, bucked his body, and leaned in to join us. We laughed, our lips still pressed together, at his slobbery attempt at his own kiss.

"Oh, you want love, too?" John asked, and he took baby from my arms. He kissed baby's chubby cheeks and bear-hugged his eight-month-old little body, which produced squeals of joy from our happy boy, and I grinned at the sight.

"Alright, for real this time, gotta go," John said, handing baby back to me.

"We'll walk you out," I offered, and when I stepped out our back door into the oppressive heat of the Texas morning sun, I remembered the date. "Oh, don't forget to text your sister happy birthday," I said.

"Nice, thanks," John replied. He gave baby and me each one last peck on the cheek, then ducked into the driver's side door of his gray sedan.

"Bye, Dada! Say 'Bye, Dada! Bye,'" I coached baby in a singsong voice.

We both waved goodbye as John blew us kisses and backed out of the driveway.

"Text your sister!" I yelled one more time and was satisfied when John gave me a thumbs-up. I wondered for a moment if his friends and family knew how often I thought of them, or if everyone assumed John's impressively thoughtful nature was inherent. Then, I noticed the pavement below my bare feet was hot enough to burn. I jumped into the grass for some relief, then trotted inside seeking the comfort of central air conditioning.

The back door closed behind me, and I set baby on his play mat in the living room to get myself a cup of water. As I stood in the kitchen enjoying my cool refreshment, I took in the stillness around me. Baby was quietly concentrating on his favorite sensory book, and I hadn't yet turned on the playlist I liked in the mornings, so the only sound I heard was my swallowing. I finished, set my glass on the countertop, and paused, letting the quiet envelop me.

It felt lonely.

I pulled my phone out of my pocket to distract myself and found its blank lock screen confronting. I swiped to open it and tapped through my various social media apps. No new notifications anywhere. I set my phone on the counter next to my glass and silently watched baby flip a flap on his touch-and-feel book as I wondered if anyone outside of the four walls of my house ever thought of me.

"SARAH, DOES THIS LOOK CRAZY?!" I yelled down the hallway. I was due across town soon for a joint baby shower, where an actor friend of mine and I were the guests of honor.

Sarah came out of her room with a quizzical smile that I knew to mean *Bitch, let me see* in the secret language of sisters.

"Stop, I have to go. Does it?" I asked, and I took a step out of my room into the hall.

Her eyes traveled the length of my body. My pink and blue cotton dress was supposed to have an asymmetrical hem, but my pregnant belly had more than doubled in size since my last try on, jutting out so far and lifting the front of my dress up so much that it looked more like a mini skirt with a mullet, and it threatened to expose my vulva.

"Classy," Sarah said, rubbing my belly, and with that one word I whirled around to rip through my closet for alternative options.

"Hey, I'm feeling disgusting, do you have a minute?" I called.

"I'm right here," she said in my ear.

"Ah!" I yelped. Evidently, she had followed me into my closet. "Creepy."

"Psshhhhaw, never mind, I *won't* help you find an outfit." She turned on her heel to go.

"Wait!" I looked at the time on my phone. It was already twelve-thirty. "Actually, would you mind making me a sandwich, so I don't pass out and barf driving to this thing?"

"You're going to do both?" she teased.

"You're going to feel so bad if I do both," I replied.

She laughed, but I was really hungry.

"Tuna sound good?" She gave me a knowing smile.

"Oh my God, tuna sounds amazing!"

My sister was so supportive. I sent a quick text to my Paula, my co-honoree, to ask what she was wearing to the shower. She replied that she was in a purple maxi dress and already sweating, which made me feel better about my accidental mini skirt. I pulled on a pair of biker shorts under my dress and called it good.

My friend Paula from acting class was gorgeous and talented, and pregnant at the same time as me. I hadn't known her very well when class started, but since we suddenly had so much in common, we began spending more time together. At our second coffee date, we talked in equal measure about pregnancy symptoms and teaming up on an acting project after our babies were born. I thought it would be interesting to compare our respective motherhood journeys in film form; she agreed, saying it would be cool to have something creative to look forward to. We made a tentative plan of execution and, before long, added a third actress to our coffee dates. Stephanie was also from class, and also pregnant; she and her husband would be welcoming surprise baby number three, and we thought her perspective as a veteran mom would round out our trio nicely. I wanted to make a buddy comedy like *Three Men and a Baby*, except with three women and three babies, and I was thrilled to have collaborators who seemed as keen as I was to bring a film project to fruition.

Stephanie would be at the shower, too, but as she already had everything she needed for another baby, she had graciously declined being a third honoree, insisting that us first-time moms-to-be should have our moment to be celebrated instead. Kind, generous, and still pursuing her art after motherhood—Stephanie was the kind of mom I wanted to be.

I shoved the last quarter of my tuna sandwich into my mouth and chewed as I pulled my seatbelt across the front of my body, grunting with the effort. I positioned the shoulder belt between my boobs, thanking the forgiving cotton of my pink and blue dress for smashing flat, and smoothed the lap belt under my bump. Panting now, I blasted my AC. Finally, swallowing my mouthful, I drove to the shower. Pregnancy made everything such an ordeal.

I'm here, I texted Paula as I put my car in park. *I'm inside* came her reply, and with it, a tiny jolt of excited anticipation.

The party was beautifully decorated in pastel pink and blue—pink for Paula's daughter and blue for my son—with a banquet table full of delectable-looking pastries. I commended our friend Angela, another actress, on her hosting skills, and she handed me a specialty mocktail with a hug. People began pouring in then, taking their mocktails and readying themselves for party games, and I was touched at the number of women in attendance. Most of our other actor friends were younger and absolutely none of them were in the having-a-baby stage of life, so it was surprisingly emotional that the room felt alive with support.

I took a seat on the couch next to a different Stephanie, who had been the first person in my acting circle to find out about my pregnancy. I thanked her for coming with a hug, and she told me how excited she was for me, especially because I was going to make a *really good boy mom*. I grinned and thanked her again, excited about my little boy, but after a moment's thought, I wondered what she meant. Would I not make a good girl mom? I opened my mouth to ask, but my cell phone buzzed in my hand with a text from another friend, Shayla, apologizing for missing the shower and scheduling a time to go for coffee so she could give me my gift. I smiled and tapped my phone screen to send her a reply.

"Shawna, go sit in your chair!" Angela chided and the rest of the party giggled. I looked up to a sea of smiling faces and Angela pointing across the room, where two backless barstools flanked a gift table.

"Oh," I said to scattered laughter. Paula was already there, balancing on her stool.

My belly was huge and threw off my center of gravity, giving my back trouble whenever I sat unsupported, and the stools were tall, which meant that my crotch would be at face-height for the partygoers, but everyone was staring at me enthusiastically, so I didn't want to be a bother. *Good thing I put on bike shorts*, I thought.

I put my phone in my bag and crossed the room of well-wishers. I looked at Paula, and she looked at me, and we shared a knowing chuckle as I clambered onto my perch to open gifts while our community cooed their support.

IN THE QUIET OF THE KITCHEN, our refrigerator clicked on, bringing me back to the stark reality of my day-to-day. I hadn't seen any of those women since the shower.

The sound of the refrigerator also startled baby, who squawked and crawled toward me when he realized I was more than an arm's length away. I smiled and scooped him up, holding him on my hip for a selfie, then texted the photo to my sisters. Baby immediately grabbed for my hair.

"Okay, ouchie," I told baby, pulling my hair from his grip. I noticed my glass on the counter where I had placed it and moved it to the dirty dish pile next to the sink. The water I drank had moved through me, so I walked a few steps to the living room and placed baby down again on his play mat. I wanted to pee without an audience. It wasn't urgent, but it was something to do.

No use, though. Baby cried and crawled after me as I stepped away, demanding to come along, so I picked him up and made my way to the downstairs half bath, settling him on my lap as I sat to pee.

"Is this better? This is what you wanted, huh?" I asked, putting my forehead to baby's.

He shrieked and grabbed my nose with his little hand.

"Ow," I chuckled, and I scrunched my face away from his grasp as I wadded up a fistful of toilet paper.

I had sent Paula and Stephanie each a text message when John, baby, and I moved to our new neighborhood. I was living much farther away from them both, in a suburb of Austin, but a quick internet search produced a cute coffee shop located between us, so I suggested we try it out for our next project meeting. They both congratulated me on the house and said the coffee shop looked good, but no plans solidified.

I knew firsthand how busy life must have been for them both with their new babies, so I couldn't take it personally. I was bummed, though, because it seemed like three women with so much in common ought to have made for a solid creative alliance. Since they were on my mind, I pulled out my phone and sent two quick texts checking in. It wasn't even eight o'clock in the morning yet, but they were moms, so I was sure they'd be up. Then, I texted my friend Shayla.

Shayla was my only friend who had visited when I was newly

postpartum. She'd texted me her congratulations while I was still in the hospital and demanded I let her come over so she could meet the baby and give me my shower gift at last. She came by three weeks later, and though I was exhausted and didn't really feel up for a visit, I loved that she was so excited. I dressed baby in a tiny polo shirt onesie for the occasion, and Shayla gave me a big hug when she arrived, then immediately asked for the bathroom so she could wash her hands.

"Oh, you are good," I said, to her amusement.

Once clean, she handed me a gift bag containing an adorable newborn outfit, then sat down on our couch with her hands out. I laughed, but when I moved to place baby into her arms, she had a moment of panic.

"Ahh, wait, what do I do?" she asked. I giggled again, flashing back to the very first time I held Sarah's baby, and just like my sister had with me, I unceremoniously plopped my baby into Shayla's lap. *What a full circle moment*, I thought. And, realizing that baby was in the arms of a nonfamily member for the very first time, my eyes welled up with tears. It might have been the new mom in me, but the moment felt monumental.

I hadn't seen Shayla or texted with her much since that early postpartum visit. She was busy with acting jobs in Austin, and I was busy with baby in the suburbs. It was no one's fault, but I wondered if she missed me like I missed her.

"I had so many friends," I muttered to myself. "What happened to everyone?"

Baby babbled again and squirmed on my lap to communicate his boredom. "Okay, hold on," I told him. I shifted him to my hip with my left hand and tucked my phone into my bra with my right, freeing it to pull up my leggings as I stood. Baby didn't want to sit on my hip, though, and he squirmed again when I tried to wash my hands. He began fussing as I moved back to the kitchen, until I walked a few steps and set him down on the kitchen floor.

"Alright, go nuts," I told him, and I checked my text messages as I opened the refrigerator to start on breakfast.

No replies, not even from my sisters. I knew Sarah was already at work, but Erin was a stay-at-home mom like me, living a few states away in Kansas. I suspected she must have been busy with breakfast for my toddler niece and baby nephew.

I guess I should get busy, too, I thought, and I swiped through my phone to find my music app. I tapped play and was hit by a wave of nostalgia when the first three piano tones of Britney Spears's ". . . Baby One More Time" rang out. My sisters and I loved a good Britney song. A small smile spread on my lips, and I thought of Erin again, specifically of her offer to come help after baby was born, which I had declined during my pregnancy.

"Honestly, it's so hard," Erin told me. "I wish I would have had someone here with me postpartum. I want to help you." She wanted to visit when baby was a week old. That way, she said, we'd be home from the hospital and just beginning to get truly sleep-deprived. She could hold baby while we slept.

Having my big sister come stay for my child's birth sounded nice, but Erin had recently announced her own pregnancy, her second, and she was due a mere six weeks after I was. It was exciting news that meant baby would have a cousin close in age, but it rendered her early postpartum visit risky and inadvisable. I couldn't imagine accepting an offer of help considering she'd have to fly while heavily pregnant to make the trip.

It was okay, I told her at the time. In the isolation of new motherhood, though, I found myself wishing she had come. I needed a friend. In fact, I really wished we could live closer and raise our babies together.

Sarah lives close, I thought as I pulled out eggs and leftover black beans, and cracked baby's egg into a bowl. My milk was still his primary food source, but we had begun to venture into the wonderful world of eating solids. Black beans and eggs were his least favorite, but they were nutritious, so I pushed them hard.

I looked over my shoulder at baby, who babbled happily on his play mat as he smashed shrill notes out of the light-up keys of his toy piano. His music clashed with Britney's, but noise drove out the stillness of isolation, so I didn't mind. I grabbed a silicone whisk from my canister of utensils and began to scramble while I ruminated about my sister.

Sarah was a key source of comfort before baby, a piece of home, but I'd witnessed a change in her during my pregnancy and after baby was born, the last few months of our shared lease, that I didn't understand. There had been drama with Mom about Thanksgiving, of course, but it seemed like Sarah was upset about something else, too. I wasn't as close with her husband, Dave, and it was possible that bothered her, but he and I got along just fine on a daily basis, so I couldn't see how. I adored Lillybelle, but I had to admit that it wasn't always easy to live with an elementary school–aged child without parenting her on occasion; maybe I had overstepped. Or maybe I had leaned on Sarah too hard for comfort, or she felt abandoned by me once all my attention shifted to baby, or she thought I was judging her parenting somehow by making different choices than she had. Whatever the cause, I felt deep regret that we seemed to be growing apart.

By the time baby hit three months old at the end of January, I'd been experiencing the type of bone-deep exhaustion that could have been classified as torture, so John and I didn't spend much time hanging out anywhere other than our room, or the upstairs loft space right outside of our room. With baby's nighttime sleep being so all-consumingly inconsistent, we didn't want to bother Sarah, or her family. They weren't the ones who signed up for a newborn, after all.

One Friday, baby woke at his typical, punishing five-thirty in the morning after a particularly wet and fussy night. I hadn't slept at all, not even during John's shift with baby, because I had to jump up every few moments to grab extra wipes or fetch gas drops. John would have to leave for work before long, though, so I knew I was going to need a lot of caffeine to meet the day. I left the boys cuddled in bed and padded downstairs, where I caught Sarah, alone, scooping fresh coffee grounds into a clean filter.

"Ooh, can I get in on that?" I begged. She smiled and I missed her instantly.

"How much do you want?" she asked.

"Just double what you usually do, I'll drink it," I said with a sigh.

"Rough night?" she asked.

"I might die," I joked. She sucked air through the side of her gritted teeth and gave her head a shake. It was a gesture I knew to mean *that sucks*, which I had seen her make a million times before.

"Hey, what are you guys doing tonight?" I blurted it out before I even realizing I wanted to know.

"Oh, uh, I don't know. Nothing," came the reply. "Why, do you want to do something?"

"Yeah," I chirped, and I meant it so, so much. "I mean, we

obviously can't really do anything, but we need to eat. Want to, like, order pizza?"

Sarah took a moment to wipe a few crumbs from the counter to her left, turning her back to me, and it occurred to me that she was stalling.

"Umm . . . we can do dinner," she said at last. Then, turning to face me again, she added that she already had a meal planned and could just make enough for us to eat, too. I nodded my agreement and thanked her for cooking, trying not to notice the way our communication had stiffened, and then, thanking her again for making coffee, I took my cup and left her to enjoy the last of her alone time before the rest of the house woke up and needed her.

At dinnertime, all six of us gathered around our dining room table to eat. Baby sat on John's lap, and we laughed at stories from Sarah's new job. I so desperately wanted everything to be back to normal, but the evening felt more obligatory than I had anticipated, and my eyes were sore enough from lack of sleep that they felt like they could bleed out of my head. When I couldn't take it any longer, John and I excused ourselves to bed, ending our roommate dinner just after six in the evening.

We were halfway up the stairs when I heard eight-year-old Lillybelle yell in disgust, "I am NEVER having a baby!"

"Shh," came Sarah's quick, hushed reply.

Lillybelle lowered her voice significantly, but I always had excellent hearing. "Do you really have to go to bed at six o'clock when you have a baby?!" she whispered.

"No." Sarah said it with a quiet scoff, and because I know the secret language of sisters, I understood what she really meant: *They're being overprotective and ridiculous.*

In that moment I knew I was right; our relationship was strained, and it was clear from her simple judgment that Sarah felt it, too. Our family didn't discuss feelings openly growing up—not in a calm or direct way, anyway—so I didn't know how to talk to her about it, choosing to continue to avoid the topic altogether. She had her family and I had mine, I told myself. Sarah and Dave closed escrow on their own home just three weeks after we did, and I was as excited for them as I was for us. I loved her dearly, so I hoped she and I could find a new dynamic once we had a little space to live our own lives.

Unfortunately, it hadn't worked out that way.

By March we had sleep trained, and baby was finally sleeping for four-hour stretches, which meant John and I were finally sleeping for four-hour stretches, which meant I finally had enough energy to get started on creating family traditions in our new home. Easter was coming up, and though baby wouldn't be able to egg hunt, I wanted to make sure we celebrated. I called Sarah to solidify plans and offered to host.

"Oh, is that a thing?" she asked.

I was puzzled. "What? Easter? Yeah, it's totally a thing. We always had an egg hunt growing up, and Grandma would make a big Easter meal, remember? Deviled eggs, candied ham?"

"Wow, I do not remember that at all," came the reply.

"You're kidding! You don't do a basket for Lillybelle?"

"I mean, yeah . . ." she began.

"You did a basket last year! And an egg hunt." I remembered hiding eggs with my own two hands for Lillybelle to find, so Sarah's apathy seemed bizarre.

"Yeah, okay. It's coming back to me," Sarah said with a laugh. I laughed, too.

"Okay, cool. Well, if you guys want to come over here, I don't mind cooking so you don't have to worry about it, and Lilly won't have any egg hunt competition because baby can barely crawl, so she'll be stoked, and I heard our neighborhood does something cute, too, like a whole big egg hunt thing. So, we could do that if you want, or keep it just us, either way."

I thought a holiday celebration like the ones we both loved so much as kids sounded fun, but Sarah hesitated. Then she informed me that, actually, because she didn't think Easter was a big-deal holiday, she had already made plans with her new friends from her new neighborhood. There were a lot more kids Lillybelle's age, she said, and that would be more fun for her. Plus, the new neighbors were going to get a keg and do a cul-de-sac crawfish boil, which seemed so quintessentially Southern that she couldn't miss it.

My sister was in a different stage of motherhood than I was, but I knew we couldn't have a close familial bond if we didn't cultivate it. And, despite living a mere eighteen-minute drive away from me, Sarah seemed to have zero interest in raising our babies together. I was devastated. It felt like there'd been irreversible damage to our relationship. And I wasn't sure how to start repairing it, if repair was even possible.

Baby's eggs were done, so I swallowed the lump in my throat and clicked him into his high chair. I handed him his bottle of milk first. I hated feeding him solids; my stomach leapt into my throat the moment his chubby hand palmed the first morsel. I was afraid, every single time without fail, that he would choke. I made a habit of turning off all electronics for every mealtime, including any noise-making toys, so I could sit in silence and watch to make sure each bite made it down the right pipe without incident.

Baby loved eating, though, and who was I to deny an eight-month-old one of life's simplest pleasures? I plunked a blue plate full of eggs and smashed beans and mashed bananas down on the table in front of me as baby swallowed the last of his bottle.

"Hungry boy," I cooed, and he gave me a drooly, four-toothed grin. I spooned some egg onto his high chair tray and watched his eyes go wide with excitement. He concentrated hard on a big lump, readying his thumb and forefinger for the task ahead, but before he could get the piece into his pincher grasp, I decided it was too big and quickly smooshed it in half. He looked at me, grinned again, then took the larger of the two halves in his hand and brought it to his mouth.

"Yum," I said with a grin. My insides were in anxious knots, but man, was he cute! *Who wouldn't want a close familial bond with this kid?* I thought, and the thought made me sad.

AFTER HIS MEAL I TOOK BABY out to the front of our house so he could practice crawling around and I could ease my feeding anxiety with some deep breaths of fresh air. It was hot out, but our covered porch provided a big shaded area that baby could explore without my having to worry about the pavement burning his little knees.

Our house was situated on a greenway, which acted as a shared front lawn for a dozen or so houses that faced each other on our block. When I opened our front door, I made eye contact with the man who lived directly across the way from us. He was sitting in a camping chair, cracking nuts. I smiled but he did not, so I immediately averted my eyes and sat down with baby to examine the concrete of our porch, conveniently blocking myself from his gaze with our decorative shrubbery. I could see through the bushes, though, so I watched as the man was joined by a woman I assumed to be his wife. They talked and laughed and cracked nuts together, and he looked perfectly nice, so I wondered why he had been so unfriendly.

Baby was occupied looking at a leaf I plucked for him from the dirt beneath the nearest bush, which gave me time to nonchalantly watch a third woman join the first two, bringing her own camping chair from her house. The three of them chuckled and visited, so I figured I must have misunderstood the man's non-smile. I wanted to scoop baby up and go say hi, but I felt shy and insecure. I was new to the neighborhood, while they all knew each other. John and I had fallen in love with our house when we were looking to buy, thanks in large part to how friendly the neighborhood had seemed, but suddenly I couldn't remember if we had actually witnessed any friendliness, or if our realtor Amanda had just assured us it existed. Sarah's new neighborhood seemed to be friendly as hell, so I wanted to believe it was possible for us, too. I gathered baby into my arms and stood, pretending to look at our front porch pillar, waiting for the strangers across the way to become neighbors.

Out of the corner of my eye, I could see from their body language that they saw me, and that they were talking to each other about me, but they didn't wave or say hello.

I guess it's on me, I thought, and as I slowly turned to present baby with the second pillar on our front porch, I pretended to be seeing them for the very first time. It was like an acting exercise, wherein I attempted to convey surprise and delight with my body language and facial expressions to convince the neighbors what an airhead I was. *Oh! You're here, too? I had no idea! But I'm thrilled!*

I knew I was an excellent actress, so I was pretty sure I pulled it off. I waved, and they waved, but they didn't get up from their chairs or beckon me over from across the green space, so after a few more awkward moments—likely awkward for me and nobody else—I made a mental note to take in the air from the backyard from now on and went back inside.

My shoes clacked on the tiled entryway as I walked through my front door. I hadn't noticed how hot I was, but the air conditioning felt so good that I sighed an audible "Oh wow" as I pushed the door closed. *Inside definitely feels better*, I thought. With a twist of my wrist, the lock on the door clicked into place, and then baby and I were in silent stillness once again.

Baby bucked in my arms, so I kicked off my shoes and walked a few steps to place him on his play mat. I dug into the stretchy pocket of my leggings to retrieve my phone and was depressed to see I still had no new text messages. I swiped through my apps, but it was no use: I had no emails, no phone calls, no notifications that anyone, anywhere, had tried to communicate with me in any way. *Not even a scammer? Come on*, I thought with a chuckle.

I had never *thought* so much in my entire life.

When I was pregnant, it felt like the whole world was excited for me to be a mom, but as soon as I became one, I was forgotten. Worse than forgotten, actually—it felt like I was expected to take my place on the fringes of society. *Ohmygawd, yay, have a baby! Just don't bother us after you do.* I knew logically that everyone had their own lives—that it was nobody's responsibility to check in on me, to make me feel welcome, to be as excited about creating memories with baby as I was—but logic didn't change the way I felt: alone. Where was that famous "village" I had heard so much about? My life had changed so much in a few short months, and while I was desperately trying to adjust, the whole entire world just kept on turning like nothing had even happened.

"Let's read some stories, bub," I said to baby with a sigh, then picked up a stack of board books that lived in a basket near the couch. I sat next to baby on his play mat and let him crawl all around me as I read aloud.

Baby's books were simple but always beautifully illustrated, and I loved watching his eyes to see which images would catch his attention most. Today, it was a colorful, swirly lollipop that a caterpillar had eaten through, and baby was so intrigued that he put his left hand on my arm and reached for the book with his right. I giggled and teased like I was going to turn the page, but baby wouldn't let me, grunting and pawing at the spot where my hand held the book. I laughed and tried again, but baby employed his second hand, moving it from its spot on my forearm to the page, and then threw his whole weight into grabbing the book. Curious what he would do, I guided him into a seated position, then let the book go. He shrieked with glee when he realized he now had sole possession of the book and slapped the glossy cardboard with an open palm. Then, breathing hard and drooling, he collapsed forward and put his mouth on the page's colorful imagery.

"Eww," I laughed, taking baby by the shoulders and straightening him to seated. "That's not food! We don't eat books," I added in a singsong voice.

I mopped up his spit with the hem of my shirt, then pulled him onto my lap. I held his fuzzy head in my hands and rapid-fire kissed his chubby cheeks and neck and hugged him close while he giggled.

"You're so cute! I can't handle it!" I told him in jest.

I leaned back where I sat on the living room floor, resting the weight of my upper body against the front of our couch, and bent my knees until my feet were flat and baby was cradled perfectly in the gap formed by my legs, like a chubby puzzle piece.

"You fit me," I told him with a tickle of the belly.

Baby yawned, signaling that it was nap time, so I hugged him close and kissed him again. I walked him upstairs to his room, slowly, calmly, and changed him into a fresh diaper. I flipped the switch on the wall next to his bed and swayed with him in the dark, noisy cool of his room. He sighed, and I heard him smack his little lips when he laid his head on my chest, and my heart ached with how much I loved him. I laid him in his bed and left the room, and when I closed his bedroom door, loneliness caught in my throat.

Then, in the quiet isolation of motherhood, silent tears fell from my eyes. Baby didn't deserve to be treated like an afterthought. I didn't want him to feel alone. I wanted to surround him with relationships that made him feel good. I wanted him to be around people who wanted to be around him, not out of obligation or habit, but because he was important to them. And the only way he was ever going to foster those kinds of relationships was if he watched me do it first.

I was so nervous I could hear my heartbeat in my ears, but determination to show baby a better way won out. I flopped onto my bed and swiped away the lock screen on my phone. I flipped to my Messages app, clicked on Sarah's name, and typed out a text message: *Hey! I miss you and I feel like things have been weird with us. Can we talk this weekend?*

If I wanted us to have a close relationship again, I knew that facing some hard, scary feelings was the only way to get there. I didn't know when or how she'd respond, but I at least had to try.

I set my phone aside and flopped over onto my back. Maybe I wasn't being left behind. Maybe it was in the silence motherhood afforded me that I was finally able to face truths about the relationships in my life: the ones that had been strained, and the ones that might be lost. Maybe, if people fell away while I adjusted to my new reality, it was because they just didn't fit me anymore. I hoped that wasn't true of my sister, but I decided right there on my bed that if it was, I would face it.

A new text message buzzed my phone and my heart skipped a beat. I flipped it over so I could see the screen and grinned with delight. The text message was from John.

Hey baby, I miss you! Any pics of you and bub?

CHAPTER SIXTEEN

THE CURRENT

An unmistakably urgent cry crackled through the white noise static of our baby monitor, and I was on my feet. The sky outside my window was dark but for a hazy line of orange at the horizon, so it was still too early to rise. I stopped at the mini fridge next to my pumping station for a fresh bottle, then made my way to baby's room. Keeping the lights off, I cooed softly when I entered, and when he saw me, he smiled. I gathered him up and sat quietly for a bottle, which he ate quickly. *Ah*, I thought, *he must have been hungry.*

I held him to my chest and rested my cheek on his little head, then patted his back for a burp. I stood and gently swayed him and marveled at how big he'd grown in his nine months. After cuddling him for a moment, I placed him back in his crib, hoping he would go back down for a little more rest. I tiptoed backward out of his room, but when the door opened with a creak, he giggled, and I knew he was up. I sighed, rolled my eyes, then flipped the wall switch to turn on the overhead light. He giggled again and gave me a gummy grin through the bars of his crib.

"Good morning, handsome boy," I greeted him in a singsong.

He wrapped two chubby hands around two bars and pulled himself up to standing.

"Oh my goodness!" I said loudly, and then remembered that John was still sleeping. I didn't even know what time it was and suddenly felt horribly worried that I had begun a 2 AM lights-on party.

"You can pull yourself up," I whispered. "When did you learn that?"

I gathered the boy up and took him downstairs to check the clock on the stove. It read 4:38, two hours too early to start our day, but baby was wide-awake, so I sat him on his play mat and started my coffee. He groaned a bit, annoyed that I'd abandoned him, and began scooting in my direction, so I talked to him from the kitchen. My voice didn't calm him, though; it seemed like it was going to be more of a high body-contact kind of a morning. I picked him up and perched him on my hip while I poured my coffee creamer, then was hit with a sudden urgent need for the bathroom. I sat him down again and tried not to pee my pants on my way. Baby wailed and crawled toward me.

"I'm right here, I'm just going potty, you're okay," I called, then cringed. I hated telling him "You're okay." It was meant to be reassuring so that he'd stop fussing, but he was fussing because he wanted me. "You're okay" was essentially saying "I don't think you have any reason to be worried," and it wasn't my job to tell him what should or shouldn't feel worrisome. I made a mental note to catch myself next time.

Maybe he pooped, I thought, as I hurried to wash my hands. I checked his diaper but found it saturated with just a regular amount of overnight pee.

"Oh, just wanting Mama a little extra hard this morning, okay," I said, and I tickled his belly as I changed him. We played with toys and read books and I drank my coffee until the clock read six-thirty and John woke to start his day.

My boobs were about to burst with milk, so I practically threw the baby at John when he joined us. I made myself a fresh cup of coffee and ran upstairs, where I pumped for a luxurious thirty minutes instead of my typical twenty, just to get a little extra alone time. I closed my eyes and the minutes passed in seconds. I didn't feel guilty, though, because my boobs made three whole ounces before John brought the boy upstairs so he could hop in the shower for work.

In the meantime, I zipped baby into his sleep sack for nap time. It was an odd hour for his first nap, but we had already hit his first wake-window max and he was rubbing his tired, red eyes with his fists. In his room, I swayed gently as he settled in my arms, and I thought for a moment that he needed more soothing than usual before he could sleep. A memory of bouncing him for forty-five exhausting minutes flickered onto the screen of my mind like a war flashback, though, and I shuddered at the thought of returning to those tactics, so I went ahead and gently placed him in his crib and crept out of his room.

When I closed the door, he cried, and I balled both of my fists, biting the left one in frustration. I opted to give him a few moments to see if he would figure sleep out for himself, like he knew how to do after sleep training, but he didn't this time. He escalated, crying harder than I'd heard him cry in a very long time. I rushed in with concern, but when I scooped him into my arms, he giggled. I felt his cheek for warmth, but he seemed fine. I checked his diaper for poop, but he was clean. I offered a bottle, but he didn't want it. He was happy and smiley and alert.

Okay . . . I thought, *I guess we're not napping.*

I took baby back downstairs and reread the same books and replayed with the same toys. John kissed us both goodbye and gave baby a few sky-high tosses on his way out of the door. I wished he didn't have to go.

The day had brightened by then and looked warm and inviting, so I strapped baby into his stroller and pushed him around the neighborhood for a change of scenery. We'd walked all the way to the far end of the golf course on the pedestrian path that connected our street to the older part of the subdivision, about a mile from our house, when baby screamed. I stopped and opened the stroller visor to see what the problem was, and when we made eye contact, he stopped and gave me a gummy grin instead.

"What are you doing?" I asked with a little laugh. "Should we go home?"

When I started to walk again, he screamed again, tensing his body against the stroller straps.

"Hey, hey, hey," I cooed, rubbing his chest, attempting to make eye contact again. He was too mad, though, and continued voicing his distress loud enough that neighbors on their morning walks began to look at me.

I unbuckled him and brought him to my chest, patting his back, unsure what the issue could be. He cried and moved his head back and forth, bringing a balled fist to his mouth.

"Oh, fuck," I said. He was hungry, and I hadn't brought any milk. I clicked him back into his stroller restraints to much loud protest and jogged the mile home, my tits jostling loosely in my nursing bra the whole entire way.

Back home, with baby in my arms happily drinking his bottle, I settled onto the couch. My eyes were gritty with exhaustion from the lost hours of sleep, and a headache was beginning to grip my temples. I mopped the sweat on my brow with the back of my hand and made a mental note to take some painkillers before my headache got out of hand.

As baby finished the last dregs of his milk, he tooted, his eyes staring up at mine, his mouth curling into a creamy grin, and I laughed as he chewed on the nipple of his bottle, seemingly delighted with himself.

"There it is," I said.

I laid him down for a diaper change, and when I wiped him clean, I noticed red irritation all over the folds of his bottom. "Aw, poor guy," I told him. I hadn't seen any diaper rash when I changed him earlier, so it must have been too dark for me to notice. I wondered if that was what all the fussing had been about.

I applied a thick layer of diaper cream, hoping we had resolved the issue at last. Once his pants were secured, I pulled him by his arms until he was standing and kissed his cheek and his chubby neck while he squealed, his eyes wide and darting all around the room. My stomach growled, and I realized it must have been at least lunchtime. I picked baby up and secured him on my hip, walking into the kitchen. I stopped in my tracks when I saw the angry red light on the stovetop clock: It was only 9:15 in the morning.

"Fuck me," I said.

That also meant baby had been awake for close to four hours. I looked at his little face, noticing that he held his eyes wildly wide, and I recognized the adrenaline-addled expression of an overtired baby. He typically only lasted a two-hour stretch of wake time, so he was severely overdue for a nap and I was risking a bout of crankiness.

I did a mental nap time checklist: baby was clean, dry, fed, and tired. I took him upstairs, walking slowly and speaking gently, turning off all the hallway lights as I moved. We went into his bathroom, where I drew a bath and added the lavender essential oils we typically reserved for nighttime only, a luxury for the senses that signaled bedtime. Once submerged, baby splashed and flailed his limbs in a jerky motion, so I wet a cloth, letting it get heavy and warm with bathwater, then laid it on his tummy. He settled a little, and his eyes began to droop, so I sang a soothing song as I slowly lifted him into the warmth of my embrace. I dried him and dressed him in his room to the lull of white noise. I zipped him into his sleep sack, turned off the lights, and to my great relief, he sighed and rested his head on my chest. We swayed a little, and I gently rubbed his back as he began to breathe heavily. *Don't rush this time*, I thought, and I waited until he felt heavy in my arms to lay him down in his crib. He smacked his lips and turned his head as I slowly backed away. I closed his bedroom door and stood a moment with my heart pounding in my chest as I braced for him to cry out. All was quiet, though, so I wiggled in a silent happy dance and, exhausted, made for my bed.

An airplane buzzed dimly somewhere overhead as I tucked into the coziness of the covers, and I imagined where its passengers might be flying. A beach vacation, perhaps? The plane would fly over clear blue waters, landing on a warm, sun-drenched strip surrounded by palm trees. People would pile out into the golden light, luggage in their hands, and skip merrily toward the boardwalk. I could see the blue waves crashing and smell the salty sea air. I imagined digging my toes into the hot, tan sand off the California coast, and I missed home. I wondered what my mom was doing, and if she had ever drawn me a lavender bath, as my heavy eyes closed, enveloping me in serene calm.

MY EYES SNAPPED OPEN TO THE shrill pierce of baby's cries. I looked at my phone and my heart sank: It had been ten minutes.

"What the hell is going on?" I wondered.

With a sigh, I pushed my tired body up to standing and ran my fingers through my hair, twirling its messy strands, along with my frustration, up into a knot on top of my head. I rubbed my temples and rummaged around in my side table for some Advil, dry-swallowed two pills, then took a deep breath and set off to comfort baby.

I opened the door to his room and flicked on the overhead light. His face was red and wet from tears, and I felt a pang of guilt, wondering how long he'd been crying for me.

"Hey? Hey, hey, hey." I picked him up and stripped him of his sleep sack as I shushed his cries to no avail.

I gently turned his head toward me, but he didn't want to meet my eye, which worried me. I took him into the bathroom for a quick temperature check, but he was within normal range. I checked his mouth next, running my finger along all his gums, squinting my eyes to peer past the drool, but no new teeth appeared to be erupting. I sat down and examined his hands and feet, looking at all ten fingers and all ten toes, but found no injury or irritation. He cried as I stripped him naked and scanned my eyes over every inch of his creamy skin for a sign: a bug bite, a sore, a spot of eczema that might be itching, a rash. Nothing. There was nothing wrong with him that I could see. He was perfect but for the crying. I was ready to pull my hair out.

I sat him on my hip and walked him downstairs, which seemed to calm him. I needed more coffee. Would this be cup number three? Or four? I couldn't remember, and I didn't care. I sat baby down on his play mat, accepting that he was just going to have to suffer a little bit of crying for a moment while I steeled my nerves. To cut the noise, I turned on an episode of *Daniel Tiger's Neighborhood* and oriented baby's body so that the TV was in his eyeline.

Nine months, I thought, as I went to the kitchen. *I made it nine months before resorting to screen time.*

I added cream to my cup and watched as baby smiled up at the TV. *God, he's cute*, I thought. His eyes were curious and searching, but when his mouth erupted into a grin, it spread wide across his face, crinkling his curious eyes with glee. I loved seeing him smile. But after a moment I felt guilty that he was smiling at a cartoon. I took a swig of coffee and sat on the couch behind baby. I turned his play mat to orient his face toward mine, and clattered a rattle toy to get his attention. He engaged for a moment, grabbing the rattle, then curiosity got the better of him and his gaze returned to *Daniel Tiger* once again. I sighed, turned the TV off, and began rereading books for the third time as he began to scream.

I picked him up and forced him to look at a binge-eating caterpillar, but he was *mad*. He cried, grabbed at the book, grabbed at my hair, and twisted his little body out of my grasp, sliding down my legs until he was on the floor. Once on his hands and knees, he attempted to scoot his way back toward the TV.

"Fine," I said with a little too much frustration, and I turned *Daniel Tiger* on once again.

I felt guilty and my face grew hot. I grabbed my phone and called John. The dam burst as soon as I heard his voice, and I asked him, through sobs, if he could leave work early. He couldn't, which meant I had to suck it up, so I asked him to at least come straight home when he was off at five, if he could. He could, he said, and I nodded my head and wiped my tired eyes. I hung up and felt very alone, but there was no help in wallowing, so I stood and readied a bottle for baby. I had no idea if it was time for another bottle because I'd lost track of when he'd last eaten, but I figured some milk wouldn't hurt him. He ate, which I was glad for—I'd done something right, at least—and I changed another diaper before deciding to try the backyard for a new setting.

The sun was shining warm, happy rays, birds were chirping sweet, happy songs, and the scent of honeysuckle floated through the air along a gentle breeze that blew life into my face.

"Why didn't we do this sooner?" I asked baby, and he squirmed with a whine to be put down.

I sat him on a picnic blanket in the grass and gave him a pile of leaves to look at. Then I took a delicious, deep breath and looked up at the cloudless blue sky. It was a gorgeous day. I chuckled to myself about the ridiculous set of events so far that morning and glanced down at baby. He was practicing his pincher grasp with his right hand, grabbing at his left, where a black spider had crawled. I screamed, smacked his little hand, and then scooped him up into my arms as he cried again, rightfully so.

Great, Shawna, I chided myself. *Not an overreaction at all.*

I kissed his hand and apologized, abandoning my picnic blanket to the creatures of the wild, and walked us both back into the house for more *Daniel Tiger.*

But not even *Daniel Tiger* could get baby to stop fussing. I picked him up, securing him to his usual perch on my hip, and took an avocado and some leftover mashed sweet potatoes out of the fridge.

"Want to try some food?" I asked. "Can't make you much madder than you already are."

I clipped baby into his high chair and tapped some mash onto his tray with a baby spoon. He touched the macerated orange and green before him, discovering that each pile was squishy, but didn't move any food to his face. Impatiently, I grabbed the baby spoon, scooped a bit of mash from each pile, and held the offering aloft in front of his face. He used his fingers to pinch himself some sweet potato and, finally, gave it a taste. His eyebrows raised as he smacked his little lips and, to my surprise, went in for another fingerful. I directed him to the piles on his tray and laughed as he grabbed a fistful of the stuff, shrieking and giggling as he brought his hand to his mouth. He seemed to like the sweet potato better than the avocado, and after sucking his hand clean, he bent low and put his mouth directly onto the pile of orange.

I snapped a photo, laughing. I only looked down at my phone for a moment to text the photo to John, but when I looked up again, baby's eyes were wide, his brow was furrowed, and his mouth was pursed into a tiny heart.

"What are you doing?" I asked in a singsong I was sure would produce a drooly smile, but baby bent his head low, his eyes still wide, and emitted a little gurgle.

"Oh my God!" I shouted. He was choking.

I ripped baby out of his chair and pried his little mouth open to see a mess of orange glop. I scooped out everything I could, flipped him upside down, and banged between his shoulder blades with the heel of my palm. It took three bangs but he cried at last, music to my ears, and I hugged him tight to my chest.

"It was mashed up," I cried, replaying the moment in my mind. "Oh baby, I'm so sorry."

The clock on the stove read 12:22.

I felt a stab of hunger then, a reminder that I hadn't consumed anything other than coffee all day, so I poured myself a glass of water and got a yogurt from the fridge. I grabbed a banana, too, and when I peeled its yellow outer layer and took a big bite, an image of me choking to death flashed into my mind. With no one around to scoop out my mouth and bang between my shoulder blades, I would die sprawled out on my kitchen floor while my devastated infant cried for help, and John would come home to a cold, dead wife and a traumatized child and have to live with that horrifying imagery for the rest of his life.

Consciously pushing the scene out of my head, I finished my makeshift meal and turned back to baby.

He was filthy from his food attempt, so I took him upstairs and ran another bath. He splashed a bit as I cleaned him up, but not with the same zeal he had that morning. I knew he was absolutely exhausted.

"Baby, let's go to sleep," I encouraged as I dried him off and applied his soothing nighttime lotion, concentrating on his little arms and legs, where he typically got the driest. I discovered that his pinky toe on his right foot had been encircled by a strand of hair. It wasn't tight, but I had no idea how it had gotten there. I picked the hair from his toe and unfurled it. It was long and had obviously come from my head.

Leaving baby on his towel on the bathroom floor, I stood for a moment to look at myself in the bathroom mirror. My hair was still pulled up in a top knot but two fuzzy puffs had developed on either side of my hairline, like devil's horns.

"What the hell? When did that happen?"

I pulled on each tuft of hair with each of my hands until they stuck straight up in the air like spikes. *Cute,* I thought, then my gaze dropped to my red-rimmed, tired eyes and the dark, puffy circles underneath them. I decided to stop looking in the mirror.

Instead, I looked back down at baby, who now sat at my feet and had, in the time that it took for me to look at myself in the mirror, found a bag of cotton balls and dumped them all over his lap and across the bathroom floor. I sighed to the heavens, tipping my head all the way back, but there was nothing else to be done. I bent down and scooped the cotton balls back into their bag.

Once in his room, I broke sleep training rule number one and fed baby a giant bottle to put him to sleep. He ate all six ounces and conked out immediately, in a move that surprised no one.

You're stubborn like your mother, I thought.

I stood and rocked my boy in my arms. I could just make out the slope of his tiny nose and the curve of his cupid's bow in the dark of his room. He smacked his little lips and my breath caught in my throat because, for a moment, I was transported back to my hospital room, where I saw him make that move for the very first time.

I love you so much, I thought. It didn't seem possible to love someone as big as I loved him. I wanted, for a moment, to sit as he slept in my arms, to let him nap on my lap like he did when he was tiny, but he never slept for very long in those days, and he needed a solid chunk of sleep to offset our early start. I laid him in his bed and slipped out of his room.

My mind wandered to Thesla as I crashed into the soft comfort of my bed, too wired from coffee to try to sleep. I wondered what motherhood had been like for her, if John had ever had the same sort of day that baby was having. Then I remembered John talking about Aba, his abuelita, which meant Thesla had her mom around for support when she became a mom. I was glad for her. That was probably easier.

I picked up my phone to scroll social media but baby cried again, signaling an end to his nap.

"Are you kidding me?!" I yelled. I cupped my hands over my eyes and lay there, mad at the world. I had no idea why nothing was working.

BABY'S FEET WERE STUCK ON HIS sleep sack, preventing him from standing fully, and he was reaching for me, his face full of frustration, by the time I flipped the light on in his room.

"Hello," I said, trying not to sound as annoyed as I felt. When I picked him up, he arched his back so hard that he threw himself out of my arms. I caught him by the leg just before he hit the ground, and landed him safely on his back. He cried and picked at my hand with his.

"What are you doing?!" I demanded. I zipped him out of his sleep sack, then took my hands off his body. He flipped over onto his belly and tucked his hands and knees up under himself and rocked in place.

"Okay, come on," I insisted, grabbing him.

He fought me all the way down the stairs, but he needed a diaper change, so I didn't care. I sat him on his play mat to gather my materials, and he flipped onto his belly to try crawling again.

"Sorry, buddy," I said, and laid him down on his back again.

He wailed and kicked and twisted his body away from me, so I put my head in my hands and let him. He won. I was defeated.

I turned the TV on again and went to the bathroom to cry. Baby saw me go and began to protest, scooting himself in my direction, so I shut the bathroom door. I couldn't do it anymore. I texted Sarah, but I didn't know why; she hadn't even replied to my last text. I texted John, but that was futile, too; he had meetings all day. Then I texted Erin, who replied right away, but when I typed out a paragraph complaining about my baby, I felt horrid, like I was the worst mother on Earth. I deleted the message and sent a fake, positive update instead, adding a cute selfie from the day before to boot. She sent a cute selfie back, and for the millionth time, I wished we could be in same place, raising our babies together. I washed my hands, plastered a smile on my face, and then opened the bathroom door.

For the rest of the afternoon, baby fussed and tried to figure out crawling. I didn't bother with any more books or toys, but I did manage to complete a diaper change despite much complaint and protest. I didn't care. I had no more capacity for his emotional storm and it felt as though I never would again.

John returned from work promptly at five-forty, carrying our picnic blanket as he entered.

"I hope you shook that out," I said. I shuddered, recalling the spider, as John gathered our baby boy into his arms for dada kisses, tossing his little body high into the sky to make him squeal. And, also for the millionth time, I felt grateful to have made a baby with such a hands-on, devoted man.

I gave John a kiss on the cheek, informed him that we'd be ordering in for the evening, then handed him baby's bottle and went upstairs to pump for a luxurious thirty minutes of alone time. My insides churned as my pump did and I wondered how many other moms in the world had had a hard day like mine, and if they were, like I was, feeling duped by the prettily romanticized version of motherhood we had been sold the world over. I felt guilty for thinking it, though; I really did love baby so much.

After my pump produced a measly two ounces, I rejoined the boys downstairs for a family walk. The evening air had a crispness to it, and the same sweet smell as earlier in the day, so I closed my eyes and took a nose-full. Neighbors passed by and nodded their polite smiles as baby chattered to himself. I told John about our day of no naps, and about how the uncharacteristic chatter was more evidence that baby was overtired, and secretly worried it would mean a difficult night's sleep.

We took baby home and ate our takeout, then John did bath and bedtime while I sat for another pumping session. I watched on the video baby monitor as John rocked our sweet boy for a moment before placing him in his crib. Baby turned his head and smacked his lips like always, drifting off to sleep. I sighed with enough relief to last a thousand lifetimes and finished my pump, but as I stood to plug the baby monitor in to charge, I noticed movement. Baby had grabbed the bars of his crib with both of his hands and was again attempting to pull himself up to standing.

"Oh my God." I tipped my head back and yelled to the heavens above. Had baby been practicing his new skill all day long instead of sleeping? I laughed at the absurdity.

"What?" John asked.

"He's gonna be up all night," I warned. I brushed my teeth and gave John a kiss and lay my weary body down to rest.

"OH . . . MY GOD," I SAID AGAIN, sitting straight up in bed.

"What?" John looked from his book to me.

"This whole entire day was one giant clusterfuck of opposites," I said.

John laughed. "What?"

"Yeah, it was cute one second and then infuriating the next, it was like happy-sad, easy-hard, neutral-ridiculous, just this ebb and flow of *ahh, this sucks so much* into *ahh, I love him so much.* It's like everything all at once, and this—" I looked at his face to make sure he understood me—"IS the experience."

"What experience?" He clearly wanted to follow my train of thought, but he wasn't a mom.

"Motherhood. It's not a Hallmark commercial. It's sometimes sweet and pretty like that, and sometimes it's mind-numbingly boring, then baby barfs in your face. It's not 'moms are bat-shit crazy, butt of the joke, irrational women' like 'uh-oh, hormones,' it's just that all of us thought we were signing up for Hallmark, but we just got more life."

"Huh," was John's reply.

"And in real life, nothing is Hallmark! My husband's not perfect—sorry, no offense."

"None taken," John said with a shrug and a grin.

"And I love baby more than life, to the depths of my soul, more than I ever thought possible, but OH MY GOD being a mom is so much work! It's not warm, fuzzy love all the time! It's wiping poop! And everyone who was excited for you to have baby disappears, and I've disappeared, but not because anyone is a bad person, we just don't know how to be there for each other because we don't really know the truth of what parenting is because we're not telling each other and we've been fed lies by the government or something." I buried my face in a pillow and bellowed.

"You had a lot of time to think today," John said.

"I'm alone a lot," I said into the pillow. "And then," I went on, sitting up again, "all of society has these set parameters for how a person is supposed to feel about all of that: You're a mom, you wanted this, shut up and be grateful. I'm not Shawna anymore; I'm just a mom. I'm just Shawna the mom!"

John laughed and pulled me close, hugging my head to his chest. "I think you need to go to sleep," he said.

"I do, but I haven't even gotten to the real kicker yet." I pulled away from his grasp, squaring up to face him.

"What's the real kicker?" He adjusted to face me, too.

"You go into this thinking 'I'm having a baby!' but really it's 'I'm going to peel myself open, heart, mind, body, and soul, so that a new consciousness can emerge, and then, I have to heal all of my shit in real time so that I don't mess him up too badly.' And you have to do all of this in a world that is straight-up hostile to moms and kids." I clapped my hands and exhaled, flopping flat on the bed, resting my case.

"That's a lot," John said, lying down, too.

"I know. It's everything. All at once," I said.

"No wonder we're exhausted," he said.

"Do you feel like that, too?" My eye traced the silhouette of his profile as he thought.

"Maybe." He looked at me. "I don't think I think about things that hard."

"What's that like?"

"Quieter."

I laughed, and he pulled me close. As we kissed, the video baby monitor hummed with white noise on my bedside table, and I knew that baby had fallen asleep at last.

CHAPTER SEVENTEEN

THE CULTURE

As my coffee maker belched its final drops into my mug, a mechanical, melodical trill rang out that I couldn't place. I added cream to my cup, hoping its contents would stir patience into my soul, when the tinny sound trilled again. I paused mid-sip and turned my head to listen. The noise rang out a third time, and my phone lit up where it lay on the counter.

"Someone's calling me?" I asked no one. I hadn't known my ringer was on.

I picked up my phone, and the joy of receiving a call vanished when I read my caller ID. I debated denying the call, filtering through plausible excuses in my mind, but ultimately, I really wanted to talk to another adult.

"Hi, Mom," I said, pinching the phone to my ear with my shoulder.

"Hi, just checking in. What you got going on today?"

When I heard her warm, friendly tone, I realized I hadn't heard from her in months. She'd tried so hard to orchestrate being with me when I was immediately postpartum, only to ghost me for months on end after baby arrived. I had to admit, though, it was nice to hear her voice.

"Nothing, we're playing. Baby is going to have a nap in a minute, and then we'll go on a walk and do lunch, and then he has a doctor's appointment later today for shots."

"So, are you a stay-at-home mommy now?" Her high-pitched upspeak seemed condescending.

"Yep. We would break even with the cost of daycare, so I'm staying at home with him." My words were clipped in response.

"Aww," Mom said. "Who knew you were my little June Cleaver!"

A memory from Mom's visit when baby was three months old came to mind. John had just returned from work and had taken baby so I could relax my tired arms. He rubbed my back, in between my shoulder blades, then squeezed the back of my neck as my eyes rolled up into my head in bliss. He chuckled, gave me a kiss, then took baby upstairs with him to change out of his work clothes. I watched him go, and when he disappeared up the stairs my gaze returned to Mom, who had witnessed the interaction from her chair across from mine.

"What?" I asked at her incredulous smile.

"Nothing," she quickly insisted with a shake of her head. "He's angelic. What an absolute doll."

I laughed and rolled my eyes. "He's a regular person, Mom. But yes, he's sweet," I conceded.

"Your dad was sweet."

It came from out of nowhere, an emotional missile that knocked my jaw to the floor. Mom didn't usually have anything kind to say about Dad.

"I've never heard you call Dad sweet," I said.

"He was. He was my John." Another missile, this one to the heart. "I had high hopes. I wanted us to be the Cleavers."

"Who?" I asked.

"The family from *Leave It to Beaver*." She smiled wistfully.

"What?" I laughed, desperate to make light of the moment.

"It's a TV show from when I was a kid. I showed you when you were little. I thought I'd be June Cleaver, baking in my pearls in my pristine home." Mom pressed the memory between her lips.

"You bake. At Christmas," I joked.

"Ha ha. Not like June. She was the perfect mom. When I had babies, I thought I would be her."

Ah, I thought now, six months later in my kitchen. *So you were duped, too.*

"Yep, baking in my pearls," I said into my phone, and quickly snapped a no-makeup, dirty, top-knotted selfie to text to Mom.

"Oh, looking fabulous, darling!" Mom said, adopting a posh accent in sarcasm.

"Hey, sorry, I gotta run, he's getting fussy," I lied. It was his nap time, but he was fine.

"Okay, send me pictures," she requested.

"Okay, don't post them on Facebook," I reminded.

She scoffed, I laughed, and we hung up the call.

Baby went easily down for his nap, so I stood in my kitchen and looked June Cleaver up on my phone. Her bouffant was blond and her smile sweet, and she did in fact wear pearls. She was the matriarch in a house full of boys, and her show was story after story of her youngest child's hijinks told from his point of view. I laughed.

"June Cleaver was a side character," I said out loud.

What a disappointment it must have been for Mom to birth her babies and realize the woman she wanted to emulate only existed to fill a role in someone else's story, as a part of someone else's whole. When a woman becomes a mom, she's the main character, the one experiencing all the gory details. But as side character, we didn't get to witness June Cleaver's pregnancy fears, or her postpartum era, because the boy at the center of *Leave It to Beaver* wouldn't have seen them either.

I imagined poor June bending too low, too fast, into a squat and tearing a stretch mark next to her labia as I had. I giggled, thinking of her horrified face as she reached to feel the deep trench of her new scar, like me. And later, after their baby was born, was Ward Cleaver just as wise, patient, and hands-on a father as Beaver thought? Did he get up at 3 AM for the third night in a row because little Beaver was going through a developmental leap-induced sleep regression?

June Cleaver was an ideal precisely because she wasn't real. *Poor Mom*, I thought.

After his nap and a bottle, I strapped baby into his stroller for a walk. He babbled and played with his rattle toy as I strolled him past the colorful homes in our neighborhood and let my mind wander. Before I got pregnant, I daydreamed about having a baby, and in my daydreams, I envisioned a happy little family. Had I aspired to become only a part of whole, like Mom had? Was I raised just to play my role as a wife and mother without my knowing?

I had always liked Clair Huxtable from *The Cosby Show*. She was a beautiful, successful attorney who worked as a partner in a New York City law firm. I liked that she was intelligent and confident and never accepted any disrespect, least of all from her husband, Cliff. She was the disciplinarian in their home, as mother to their five children, and though she was firm, she was fair and loving. She was funny, too, and I remembered one episode when she serves her son Theo some eggs, and when he protests, saying he wants them scrambled, Clair mashes the already-cooked eggs up with her spatula.

Oh right, I thought. *Clair had grown kids.*

While the dynamics of her family played out with hilarious realism, the story began *twenty years* into her motherhood journey, when she already was a seasoned pro. I laughed, imagining poor Clair, newly postpartum, sitting up in bed in the middle of the night trying to calm a colicky baby while her husband delivered other people's newborns at the hospital. Since Cliff was an ob-gyn, I wondered if he had been helpful during her labor, or if he had tried to take over and mansplain the process to a painfully contracting Clair. *She would have put him in his place*, I thought.

Clair Huxtable was a great, admirable woman, but just like with June Cleaver, we didn't get to see her in the throes of new motherhood, assessing her postpartum lochia or finding relief with a numbing witch hazel spray, because her role as mother was a side story.

Once home, I secured baby into his high chair for a lunch of tiny bits of chicken and mashed-up peas. I still hated giving him solid foods, especially after the sweet potato incident, but it had to be done. I watched closely, my anxiety spiking with every mouthful, and I wondered if Clair or June had walked through the signs of choking in their minds at every solid-food feeding with their ten-and-a-half-month-olds. I wondered if they had felt gripped with worry about whether they were doing things right, like I did.

OUR PEDIATRICIAN'S OFFICE HAD A CHEERFUL underwater mural featuring various aquatic parents and babies on the wall behind the front desk, and it always felt so welcoming to me. The staff was less friendly, though, which was unfortunate, because I really could have used some moral support when taking baby in for a round of vaccinations. The receptionist barely cracked a smile as she checked us in.

"Thank you so much," I sang, hoping my warmth would thaw her cold demeanor.

"You can wait in well-baby, Mom," was her monotone reply, indicating the area of the waiting room partitioned off for healthy patients.

"Say bye-bye." I waved baby's hand, but the receptionist averted her eyes, so I felt like a nuisance.

After a few moments, an equally unfriendly nurse, the one from baby's blowout incident months prior, called baby's name and escorted us to the back to begin his appointment. I wondered if she recognized us, and, if so, if she noticed how quickly and efficiently I was moving baby through the weight/height/head-circumference portion of our appointment. If she did, she made no mention of it.

"This way, Mom." She directed me to an empty appointment room without so much as making eye contact.

"Uh, do you know if he'll get his vaccination in his arm or his leg?" I asked. I wanted to emotionally prepare.

"The doctor will be in shortly to go over vaccine information, Mom." She began to close the door.

"Oh, sorry. Do you know if it's just one poke, or two? I'm nervous." I chuckled to ease the tension.

"You can ask the doctor, Mom," came the reply, and with it, a slammed door.

"She's working in the wrong profession," I said to baby, who giggled.

It turned out to be three pokes, two in the leg and one in the arm, and I had to act like my heart wasn't exploding in my chest as baby screamed so hard he made no noise and looked to me for answers. I rubbed his chubby little leg and cuddled him close and offered a bottle of fresh milk to calm him.

"Good job, Mom," said our pediatrician, and I beamed at the praise even as I cringed at the moniker. Baby's appointment was my adult interaction for the day, but instead of being a person, I was just Mom, a side character, reduced to my role and largely ignored.

When did "Shawna" cease to exist? I thought, and I wondered if there were any shows that depicted a woman's loss of identity at her baby's pediatrician appointment.

On the drive home I thought about Kitty Forman, the mom on *That '70s Show*. Like me, she was a neurotic fan of praise. The show wasn't Kitty's story, so she was another mom-as-supporting-character, there for comedy's sake. She drinks heavily and laughs awkwardly to cope with her lack of identity outside of motherhood, while her children age through their teen years and out of her home. Kitty is frequently the butt of the joke, even calling herself crazy on occasion, but ultimately, she earns the love and respect of the group of kids growing into themselves in her basement as, over the years, she serves as a soft, nurturing landing spot for each of them.

I wondered what the show would look like from Kitty's perspective. Would her grumpy husband still seem like a lovable curmudgeon, or would his hilarious ire tiptoe into abusive territory? Did Kitty enjoy doing all the thankless cooking and cleaning and breadwinning? What was it like for her to have a two-year-old and a newborn, and an angry husband to boot; was that when she forgot who she was and began self-medicating with alcohol? When did "Kitty" cease to exist?

I tried to think of a show that portrayed the psychological heavy lifting necessary to process becoming so-and-so's mother at the expense of being oneself, but nothing came to mind. Maybe the complexities of a woman's disintegrating personhood juxtaposed with her adoration for the tiny baby she made sounded too boring to be turned into a television series.

Baby had fallen asleep in his car seat as I drove, a pitfall I typically tried to avoid, as it meant a choice on arrival between moving and potentially waking him or being trapped in my car while he slept his full two hours, but my wandering mind had distracted me. I dug my phone out of my purse, opting to be nap-trapped so he could rest.

Not two minutes into my doomscroll, I came across a social media post decrying women who made the fact that they had babies their whole personality. I scoffed. My cheeks grew hot with exasperation, or maybe it was embarrassment. I hadn't intended to make baby my whole personality, but becoming a mother was the biggest thing to ever happen to me. Birthing him transformed my body. Loving him transformed my heart. Caring for him transformed my relationships. And deconstructing my identity to rebuild myself into his mother transformed my mind. I felt different on a soul level because of him, and he was the most important person in the world to me. And, to top it off, I lived in a society that relegated me to my role as his mom, reminding me daily, via in-person interactions, social media, and actor portrayals, that my story had become secondary to his. How were moms not supposed to embrace motherhood as their new identity if they also weren't afforded personhood?

What an asinine take, I thought.

There was one TV mother I could think of who didn't make being a mother her whole personality. Lorelai Gilmore still had a dating life, a town full of friends, and a career she loved. She was as much the main character of *Gilmore Girls* as her daughter Rory was, so the story is told from her perspective, too. But Rory is sixteen when the show begins, so we don't get to see Lorelai grapple with retaining her identity amid the twenty-four-hour demands of newborn care. And though the show is premised on the fact that Lorelai had eschewed her former life of privilege to welcome her baby into a life of her own making, we don't get to witness the teenaged identity shift she underwent to bring Rory into the world.

I imagined sixteen-year-old, chatty Lorelai learning to breastfeed all on her own. I thought of her figuring out how to decipher baby Rory's cries. I wondered if she took the baby everywhere she went or if she discussed her child's developmental milestones with anyone who would listen.

Of course she did, I thought.

It occurred to me, also, that if Lorelai hadn't identified so completely with her role as Rory's mom, with her desire to provide an emotionally validating life for her child unlike the one she had known, she wouldn't have left the comfort of home so quickly. Becoming Rory's mother allowed Lorelai to become herself.

AS I FLICKED MY THUMB ACROSS the screen of my phone, scrolling for better sources of dopamine, something moved in my periphery. I looked to my right and was startled to see a car pulling into my driveway, next to where I was parked, at 3:55 PM. It took a moment to register that the handsome, smiling face I saw was John's. I smiled wide and rolled my window down to greet him.

"Hi!" I whisper-shouted.

"Surprise!" he whisper-shouted back. He exited his car and leaned into mine.

"He's sleeping," I explained.

John nodded and craned his neck to get a look at baby's cute sleep face.

"Why are you home?" I asked.

We were invited to a party at the lovely home of a colleague, John informed me. It was a last-minute, casual thing, the local college football team was playing a rival, but he knew I had been cooped up at home with a baby all week, so he wanted to give me time to shower and get ready if I wanted to go. I didn't want to go; I was exhausted, but a party invite had become a rare occurrence since baby's arrival, and John seemed excited, so I heard myself saying yes.

"Cool." John slapped the door frame in affirmation. "Well, head inside, take a shower. I'll sit with him."

"Okay, wake him up if he's not awake by four-thirty, and he'll need a bottle and a diaper and a new outfit," I instructed.

"Not my first rodeo," John said with a bright grin.

I opened my driver's side door and stood, leaning into him for a deep kiss, inhaling his earthy, sweet musk.

"Get outta here," he purred, sliding his hands down from their position on the small of my back. I giggled and snuck one more kiss before peeling myself away.

A tired, pudgy mom stared back at me as I gazed at the reflection in my bathroom mirror a few minutes later. Her hair had been pulled into a greasy bun on top of her head, but that didn't stop the tufts of baby hair from sticking up where they grew in at her temples. Her eyes were red and her skin was dull. Her Kohl's Cash t-shirt was loose but too small to be purposefully oversized, so the effect was disappointingly frumpy.

I turned on my shower and stripped naked to examine my reflection further. The red lines that zigzagged across my low belly had begun to fade to an iridescent pink, and the fat that stretched my creamy stomach had begun to hang in a slight apron made more pronounced when I bent at the waist. My breasts had deflated from their swollen, painful newborn days, but had inexplicably retained their shape despite the daily work they put in.

"Go, you guys," I told them, and I thought about Miranda Hobbes from *Sex and the City*. There is an episode of the show when Carrie visits newly postpartum Miranda, who is frazzled trying to remember all she needs to do to care for her newborn. And to Carrie's horror, in Miranda's debilitated state, she whips out her shockingly swollen, hideously veined postpartum boobs. The episode was told, much like the series, from Carrie's point of view, so Miranda's titty shot was filmed for comedic effect.

As a freshly postpartum woman, it was jarring to experience my boobs swelling so hard that they felt like they could explode off my body, and I wondered what emotional catharsis we might have reached had Miranda been the one reacting to her own body. Could the moment have had humor and heart? I imagined her catching her reflection in her bathroom mirror, wearing nothing but a postpartum diaper, examining the changes to her breasts and belly with a tear-streaked face. Then Brady would cry, snapping Miranda back to the moment, and she'd attempt to say soothing things to him as she assembled her breast pump.

It would have been interesting to watch cynical, hard-assed, brilliant Miranda grapple with a cataclysmic shift in identity that threatened to take her away from her lunches with the ladies. But motherhood was a side plot for a side character in Carrie's story. Miranda was tired and overwhelmed, but she quickly hired a nanny and went back to discussing sex as though nothing much had happened.

No wonder I had envisioned a baby who could slot conveniently into my life, I thought.

THERE WERE DOGS AT THE PARTY, so baby immediately demanded to be put down. He wasn't very good at walking yet but could bear crawl with the best of them, so what was supposed to be a social event became more of my everyday: me, by myself, following baby around to keep him from eating or breaking things. John was having a great time, chatting with a friend from work, which was annoying—doubly so when I recognized his buddy as a man who had burned his bridge with me some years prior when, during a heated moment in a game of cards, he asked me if it was "that time of the month." When I noticed an acquaintance I hadn't seen in months across the room, I interrupted John's social hour, handing him the baby, and sat down on the couch to have a conversation of my own. The woman was younger than me, and child-free, and when she asked me how I liked being a mom, I couldn't help but gush.

"It's so crazy. It's hard to describe," I said with a smile so wide it hurt my cheeks.

She nodded. "Because you're so tired?"

"No. I mean, yeah, I am, and that was a huge thing in the beginning, like absolute torture. But no, it's crazy because my entire worldview has changed, and everything I thought was really important doesn't matter anymore. And now I care about things I never even thought about before." I was proud of explaining such a monumental life shift so succinctly.

"Ohh." I could hear her disinterest, but I couldn't stop myself from elaborating.

"Like, he's a whole person with his own thoughts and feelings and point of view." I maintained eye contact and nodded with vigor.

"Yeah," was her simple reply.

"He's a complete human unto himself, already, from the moment he was born. It's so incredible!" I giggled.

"Oh! I didn't realize he was a human. Oh my gosh! Wow." From her sarcasm, I sensed that she didn't care about my psychological epiphanies.

"It's kind of hard to describe," I said.

She nodded, and I pressed my embarrassment between my lips and tucked a strand of hair behind my ear. I asked her about work, but neither one of us was very invested in our chitchat anymore, and after a few moments she turned to another conversation, leaving me sitting awkwardly on her other side.

Who was I before motherhood? What did I think about, what kinds of things did I talk about? I couldn't remember anymore, and I didn't really care. I wasn't interested in who I was before I had baby; there was no going back to her anyway.

"Aww, you're changing a diaper?!"

My head whipped around to locate the source of the praise in time to see our party hostess clap John on the back and tickle baby's belly while John shrugged our diaper bag onto his shoulder. "Dad of the year over here!" she announced to the party.

That's about right, I thought with a chuff. John was praised for fulfilling the duties of his role as father. I simply *was* my duties, a meeting of societal expectation that warranted no acknowledgment.

I looked around the party, at a room full of nonparents in their mid-twenties, and felt invisible. I wasn't a woman of the world any longer. I hadn't read anything interesting, traveled to any new destinations, or met any exciting people that would make for an amusing anecdote amid polite conversation. I *had* studied child development, traveled the recesses of my own mind, and met divinity in the humanity of my tiny baby, but no one cared about that. The entire gathering existed because of me, or women like me; every person on Earth emerged from the wombs of our foremothers, my sisters in arms, yet no one seemed to want to hear our stories or glean our wisdom. Why?

Maybe it's because people have hard feelings about their own mothers, I mused, and I thought about my mom. My feelings about Mom had long been complicated. She gave me life, food, and clothing but not emotional safety. I was expected to hear Mom's stories as a child, to have empathy for her plight, and I was punished when my internal compass pointed in a direction different than the one she wanted to steer me in. After I grew into adulthood, Mom still expected me to understand her perspective, grant her forgiveness, and continue to give her access to my heart, even though she had proven herself to be reckless with its keeping. I loved her, but I couldn't hear her stories; it wasn't my job to witness her humanity. That was a responsibility for society.

Was that why Mom had so much pain and rage? Did society not see her? I wondered what life would have been like if real motherhood stories, instead of just June's, had been shared with Mom.

Would she have felt less duped? Better about her own life? And if she felt better, would I have experienced her as an emotionally safe person? *What a dream that would have been*, I thought.

I pulled out my phone, since no one at the party was talking to me anyway, and searched for film and television stories about motherhood created by women. A few populated, some with women producers but male writers or directors, and most focusing on the task of child rearing or the lead-up to birth. There was one series that seemed to explore a woman's internal landscape, created and written by a woman, and largely based off her own life experiences as a brand-new mom: *The Letdown*, an episodic comedy about a new mother facing the harsh realities of early motherhood.

Yes, I thought. This was the type of motherhood story that needed to be mainstream. If women had control of the motherhood narrative, we could teach society about ourselves instead of relying on society to tell us who we are and how we should be. We wouldn't romanticize motherhood, or mythologize it.

I looked to my left, at the back of the blond head of the acquaintance whose words and attitude had made me feel small. She didn't know what it was like to be a mother, but I knew that if she were ever to become one, she would encounter the same patronization she offered me, and the thought made me sad for her. *More women need to tell motherhood stories*, I thought, and there, on the corner of the couch, in the corner of the room, with not one person paying any attention to my existence, a new pathway took shape in my mind.

CHAPTER EIGHTEEN

THE GUIDE

When I was eight years old, I attended an assembly held in the massive cafeteria of my elementary school. The air smelled like stale French bread pizza and industrial-sized ranch dressing, but a troupe of actors was performing a stage play, so I was enthralled. The players told a tale of the triumph of good over evil via a story of a boy who wanted to make a friend but first had to stand up to a bully. The actors expressed excitement, grief, transformation, and joy through easy-to-understand slapstick and exaggerated facial expressions. The performance was riveting; I didn't want it to end. Then, after a final company bow, the most curious thing happened: The acting troupe's leader took possession of a nearby microphone to explain that his company had one additional story to tell. The other students around me clapped and shouted their approval.

"For this next story," said the man with the dark, curly hair and matching mustache, "I am going to need FIVE audience volunteers."

The kids around me went berserk. Everyone was screaming and bouncing and losing their minds, waving their arms, begging to be selected. I wasn't, though, because I knew the man was talking to me.

He jumped off the stage and wove his way through the crowd before selecting the first kid volunteer, in the first row. I didn't *want* to be chosen; I *knew* that I would be chosen. So, though I was in the second-to-last row, I folded my legs beneath me, crisscross applesauce, and put my right hand in my lap. I straightened my spine, sat up tall, and bent my left elbow to lift the five fanned fingers of my left hand to head height. I didn't wave or scream or beg. I sat still, smiled sweetly, and locked my gaze onto the acting troupe leader.

The man moved slowly, his eyes scanning from face to eager face, as he chose three more children to be participants. Then, he turned his curly-haired head to the right, and his eyes met mine, five rows away. He smiled and the fuzz of his mustache arced wide across his top lip, producing an expression that felt warm and accepting and safe. He took ten steps, his eyes locked on mine, his left hand gripping the microphone just below his chin, and he pointed his right pointer finger at me.

"Number five!" he said into the mic. I jumped up, ecstatic, and followed the man and my four new costars backstage, where I came alive.

THE CLOCK ON MY PHONE READ 12:15 AM. We had left the football party that evening at nine o'clock on the dot to get baby in bed by nine-thirty, two hours past his usual bedtime, and I had chattered to John the whole car ride home about how weird it was to feel so incredibly alone in a room full of people. When we finally tucked into bed, I was emotionally exhausted and worried baby would be up all night thanks to his late bedtime. I checked the monitor: Baby was sleeping fine. No, it was I who couldn't sleep; there was an ache deep in my chest that required my attention.

I pressed both my hands to my chest, between my breasts, where my love for baby felt most tender. It felt like a privilege to be his mom. I loved him so much that the ecstatic feeling teetered into pain, and I ached both with the need to protect him and keep him safe and with the fear that I would never be a good enough mom for him. I desperately wanted to soothe the ache, but tonight, in the darkness of my quiet bedroom, after having spent an evening in the company of people who could not or would not understand me, I wondered: What if the ache wasn't meant to be soothed?

My throat felt dry, so I took a drink of water from the glass on my bedside table, grateful that my mom had taught me to always take a glass of water to bed with me as a child. I settled back into the covers, closing my eyes and willing sleep to take me, but I couldn't stop thinking about Mom. She had wanted to be June Cleaver: the perfect mother with the perfect family. So, when I was perfect, a good girl, Mom was happy. But when I was far from perfect, which was often because nobody is, Mom was punishing.

When I first told Mom I would one day be an actress, she was enthusiastic, encouraging me to be anything I wanted to be. But as I grew, my Hollywood career aspirations never wavered, and Mom began to worry. Her support for my dream began to dwindle. I needed to be cautious, Mom warned. I needed to be practical. I needed to go to college, focus on my studies, have a backup plan, and adjust my expectations. When I informed her that I wanted to be an actress no matter what, even if all I ever managed to be was a struggling artist, she was furious. She told me I was wasting my potential. She told me she wouldn't support me financially if I ever got into trouble, unless I had a college degree first. It never mattered to Mom that I *knew* I was meant for acting. She just wanted me to be a good girl and do as she said.

But what if that wasn't all it was? *What if she had an ache?* I thought. My heart raced, and I wasn't sure I was going to be able to get to sleep at all. What if that ache was why Mom had been trying so hard to keep me from the pain of a difficult artist's life?

My own ache was a feeling that oscillated between the physical and the metaphorical, most acutely felt in the dim, quiet isolation of the midnight hours I spent alone with my thoughts and my pump after baby was born. All day long I set about the mundane tasks of daily life, but at night, the ache roused in me some deep, dormant beast that was desperate to keep baby from ever having to experience pain. When baby first came home from the hospital, I stayed awake as long as I physically could in anticipation of his needs. I wanted to be such a good mother that baby would never even have to cry out for help. Instead, I kept him up all night until my anxiety became his poor sleep habits.

That wasn't protection; it was overprotection, I thought.

When baby cried nonstop at six weeks old, I wanted to stop the crying. But that wasn't what was best for baby; he needed me to listen to him, to interpret what he was trying to tell me. And later, when baby struggled to get to sleep at four and a half months old, he didn't need me to bounce him all night long, though I tried;

he needed me to stand closely by as he safely worked through the frustration of learning a necessary life skill. My love ached for him at each of those developmental milestones. If I could have, I would have done his learning for him, to save him from the pain of having to learn himself. But saving him would have been for *me*, not him. I was trying to ease my own hard feelings about watching my baby suffer. I had misinterpreted my ache.

Maybe Mom had done the same, I thought.

On the day of my sixteenth birthday, Mom wept because she couldn't get me a car. She was so consumed by her own pain that she couldn't see that I didn't need her to get me a car; I just needed her to let me have fun on my birthday. I just needed her to be happy. Instead, because I wasn't properly attentive to how bad she was feeling, Mom snatched my arm in anger. I remembered thinking back then, when I looked down at the blood she'd drawn, digging her nails into my flesh to keep me there, that it had been my own fault for wrestling my arm away from her grasp. After becoming a mother myself, I saw the scenario differently. I couldn't imagine gripping my son's arm so tightly that I left marks. Little sixteen-year-old me didn't deserve that. Mom thought I was suffering because she couldn't get me a car, but it only seemed like that to her.

I wondered what my relationship with Mom could have been like if she had figured out how to bear her ache enough to be the mom I needed.

I never needed Mom to save me from my difficulties; I needed her to see things from my perspective, to support me in figuring life out for myself as I grew. Baby needed the same thing from me. The first year of motherhood was an intense period of hyperfocus; his care required so much of me, and nothing had ever felt so important, so all of my time and energy was spent on learning him while also navigating my big emotions. But while the era felt profound for me, as I struggled to balance his care and my transformation, baby was experiencing childhood. The foundation for his humanity was being laid. He didn't need me to freak out about how much I ached for him; he needed me to put my feelings aside and let him discover life for himself. It was my job to make baby feel understood, then get out of his way. In baby's story, I was a side character.

Of course, I thought with a laugh. *I'm playing the role of mom in his life.*

June Cleaver's depiction was spot on.

THE NEXT MORNING, THE SUN FILTERED in through the curtains that flanked the window closest to my side of the bed, waking me up. The sheets were rumpled on John's side but he was gone, which meant he had woken up with baby and let me sleep late. He really was the best guy on the planet. I stretched my body long and wide, like a starfish, then rolled over to smell his scent on his pillow. I took a big nose-full, feeling happy.

When I was pregnant and trying my hardest to distract myself from worrying about baby's birth and the associated life changes, I read an article that stated that the number one indicator of a child's ability to thrive was their mother's happiness. In essence, a mother's well-being affected her ability to be present and supportive of her child. Her happiness fostered a positive childhood environment, which lead to better resiliency, better social skills, better academic outcomes, and better physical health. *I have to be a side character for my kid but also enough of a main character in my own life to be happy,*

I thought, head still full of my middle-of-the-night rumination. It didn't sound like an easy feat, and again, I thought of my mom.

Mom was my favorite person in the world when she was happy, but she didn't know how to handle her own hard feelings, and too much of my life was spent tiptoeing around her volatility. I wondered if she had ever felt like the main character in her own life. It didn't seem like it, from my vantage point as her child, because, it seemed to me, if she had felt centered in her life, she wouldn't have had to rely on my sisters and me for help with her feelings. I wondered if the inability to bear her ache so she could play her part in my life was directly related to her lack of a support system.

For the first time ever, I thought about Mom's experience being mothered. Grandma Sally was a shrewd businesswoman, and she could be severe. I'd seen her on more than one occasion lean over my crying mother and tell her to "stop this nonsense." When baby was six weeks old, I just wanted the crying to stop. Had Grandma felt what I felt? Had Mom? Had either of them ever felt curious about what their precious baby was trying to communicate?

By the time I was old enough to witness Grandma leaning over Mom, she was in her sixties and Mom was in her forties. They had language by then; Grandma could have just asked what was wrong. Why didn't she? Was Grandma trying to relieve her own ache? Did *she* not have the support she needed? She didn't have many friends. She spent most of her time outside of work with her children and grandchildren, but when it came time to play the part of mother, when Mom was feeling pain, Grandma couldn't comfort her. How many times had Mom been told by her mother that her pain was nonsense? How horrible that must have been for Mom when she was a child.

I wondered who taught Grandma to snap at Mom like that. Growing up, I heard tales of my great-grandmother, who was an alcoholic. From what I was told, Grandma had been on her own a lot from a very young age. At four years old, she was walking with a friend when the other girl was pinned to a telephone pole by a car and killed. When Grandma returned home to her mother, Grandma's mom wasn't able to provide any comfort; though it was barely noon, she was already too drunk. And on days when Grandma's mom wasn't drinking, she was desperately mean.

Poor Grandma, I thought, flopping onto my back and hugging John's pillow to my chest.

Then my mind landed on John and his mom. I knew he had experiences similar to Grandma's with Thesla's alcoholism, but the difference was that Thesla was mostly kind and comforting when she was sober. Still, it must have been sad and confusing for little John to have a mom who was sometimes wonderful and sometimes scary. I wondered what drove those women to drink; before drinking escalated into a disease, was it an escape from the ache? Was it an inability to be their own main characters, a lack of support? Did all mothers who lacked support attempt to ease their ache at the expense of their children?

I didn't have the answers to all of my questions, but I knew I couldn't carry the wounds of my lineage forward with me through motherhood. I didn't want my pain to hurt baby. I had to find a way to heal.

But, I realized, I couldn't heal just for him. Just like I wasn't the main character in baby's life, I couldn't make him the main character in mine. I couldn't live *just* for baby; to do so would mean I was playing a side character *in my own life*. I couldn't think of a faster way to lose all sense of self. How was I supposed to teach my child to live his one beautiful life on Earth authentically, to the fullest, without first doing it myself? And what would I be teaching him about the role women should play in his life, and society at large, if I abandoned my wholeness to live for him?

No, baby needed me whole, enjoying my own life enough to maintain my own happiness, so that I could walk alongside him on his life path. And to do that, I realized, I needed an emotional education.

I PICKED UP MY PHONE AND sent a text to John. I was awake, I told him, but I needed to put my pump parts away. His quick reply made me smile: *Cool, take your time. We're just hanging out.* I liked that he liked to *hang out* with baby. Baby was my favorite little guy, too. For a second, I wanted to ignore my pump parts and join the boys downstairs, but I had been putting the task off for months and it needed to get done.

I'd quit pumping regularly when baby was seven and a half months old. His pediatrician had instructed me, when baby was six months old, to begin supplementing his diet with iron-rich foods, explaining that my milk no longer contained all the nutrients he needed, and the revelation made pumping feel less important. I had a small freezer stash, and baby was in the ninety-ninth percentile for height, weight, and head circumference, so I lost focus on my pumping schedule, skipping pumps here and there, and when my milk supply dwindled, I called it good enough. My goal had been to pump for a year, so I still sat for a pump here and there in the months beyond seven and a half, but I rarely got more than an ounce or two anymore. We began supplementing my milk supply with formula, and we would switch to whole milk in a few weeks, when baby turned one, so my pumping journey was over. I was glad to be done. Yet, somehow, I hadn't been able to bring myself to pack up my pump for storage.

I retrieved the small, white cardboard Spectra S2 box from its place under my pumping chair, then walked to my bathroom, where my washed pump parts had lain dormant for months, as I wiped the tears from my eyes.

Emotional regulation was not taught to me as a child. I was taught obedience instead of autonomy and managing the emotions of others over self-acceptance and self-compassion. But motherhood showed me that managing the emotions of others was nothing short of manipulation. And it didn't work anyway. Even in his infancy, baby had feelings and thoughts and opinions about the way he was experiencing life, an internal compass that guided him the same way I was guided to sit calmly at the assembly that day in elementary school. I didn't know better than baby in all scenarios. But to discern when to step in and protect and when to follow his lead, I had to trust in his inherent wholeness. To trust baby, I had to trust myself. And to trust myself, I had to know myself. Emotional mastery and self-knowledge were, therefore, key components of being the mom he needed.

I thought about my quest to get pregnant. I wanted a baby so badly, but I felt too vulnerable to admit my want out loud. Instead, I judged the women of the Ridiculous Women Forum for their vulnerability, secretly envying their ability to live their truths, even as I benefited from their emotionally hard-earned knowledge. If I was going to be the type of person who would allow baby to be himself,

I would need to be able to be myself first, fully, like the brilliant women online I'd grown to admire. To be able to walk baby through the difficulties of his life, I would have to walk myself through the difficulties of my own. And because I loved him, because I understood his fundamental worth, by nature of his very existence, suddenly, I understood mine as well. I was allowed to feel what I felt, just as he was. The ache, then, was guiding me to face the truth of myself.

I didn't share my birth story with anyone, not even my sisters, for three months after baby was born. I was ashamed that I had been induced. Though my birth was easy and, ultimately, I felt grateful for my experience, I had wanted to feel the natural onset of labor. I wasn't able to advocate for myself, though, and I was afraid of what others might think about me for my choice.

I thought about what I might say to baby in similar life circumstances, and after a moment, a response came to mind: *That really sucks*, I said to myself. *What a bummer that you didn't get the experience you wanted. And what a bummer that you felt like you couldn't speak up.*

It was a thought exercise about how I might support my baby through his own future difficulties, so I didn't expect it to feel so validating to say the words in my own head. It absolutely did suck to feel scared and helpless right before giving birth. *Why do you think that happened?* I asked myself, and when I filtered through the circumstances of my induction in my mind, I realized that I lacked the emotional safety I needed to be able to tell my doctor how I truly wanted to proceed. I didn't have a safe person to discuss the scenario with, someone who had some knowledge of the topic and could be completely on my side. John was there, but he knew even less about birth than I did, so though he was supportive, he didn't have the wisdom I craved. I needed a mom, unfortunately, one who wouldn't make me feel bad about myself if my choices differed from hers. How I wished I had the wisdom and support of a safe woman in my most vulnerable hours.

I guess I'll just have to be wise and supportive of myself, I thought.

I packed up the left bottle, flange, backflow protector, and duck-bill valve into the white box and was shocked to see how small and unimportant my pump components looked once stored, considering they had worked to express gallons of milk from me over the better part of my baby's first year of life. I gazed at them in a silent moment of gratitude, got started on the right-side parts, and thought about my sisters.

I loved Erin and Sarah both dearly, but Erin lived states away, and the tension that developed between Sarah and me as a result of my Thanksgiving drama with Mom had gone unaddressed for an entire year. What began as an exceptionally supportive living situation with Sarah had devolved over the course of my pregnancy and baby's newborn days into awkward encounters with an undercurrent of resentment. What had started out as enthusiasm for baby's arrival with Erin had become only occasional check-ins via text. Being so distant from my sisters was eating at me.

I thought about how close Sarah and I had been in our early twenties, before I started dating John. I was so enmeshed with her that I hadn't registered a change in our dynamic. What was good for me was obviously good for her, in my mind, so my constantly hanging out with my new boyfriend couldn't have been a problem. I had to accept that, maybe, I had hurt Sarah back then, and maybe, I had done something similar during our roommate era.

Suddenly, I remembered the ache. Sarah wasn't my mother, but she was *a* mother. Maybe my sister was grappling with an ache of her own. Maybe the distance between us was more to do with issues she was facing in her own life and not about me at all. Erin, too, was slow to respond to texts and calls, after all, and she and I hadn't had any dramas causing rifts between us. Maybe my sisters just needed understanding in a difficult stage of life.

I thought about what wisdom I might have for baby in such a scenario. *Can you tolerate the new dynamic if nothing ever changes?* I asked myself, and before I even had an answer, I picked up my phone and typed out a group message: *I miss you guys! Seen any good memes lately?* I understood that my relationship with Sarah wouldn't be immediately mended, and that Erin probably wouldn't magically have more time to respond, but I loved my sisters, and if I had to keep things light for now to have them in my life, I was willing to try. After all, my motherhood journey had made it very clear that life was always evolving, so I had to have hope that a day would come when we could talk deeply about how we felt.

I had just tucked the last pump part into place in the box and shut the lid when the hair on my forearms stood up. The air in the room suddenly felt electric, so I knew John must be near. A moment later, he crossed the threshold of our bedroom door holding baby with one hand and a fresh cup of coffee with the other, which he handed to me. *What a guy*, I thought, and I greeted them both with good morning kisses.

Looking down at the warm cup of creamy coffee now in my hand, I thought of my dad, who I hadn't thought about in weeks at least, or maybe months. I had a distinct memory of him bringing Mom her morning coffee, and remembering the look of appreciation on her face made me sad. I wondered what really happened between them.

Baby lunged forward then, launching himself out of John's arms and into mine, and I had to hold my coffee mug aloft to keep it from spilling on him. John and I laughed, bewildered, and in that moment, I remembered what Dad had told me, back when I announced my pregnancy: Kids really did make everything so much harder. But what a thrill! I was ecstatic to know baby, even if things were hard. I couldn't help but wonder why, as my dad, and as someone who had been through it before, he never checked on me. If he knew it was going to be so hard, why didn't he help? I didn't have to wonder what I would say to baby in a similar circumstance because the question came to me immediately: *Do you think you deserved help?* And the answer was a resounding *yes, I did.*

I had heard that thing about motherhood being hard from sources other than Dad, and my heart ached like it could bleed each time. Motherhood was hard, but it didn't ruin my life. It just ended the old one. When baby arrived, he cracked my world open with a seismic shift that reordered my every priority. I couldn't even remember a life before baby without concentrating hard. Becoming a mom, his mom, was so much deeper a transformation than I had ever anticipated.

Suddenly, an image came to mind of Dad standing at his preacher's pulpit in front of his congregation, and I wondered if God had ever blessed him with the awe-inspiring experience of recognizing the divinity in humanity, like I had felt having baby. I wondered if Dad looked around the world and saw every person alive as the tiny infant they once were, like I did. Did he hold reverence for the women who created the fabric of life itself? And if not, was that what went wrong with Mom? Where had he learned it? Had his mother attempted to ease her ache at his expense? There was so much I didn't know about Dad. I wanted to know him, but no one in my family liked to talk about their feelings, him least of all, so it had become too painful to ask. *Yes, kids make everything harder, that's the nature of humanity*, I thought.

Whether I did it with intention or not, I would be playing the role of mom in baby's life. I knew from my own life experience that he wouldn't remember the circumstances of his childhood apart from a handful of core memories, but he *would* remember how his parents made him feel. I wanted him to feel that his mother appreciated his emotional world, that she was curious about his point of view. That she was as authentic and honest about her experiences as possible. And my deepest hope was that my authenticity would pave the way for him to live authentically, too.

I thought I was having a baby, but really, I was signing a contract to perform a sacred duty for another soul. The ache was my guide; it would never be soothed because a love so deeply felt could always cause pain in equal measure. It was my job to handle my pain so I could help him do the same with his.

But I hadn't just given birth to baby. When he was born, I was reborn, and the same hopes and dreams I'd had since that day in elementary school when I was eight years old finally had direction. The creative force inside of me that knit together the cells of baby's body churned, craving expression of a vital truth I had come to understand to my very core: *Women are powerful.* To play the role of mom in baby's life, I needed to become fully embodied in my own, to step into my power. The ache was guiding me there, too.

I kissed baby and handed him off to John so I could pull on a fresh shirt. I opened my closet, drank the last of my coffee from my mug, and felt a wave of determination wash over me. There, alone in my room, grinning with the support of billions of women who had come before me, feeling more myself than I ever had, I embraced another role, as storyteller.

CHAPTER NINETEEN

THE ROLE

AT 10:12 AM ON A WEDNESDAY morning, on the outskirts of Austin, Texas, I stepped into my new role. I knew it was exactly 10:12 AM because I had just lovingly tucked my baby into bed for his morning nap and had diligently noted the time in the baby care app I used to track his sleep and eating patterns. It had been four days since his very first birthday, three days since his smash cake photo shoot, two days since his pediatrician told me he was a "healthy toddler," and one day since I had cried about the passage of time.

As I swung my front door open, I inhaled the soft, sweet scent of crape myrtle floating along the warm autumn breeze, then bent down to retrieve the package on my front step. I had researched for a week to select the best budget-friendly option, and finally, with the help of two-day shipping, my purchase had arrived. I plunged a kitchen knife into the packing tape at the seam of the cardboard box, sliced it through, and wrenched the cardboard flaps apart. There, padded by bubble wrap, lay my brand-new, six-foot-tall collapsible tripod.

I grinned from ear to ear. I was giddy. I was eager to get started on telling stories from the first person point of view of a mother, but when I pulled the tripod from its wrapping and twisted it to lengthen the center column, a tiny voice in the back of my mind asked me who the hell I thought I was and why the hell I thought I could still become a movie star.

"Hush!" I said out loud. I couldn't tell if I was more startled by my doubts or by my audible insistence that they quiet down. "I am a trained actor with a story to tell; I am allowed to experiment in my living room," I told myself.

I shushed my inner dialogue long enough to open the clasps that would drop the metal legs of my tripod to the floor. I closed the clasps, locking each leg into place, and let go, satisfied that the contraption could stand on its own. Then I unsheathed the accompanying cell phone mount and gave its spring-loaded jaws a yank to test their pliancy. The top of the tripod had a small, square platform embedded with a flat screw to hold a camera in place. I inspected the bottom of the cell phone mount until I found a screw guide the same width and depth as the tripod's appendage. *Aha!* I thought, pleased that I had figured out my equipment setup all by myself, and I spun the phone mount into place. But as I pried open its jaws and fit my phone snugly in between, locking it vertically, that tiny voice piped up again.

You're a pathetic loser, it said, *you haven't even matured past your childhood fantasies.*

I doubled over and put my hands on my knees like I had been punched in the gut. Apparently even powerful women dealt with crippling self-doubt. I pictured little eight-year-old me sitting still among a sea of excited, undulating children. I could practically smell the ranch dressing. I thought about what I might say to baby in such a moment of doubt. *Could you live with it if you never tried?* I asked in my mind. I knew right away that I couldn't. Performing that day in elementary school was an awakening. Little-girl me deserved to see her dreams realized. But acting wasn't just a lifelong dream; it felt more like duty. I had a duty to myself in the same way I had a duty to baby. And now, with the added goal of using my acting training to tell women's stories, I had a mission to accomplish.

I took a deep breath to quiet my doubts. I navigated to my phone's camera app and switched the setting to video. I selected a three-second timer, pressed record, and backed up into frame. Then the tiny voice asked me if I thought I was enough of a mom to speak on being a mom.

"Ahh, ya dumb bitch," I muttered.

I put my hands on my hips and considered her point for a minute. I had only been a mother for a year, and truth be told, there were a lot of days when I still didn't feel like I really *was* a mom, let alone any good at being one. I was a mom to my baby, and I knew him like I knew myself, but I wasn't in any position to be offering advice or expertise. Then, the answer struck me, and I clapped my hands.

"Alright! I don't know everything, or maybe even anything, but my goal is to be as honest as possible about the kinds of things *I* have experienced, which I'm allowed to do, so *shutthefuckup* with your doubts," I said.

I was engaging in literal, out-loud self-talk. *If people could see me, they would think I'm nuts*, I thought with a giggle.

I stopped my recording and watched the video back to check my framing. It was cringey to watch myself argue with no one, but I was centered in the video and the framing looked okay, so I ripped a piece of blue painters' tape and marked the ground where I stood. The voice asked if I recognized how fat I had gotten.

"Oh my God, shut up!" I yelled. I couldn't believe how mean my thoughts were.

I stomped past my kitchen to the half bath and looked in the mirror. My green t-shirt clung loosely to my low belly, so I tugged at the bottom hem to adjust the folds of the fabric more attractively. My shoulder-length wavy hair was tucked behind my ears, making them stick out, so I swept it up into a low ponytail, securing it with the black elastic band on my wrist. I looked at my face next: It was bare and pale, like I hadn't seen the sun in months, and I briefly considered running upstairs for my makeup bag, but I didn't have much of baby's nap time left, so I reconsidered. I looked into my own eyes and sighed.

"My face is my face," I said to myself. "And my body is my body. I'm not perfect, but that's why I'm exactly the right person to do this because nobody is perfect and that's life!"

I spun on my heel and returned to my tripod to double-check my battery percentage, when a flurry of worries I didn't even know I had came to the forefront of my mind.

You're selfish; go play with your baby. You're too old; this will never work. You have eye bags; no one wants to see that. And you need a root touch-up, yuck. Was that a zit I saw next to your mouth? Also, you have a crazy family. You're damaged. You couldn't even breastfeed. No one wants to hear your take on motherhood. In fact, no one wants to hear about moms at all. Besides, who says you'll even be able to convey the message? Honestly, pack it up, Shawna. What are you even doing?

I closed my eyes, took a deep inhale, then sighed all of the air out of my lungs. I thought about everything I'd learned about myself, and about life, since becoming pregnant with baby. I hadn't fully understood myself until I had my son, other than knowing I was an actor. And though motherhood didn't look or feel how I imagined it would, I was deeply in love with my journey. I enjoyed being a mom, as hard as it was, and I had immense respect for the other women of the world who had chosen to embark on this profoundly personal, yet beautifully universal experience, too. I felt certain that motherhood was an utter transformation for all of us.

For the first time in my life, I had an artistic point of view and stories to tell. And wouldn't it be great if other women felt seen by my stories and were moved to contribute their versions of events, too? I wanted to live in a society that was honest about the immense sacrifices women make to create life and about the personal power required to make those sacrifices. I wanted baby to know these stories, too. I knew the world could say a million hurtful things to me to shut me up, but I was rock solid in my conviction.

Why not me? After all, as the experts always said: Write what you know.

I checked the clock and noted that I had thirty more minutes of nap time, barring any unforeseen interruptions, so I had better get started. I picked up a stack of papers and read through the script I wrote.

INT. SHAWNA'S HOUSE (KITCHEN)—DAY

Shawna, a thirty-something blond woman with a mom bod, trots through the frame with a drooly, chubby baby on her hip.

SHAWNA
Shit. Shit. Shit.

Shawna's feet, which are clean but for the chipped toenail polish, crunch strewn cracker bits and dodge baby toys as she runs.

SHAWNA
Ohmygawd, ohmygawd.

The child giggles as Shawna shoves him, feet first, into a stationary activity center. The baby jumps, making the toy clatter.

SHAWNA
Ahh, ahh, ahh.

Shawna's hand grabs a loaf of bread, then a can of tuna, then some lettuce and mayo from the messy fridge. The baby screams offscreen.

CLOSE UP—SHAWNA

Shawna winces. She shouts over her shoulder.

SHAWNA
Just a minute, baby!

Her hand takes two slices of bread from the loaf, then manually cranks a can opener to get at the tuna. The baby screams again and thrashes against his activity center.

SHAWNA
Just a sec, babe.

Shawna dances in place at the edge of her counter, squeezing her inner thighs to keep from peeing. She lays her bread onto a plate and slaps tuna on top with a fork. We hear the baby cry out.

SHAWNA
Almost, my love.

Her right hand dispenses mayo from a squeeze bottle onto the tuna, and her left hand whacks some lettuce down on top. The baby cries hard. Shawna grimaces, adds the top slice of bread, and picks up the sandwich.

SHAWNA
Coming, baby.

She takes a massive bite, chewing like a maniac. We hear the baby let out a shriek much different than any we've heard before. Shawna looks over her shoulder mid-chew. The baby has found a rattle. Shawna's eyes go wide and she plunges a quarter of the sandwich into her mouth. Baby jumps and bangs the rattle on the activity center.

SHAWNA
(mouth full)
Yay! You're having fun!

She swallows hard and takes two more bites. We hear a gleeful baby scream.

SHAWNA
(mouth full)
I know, I'm coming. Just a sec.

Shawna chews twice and swallows. She takes a swig of coffee from a thirty-two-ounce purple travel mug and stretches her neck. The baby jumps and yells with delight.

SHAWNA
I know, almost there.

She shoves the remaining bits of sandwich into her mouth, puffing out both cheeks.

SHAWNA
(mouth full)
Mama was hungry!

She swallows again and again, clearing her mouth of the last of her sandwich, drinks more coffee, and exhales in exhaustion.

SHAWNA
Okay. All done. Want to come
with me to pee?

BLACK.

OVER BLACK: Baby screams.

END.

I knew my first-ever skit wouldn't be a massive viral hit—there wasn't much to the story, and the stakes weren't very high—but I wanted to make it anyway. I had experienced that moment in my motherhood tenure—the sudden, urgent realization that I had been so busy tending to baby's needs that I had ignored my own—and I wanted to capture the frenzy.

With the thirty minutes that remained of baby's nap, I worked quickly to capture the shots I needed to bring the "Mom Lunch" moment to life. I recorded my parts of the scene from three different angles, eating three different sandwiches and swigging coffee from the actual travel mug I used every day. When baby woke, after some milk and a diaper change, I recorded six different clips of hurrying through my house with him on my hip, and six different clips of depositing him, feet first, into his activity center. Luckily, he was in a good mood after his nap, so he enjoyed our little game of movie making. Then, I recorded one long clip of baby playing in his activity center, jumping and thrashing and banging his rattle, as I stood off camera and made faces at him. Throughout the day, whenever baby cooed or cried or screamed with glee, I recorded the audio on my phone. And when John came home from work, I gave him a kiss, handed him baby, then spent three hours compiling my footage and audio onto my computer, editing the clips into a forty-five-second-long video, complete with background music.

After bedtime, I showed my finished piece to John, who chuckled supportively.

"It's kind of funny, right?" I asked, with hope in my eyes.

"Yeah. It's more real, though. Like slice of life," he replied.

I thought for a moment. I heard the cliché, but I didn't think depicting real life was a bad thing. "A funny slice of life that no one really captures in such minute detail because it's just a mom eating a sandwich," I said at last.

John chuckled and shrugged his shoulders.

"Yeah, maybe," he said. "I've never really seen that before."

I nodded. "No one has, because who cares, but I guarantee there will be other moms out there who have felt like a crazy person because they couldn't even get it together enough to remember to feed themselves."

"Is that a thing?" he asked.

"That's a thing. That is absolutely a thing," I said. "Moms beat themselves up over every tiny misstep. But it's because we think we're the only idiots in the whole world. We're not. We all have these moments. That's why I made it so specific. It will make other moms feel seen."

"How do you know?" he asked.

I shrugged. I didn't know why I felt connected through time and space to the experiences of every mother everywhere, but I did.

"I can't explain it," I said. "I just know."

And with that, I pressed upload.

ACKNOWLEDGMENTS

THANK YOU, FIRST AND FOREMOST, TO the two brilliant women who helped me shape this story. To my editor, Leah Wilson, and my assistant editor, Clara Tamez: I'm endlessly grateful for your careful attention to detail and the clarity you offered with such kindness. Thank you for holding my hand through the editing process.

Thank you to Glenn Yeffeth and the entire BenBella team. It is because of your invaluable support and guidance that I was able to tell this story. Thank you to my wonderful manager and friend, Amy Pearson, for your steadfast belief in my ability, even in the face of my doubts. Thank you to my wonderful agent, Tim Moore, for your expertise and helpful advice at every step. Thank you, Mallory Hyde, for your marketing mastery. Thank you, Taylor Kiesel, for your PR prowess. Thank you to everyone at Shine Talent Group.

Thank you to my husband, John, for your steadfast commitment to me and our babies. Thank you for your many read-throughs and your thoughtful feedback. Thank you for your endless optimism. Thank you for celebrating every win, no matter how small. Thank you for seeing the very best in me, always. You're the greatest person I've ever known. Love you, always.

Thank you, KJ, for making me a mama. Thank you, CJ, for making our family complete. Thank you for inspiring me every day to be better. I love you both so much it hurts.

Thank you to my mother, whose body expanded to grow me and whose love evolved to sustain me, both in ways I will never know, because such is the nature of motherhood. I love you, Mom.

Thank you to my father, who encouraged me to tell the whole truth, and who let me cry, and cried with me, when I explained the role he played in my story of becoming a mother. I love you, Dad.

Thank you to my sisters, Erin and Sarah, for the many years of love and friendship, for the many deep talks and endless belly laughs, and for all the tears. Thanks for reading my manuscript when I was freaking out and giving me your honest opinions. I'll forever relish being one of three. I love you both!

Thank you to Liz Swenson, Sarah Sahagian, Amber Estenson, Sara Rigsby-Melody, Katie Nash, and Marsa Newby for listening, reading, encouraging, championing. Thanks for being there when I needed a friend.

Finally, my most heartfelt thanks to every single follower, lurker, and occasional viewer of the @shawnathemom Shawnaverse. Thank you for watching and supporting. I am forever grateful for the opportunity to tell women's stories. Without you, I'd just be alone in my room talking to myself, and for that you have my endless gratitude.

ABOUT THE AUTHOR

Shawna Lander wears many hats as the creator, actor, writer, and editor behind the viral internet series @shawnathemom, an online one-woman show with a global audience of over four million. When she's not exploring the funny, messy, and often underrepresented parts of motherhood and family life in her scripted episodic, Shawna is cuddling at home with her husband and two children, and their half-feral cat.